WOMEN IN ANTHROPOLOGY

Women in Anthropology

Autobiographical Narratives and Social History

Edited by
Maria G. Cattell and Marjorie M. Schweitzer

Walnut Creek, California

Left Coast Press, Inc.
1630 North Main Street, #400
Walnut Creek, California 94596
http://www.lcoastpress.com

Louana Lackey's article ("On Becoming an Anthropologist") was originally published in the *Bulletin of the National Association of Student Anthropologists*, Summer 1992.
Maria Cattell's poem "Rainbow Skin" was originally published in *Anthropology News* 38 (5): 60–61.

PHOTO CREDITS

Eunice Felter Boyer by Merle Boyer
Dorothy Castille by Hella Moritz
Maria Cattell by Hudson Cattell
Jane Day courtesy of Jane Day
Jean Harris by W. J. Hardiman
Ellen Rhoads Holmes by Lowell D. Holmes
Elizabeth Hoobler by Julie Sprott
Louana Lackey courtesy of Martha Gatewood Bell
Cath Oberholtzer by Ron Oberholtzer
Barbara Olsen by Joel Feiner
Ruby Rohrlich courtesy of Mike Leavitt
Marilyn Rose by Elisa Rose
Judy Rosenthal courtesy of Judy Rosenthal
Molly Schuchat by Simon Schuchat
Marjorie Schweitzer photo courtesy of Oklahoma State University
Esther Skirboll by Stanley Skirboll
Jacqueline Walden by Jacqueline Walden

LIBRARY OF CONGRESS CATALOGING-IN-PUBLICATION DATA

Women in anthropology : autobiographical narratives and social history / edited by Maria G. Cattell and Marjorie M. Schweitzer.
p. cm.
Includes bibliographical references and index.
ISBN 1-59874-082-2 (hardback : alk. paper) — ISBN 1-59874-083-0 (pbk. : alk. paper)
1. Women anthropologists—Biography. I. Cattell, Maria G. II. Schweitzer, Marjorie M. III. Title.
GN20.W634 2006
301.092'2—dc22
[B] 2006013216

05 06 07 08 5 4 3 2 1

Printed in the United States of America

The paper used in this publication meets the minimum requirements of American National Standard for Information Sciences—Permanence of Paper for Printed Library Materials, ANSI/NISO Z39.48—1992.

Contents

Foreword

The crisis of middle age has to do as much as anything with a catastrophic anxiety about time itself. How has one managed to come to the meridian and still be so far from the real achievement one had dreamed possible at 20? And I mean achievement as a human being as well as within a career.

—May Sarton, 1968

All the sorrows of life can be borne if only we can make them into stories.

—Isak Dinesen [Karen Blixen]

IN THAT potent decade of the 1960s, Betty Friedan's *The Feminine Mystique* was publicly exploding the popular North American notion tying an eternally blissful life to mastering the role of suburban housewife. At the same time, many of this book's authors were struggling with the consequences of such mythic ideas and the premises of May Sarton's words about life's meridian. In this book they are also testing out the presumptuous statement of highborn Danish writer Karen Blixen in proclaiming the totally redemptive features of personal narratives. Telling their reversal and transition stories of midlife launches out of expected mommy and spouse tracks into public academic life, they are not only capturing a critical moment of North American cultural history but situating their tales in the midst of an anthropology of aging and late adulthood. Many authors have begun to document a common pattern in many parts of the world of dramatic changes of role, power, and status by women as they pass into the middle and later adult years.[1] Indeed, this is more than a book of social history and personal encounter, but a nuanced engagement with the multiple streams of life that organize and energize any good study of culture. It resituates these women anthropologists within the fuller breadth of our expanding life span and connects to a notion posited by Barbara Myerhoff and Andrei Simić as life's work set in a "Career of Aging." They see late adulthood as a "period of activity, participation, self-movement, and purposefulness... conceived as the product of a building process involving the entire life-span."[2]

Especially because I am passionate about anthropology, I was particularly honored to be asked to contribute in at least a tiny way to this amazing volume. Its tales of experiences, knowledge, courage, and ideas about unusual career pathways of women anthropologists who gained professional credentialing in midlife or later resonate deeply. In certain ways in its reading, I wandered into the familiar role of exploring other lifeways, since my journey to anthropology was very different than told in this book. As a male growing up in a working-class family during the height of the Vietnam War, graduate school seemed a pleasant alternative to combat or driving a New York City cab while dispensing undergraduate anthropology wisdom. The fear of reproducing my father's life dedicated to manual labor combined with an early marriage and fatherhood to spur me toward a professional trajectory quite different from the more circuitous paths described in this book. With the strong support of my first spouse, I somehow achieved an "on-time" passage from college graduation at age twenty-one to the doctorate in anthropology five years later.

Upon reading this manuscript, what was immediately evoked from my educational experiences was a vivid and sad event I witnessed after I decided to become an anthropology major in 1968, during my junior year at one of New York City's public colleges. I was waiting outside the office of the department chair, the program's oldest male and a very politically conservative archaeologist. Suddenly, his office door swung open, and a young woman whom I had seen in one of my classes ran past me clutching her books and sobbing in anger. A female friend of mine who witnessed the scene came over and resolved my unvoiced confusion. "There's another one who has not learned that the chair does not think it is a good move for girls to go to grad school." I remember being stunned but not particularly surprised, having heard tirades in class by this professor about the tyranny of all the new changes then going on in society that challenged the established order. Fortunately, as a number of this book's authors found, there were other faculty in the department who were considerably more supportive of female students and facilitated at least some of them continuing on to graduate school.

Almost forty years later, I find myself the "senior" male directing a small anthropology program equally divided between male and female colleagues, but overwhelmingly teaching female majors, a good number of whom are reentering college after considerable periods of domestic labors or other kinds of work. This makes me particularly thankful for the appearance of this very special volume, which will not only serve as a crucial pathfinder for female faculty and students coming of professional age, but also give courage and possibility to their male counterparts who may now have pause to rethink their relationships and support of colleagues and life partners.

Jay Sokolovsky
St. Petersburg, Florida, March 26, 2006

~ Endnotes ~

1. Foner (1989), Kerns and Brown (1992), Brown et al. (1994).
2. Myerhoff and Simić (1978:240).

~ References ~

Brown, J., P. Subbaiah, and S. Therese. 1994. Being in Charge: Older Women and Their Younger Female Kin. *Journal of Cross-Cultural Gerontology* 9 (2): 231–54.

Foner, Nancy. 1989. Older Women in Nonindustrial Cultures: Consequences of Power and Privilege. *Women and Health* 14:227–37.

Kerns, V., and J. K. Brown, eds. 1992. *In Her Prime: New Views of Middle-Aged Women*, 2nd ed. Urbana: Univ. of Illinois Press.

Myerhoff, Barbara G., and Andrei Simić. 1978. *Life's Career—Aging: Cultural Variations on Growing Old*. Beverly Hills, CA: Sage.

Sarton, May. 1968. *Plant Dreaming Deep*. New York: W. W. Norton.

Preface

The Birth of the OWAN Project

The OWAN Project (Older Women Anthropologists Personal/Professional Narrative Project) was conceived in February 1992 in our hotel room in Santa Fe where Maria Cattell and I were attending the annual meeting of the Society for Cross-Cultural Research. As we talked about quilts and knitting and gardens, we began to compare our lives as women anthropologists. We found that we both shared the threads of marriage/raising kids/getting a PhD "late." Although the details of our career paths had been different, we shared the sense of reward that our academic achievements brought, the fascination of a broad and stimulating discipline, and the difficulties and challenges we encountered along the way.

We wondered if there were other women who shared our experiences and what their adventures had been. Had they encountered obstacles along the way? Were they glad, as we had been, that they had decided to return to school later in life? Would they be interested in talking and writing about their experiences?

We agreed to structure a project around personal and professional narratives that would reveal ourselves as persons as well as older women anthropologists. In a world where the currents and eddies had shifted radically in our lifetimes, but where the seas themselves had somehow remained the same, we had faced some challenges that were new and some that were discouragingly old.

A notice in the Cooperation Column of the *Anthropology News* that spring brought letters and cards from more than twenty women as we organized a symposium for the annual meeting of the American Anthropological Association (AAA). We suggested writing about the rewards and challenges, but we were especially interested in "Why Anthropology?"

We heard from women in other disciplines and men who asked, "Why not us?" But we were anthropologists, and we were women. Those were the defining parameters of the project.

The symposium we proposed for 1994, "Multifaceted Lives: Older Women Anthropologists—Professional and Personal Narratives," focused on the challenges (obstacles presented by academia and/or family members/crises) and rewards (encouragement by professional mentors and friends, intellectual stimulation) of becoming an anthropologist at age forty-five or later. We asked: Can we know ourselves as we try to know others, through cultural and social analysis—and can we know society and culture through ourselves?

Eight women—Eunice Boyer, Florence Chapman, Jane Day, Patsy Evans, M. Jean Harris, Ellen Holmes, Ruby Rohrlich, and Molly Schuchat—presented papers. Two discussants who are experts in the field of aging—Kathryn (Jay) Elliott and Otto von Mering—commented on the papers.

Interest in the session was high; we began planning a second symposium.

By now we had a mailing list of over sixty people, including several students and a few men. Although men did not fit the parameters of our project, we invited one of them to be a discussant. The 1995 symposium, "Culture, History, and Narratives of the Self: Reshaping Identities, Critiquing Society," focused on methodological, analytical, and political questions by asking: How does life history become social history? Can we know society through ourselves?

Ten women—Lucia Cargill, Dorothy Castille, Maria Cattell, Anna Lawson, Cath Oberholtzer, Barbara Olsen, Judith Polanich, Marjorie Schweitzer, Esther Skirboll, and Pat Slorah—presented papers. The discussants were Joan Weibel-Orlando and Mark Luborsky, both of whom had studied the cultural dimensions of aging, and Jason (Jay) Shapiro. Jay, a former lawyer, provided interesting insights from his perspective as an older man (an OMAN) working on a PhD in anthropology.

~ Fourteen Years Later ~

Why did this project take so long? I believe it has mirrored in important ways the trajectories that each of us followed in our life paths, often beset by factors completely out of our control. There were many starts and stops between the beginning idea and the final manuscript. Kids graduated from school, kids married, grandkids were born, husbands died, parents needed care, parents died, authors got sick, authors retired, authors moved, to say nothing of the time spent teaching and doing research. But we are nothing if not persistent. And I think persistence is what has paid off in the lives of all of the authors of these narratives.

Marjorie M. Schweitzer

~ Acknowledgments ~

We are grateful to, first of all, each other for many years of deep friendship and over a decade of persistence in carrying out this project in spite of all the personal upheavals in our lives; the many who responded to our call but who for various reasons did not become part of the project; our families for putting up with all the nonsense; our friends and colleagues who have encouraged and supported us. We appreciate the superb editorial guidance of Jennifer Collier, senior editor at Left Coast Press, and we thank Mitch Allen, publisher of Left Coast Press, for his encouragement over the years. We both owe a debt of gratitude to Jay Sokolovsky, our colleague in aging studies, for his extraordinary vision and his friendship.

Maria: I thank especially my parents, Anna Scofield Gleaton and Munsey Sinclair Gleaton, who died before this project began. Their breath of life continues to be inspirational. Mom was a late bloomer who taught me the word *opsimathy* and was herself a nontraditional student. It was Dad who sparked my love of words and pursuit of The Word. I also thank my various partners, the late Bob Moss, who supported my research in Kenya in so many ways, and the late Jack Mongar, who cheerfully read anything and everything I put in his hands—and the one who remains my friend of over half a century though we were married only half that time, Hudson Cattell. And thanks to my children for love, lemon meringue pies, computer help, and much else besides.

Marjorie: I thank my parents, Robert and Gladys Gardner, who encouraged me in everything I did; John, my husband of many years, who has always been my strongest supporter; and my children for their continuing encouragement. I thank Jehanne Schweitzer for technical advice and Gretchen and Mark Carney, Rosemary Cooke, Lorie Hiemer, Marj Robinson, David Rodenbaugh, Skippy Rollins, John Schweitzer, Roland Schweitzer, and Dorothy Scott for reading the "Gender Roles in Sociocultural and Historical Context" chapter. Their encouraging comments this past year have been invaluable. And I give special thanks to John, who put up with this long project with patience and unfaltering good humor.

We especially want to thank our authors who have stuck with us through these many years. We hope you are pleased with the result.

Voices of Women Anthropologists

Autobiography, Social History, and Anthropology

Maria G. Cattell

I BEGAN writing this introduction in a distant voice, using terms like "the authors" or "the contributors." Somewhere along the way I found myself shifting to the more inclusive and intimate "we." I could not write about "the authors" as if they were someone else. I was one of them. So "I" became "we"—though I alone am responsible for the words.

In this volume, seventeen North American women tell their stories of becoming anthropologists in mid-to-late-twentieth-century North America. Their stories are part of social history and the history of anthropology. The broader sociocultural context, described in the chapter on "Gender Roles in Sociocultural and Historical Context," is crucial to understanding our lives, for we grew up in a culture pervaded by the dominant middle-class ideology that a woman's place is in the home as supportive wife, mother, and family caregiver. We lived substantial parts of our lives before the information-technology revolution, before everyday life became computerized and digitized. We grew up before the second wave of feminism; before the Pill, *Roe v. Wade*, the civil rights movement, and *Brown v. Board of Education*; before many other transformations that today are woven into our culture—taken for granted by some, contested by others.

Before turning to this social context (in the following chapter), we explore here our personal histories to see how they fit into anthropology's historical stream, contemporary disciplinary trends and fashions such as narrativity and reflexivity, and issues related to marginalized and excluded categories of persons. We examine the women anthropologists, collectively, who volunteered to tell their life stories, to speak from their own experiences, to write history as they lived it. This analysis focuses particularly on ways our lives have been mediated by gender and age but includes other important factors such as religion, race, class, and ethnicity.

Older Women Anthropologists: Getting Age into the Discussion

It is now well established that, until recently, women were consistently denigrated, silenced, and excluded in anthropology and that historians of anthropology grossly neglected women anthropologists, even though women were active (especially in the Southwest) from the early days when the discipline was being defined.[1] Feminist scholarship has convinced most academics that anyone interested in the history of anthropology (or any other discipline) needs to pay attention to the voices of women.[2] To that we can add other categories of persons (basically, anyone but white middle-class males) who have been consigned to the margins of academic disciplines.[3] And yet, to say that the existence of many types of discrimination has been proven is not to say we do not need to pay further attention to the matter. We need to search out the stories and listen to the many voices in order to fill in the gaps in anthropological history and in the ethnographic, archaeological, and theoretical literature.

Gender is only one of those gaps. Another is age. As Jay Bernstein notes, from 1891 to 1930, "[d]octoral research in anthropology was mainly a young man's pursuit: more than 85 percent of doctorates were men, and more than 81 percent were under 35 at graduation, with half under 30. Only 7.2 percent were over 40."[4] Since 1930 the modal age of anthropology graduates has steadily gone up and the gender balance has shifted; by the mid-1990s, the modal PhD recipient was a forty-year-old woman.[5]

The modal age of this volume's narrators at the time of receiving the PhD was fifty-four, considerably higher than in the discipline as a whole. Why is this important? Why should anyone pay special attention to *older* women's stories? Because age matters, and it has received little attention in the spate of self-reflexive literature that has emerged in recent decades. Most of us were traditional students while getting our bachelor's degrees in the sense that we did it straight out of high school—except that it wasn't common, then, for women to complete their degrees at all. In graduate school we were all highly nontraditional students.[6] The fact that nontraditional students have been in the majority over traditional students since the 1970s has important implications for educational programs and student services. Our stories illustrate a strong trend in American education, and the issues we grappled with—balancing the many facets of our complicated lives while working toward a PhD—are equally important today, as women with careers in all fields make decisions about matters involving marriage, family, and careers.

We became anthropologists, in a formal sense, later in life than usual, from our mid-forties to age sixty. Because we were deterred from, or we never even considered, careers in anthropology when we were "young," we (all but one of us) raised families; some had other careers before we became nontraditional students, reentry women, opsimaths. The word *opsimathy*—which means getting a late start in education—originally carried a thoroughly negative connotation: "Therefore Opsiemathie, which is too late beginning to learn, was counted a great vice, and very unseemly."[7] Some of us found this seventeenth-century attitude to be persistent in the mid- to late twentieth century, when our families or professors regarded as "unseemly" our insistence on becoming graduate students.

They thought we were superannuated retreads who should have been content with remaining "housewives with hobbies." We, of course, did not agree.

~ Personal Narratives and/as History ~

This book began with storytelling in a Santa Fe hotel room, where Marjorie Schweitzer and I told each other our life stories. We soon found that other women who had, like us, earned their PhDs in anthropology later in life also wanted to tell their stories of the ways anthropology became part of their personalities and life stories—stories from the heart.

But these stories are more than personal history. They are social history as well. They demonstrate the power of culture and events to shape individual lives, though it is mostly in retrospect that we have recognized the forces that moved us along particular paths, especially the marriage-and-family path. The individual narratives, viewed in their sociocultural context, reveal the interactions of gender and age in our personal and professional lives—how being female and being older influenced our life choices and our careers, and how other factors such as religion, ethnicity, and class affected our life paths.

We were born from 1913 to 1947, the oldest coming to womanhood in the 1920s and 1930s and the youngest maturing during the turbulent 1960s. We are mostly white and middle class, though many of us, for a variety of reasons, saw ourselves as outsiders in our social and cultural milieus. Collectively, we have experienced marriage (and its "living together" permutation), divorce, and widowhood. All but one of us are mothers. Many are grandmothers. We have been caregivers to children, spouses, and aging parents. We live in Canada and every region of the United States. Our individual stories are unique but reveal many shared life experiences, and we are bound together by our passion for anthropology.

Our stories speak to the lives of our daughters and granddaughters—and other younger women—as they struggle with issues of independence and achievement, relationships and family life in a world that is, in some ways, very different from the world in which we grew up and is, at the same time, amazingly not so very different. Our stories speak to the lives of today's graduate and undergraduate students and also to our colleagues in the social sciences and women's studies as they examine women's lives. Through our stories, they can connect with social history and the history of anthropology as lived experience.

~ *Life Stories in Anthropology*

Anthropology and sociology have long traditions of using life stories—life histories, biographies and autobiographies, person-centered ethnographies—to examine the nexus of individual lives and the larger contexts in which those lives are lived.[8] Exemplars in anthropology include Oscar Lewis's *Five Families* and *The Children of Sanchez*, which use multiple life histories and the (translated and edited) words of the members of the Mexican families. Lewis remains a powerful but invisible presence in all but the brief introductions. Using a different structure in *Nisa: The Life and Words of a !Kung Woman*,[9] Marjorie Shostak presents Nisa's story (again, translated and edited) alternately with Shostak's discussions of relevant aspects of !Kung society and culture. Shostak, through telling parts of her own story, is far more visible than Lewis. In *Peyote Hunt*,[10] Barbara Myerhoff is constantly visible through her interactions with the Huichol shaman who is the focus of the book. Myerhoff's role in *Number Our Days*[11] is even more significant because the research involves exploration of her own Jewish heritage. All these stories are heavily mediated by the anthropologists who interview, translate, and edit.

The stories in this volume are part of this trend toward narrative life history and self-reflexive scholarship. But we are telling our own stories in our own words. We are compelled by "the desire which overtook a wide range of scholars... to write in newly meaningful ways, which refused anonymity and authority and instead sought connection, intimacy, and passion."[12] Recently, personal narrative is being used in an expanding number of fields to explore disciplinary histories including the sciences, history, literature, sociology, and others.[13] In particular, (auto)biographical narratives are part of the writing of a critical history of anthropology that includes those who have been excluded from that history, or denigrated or silenced: women, African Americans, and others.[14] Often these works use descriptors such as *erased, hidden, invisible, marginal, muted, silenced, submerged,* and *subterranean* because their common agenda is to bring the forgotten, the ignored, the excluded, and the silenced into the light. As Ruth Behar says, we are seeking "an anthropology without its exiles," a more inclusive and democratic discipline.[15]

To this end, Nancy Parezo—discussing ways that anthropology has *not* been "the welcoming science" for women—calls for "life histories and biographies, embedded in time and space, that analyze the personal investment of becoming and being an anthropologist."[16] Such narratives, she says, will reveal the workings of gender in academe and ways that women have gone about producing their identities as anthropologists, as scholars, and as women. Our lives have been witnesses to the necessity for such a project. Thus, this present volume helps "envision another history as well as another future for anthropology."[17]

Most autobiographical writings by anthropologists are "fieldwork memoirs"[18] that probe the relationship between personal experience and anthropological practice.[19] Some were written by partners who accompanied the "official" anthropologist to the field, what Papanek called the "two-person single career."[20] Many are organized around themes such as children, gender, sexuality, or violence.[21] Few go beyond the fieldwork experience into what might more properly be called autobiographies.[22]

Most of these autobiographical materials are by women—a phenomenon that Parezo[23] sees as a reflection of the fact that fieldwork has been the place within the discipline where men have seen women as necessary to their enterprise, even from the early days of anthropology.[24] But there may be another reason. Rosemary

Joyce suggests that a scientist "writes her life in her papers, and they give her voice."[25] It seems likely that male scientists have a greater tendency to be satisfied with the scientific voice of their professional writing, while women academics, too often finding their scientific voices muted or silenced,[26] seek other ways to make themselves known.[27] In any case, many women (and men, too) are raising their voices in autobiographies, poetry, fiction, and experimental ethnographies.[28]

~ *Gender in Autobiography*

As several scholars have pointed out, women's autobiographies often are very different from men's autobiographies. Men's narratives tend to be chronological and linear; women's lives are "much more likely to be tangled than purposeful,"[29]and their narratives tend to be characterized by fragmentation, marginality, and improvisation.[30] Men often follow the "quest plot" of Odysseus—the hero who journeys through overwhelming difficulties to triumph—while women most often follow a "romantic script" in which cultural expectations of marriage and family shape their lives.[31] Women who defied these middle-class norms often portray themselves in autobiographies in romantic terms, as nurturant, peace-loving women with only positive emotions—though in fact they were driven, creative high achievers.[32] Such women have "no script to follow, no story portraying how one is to act, let alone any alternative stories."[33] Further, women who discuss their work and accomplishments often reveal conflicts between the personal and the professional—conflicts seldom expressed by men.

Men tend to write with the voice of authority, while women's narratives often contain understatements and revelations of uncertainty about themselves and their work that undermine their own authority.[34] Men's narratives tend toward self-glorification; women's narratives are more diffident and often are written to prove their self-worth.[35] In what Okeley calls the "Great White Man" tradition, male autobiography is a "celebration of power," in contrast to an autobiography by someone who is marginalized and powerless, which is "a record of questions and of subversion."[36]

The narratives in this volume reveal many struggles with issues of identity and self-worth, instances of subversion—and a shaking off of the romantic script. We hope they provide examples of alternative models for women's lives.

~ *Older Women Anthropologists*

The seventeen women in this volume tell stories of becoming anthropologists in midlife in defiance of dominant cultural models, some at an age when many people are thinking of retirement. Interestingly, unlike most anthropological autobiographies, some authors scarcely mention fieldwork. We (the editors) asked each woman to include her fieldwork experience in her story—and all of us did fieldwork—but some women had other, overriding concerns and barely mention fieldwork. That decision is part of their stories; we did not ask them to change it.

These stories speak for themselves because they are personal. Yet, they are also professional. We are, after all, social scientists. We don't forget our social science when we tell our own stories because anthropology is not something "out there," but something that has entered into our very beings. Anthropology is in our blood and bones. It has become part of our selves; it is our way of life. We cannot see the world and our own lives as separate from what we have learned through doing anthropology and being anthropologists. Our personal stories turn our anthropological gaze upon ourselves as we examine intersections of the private and the public, the personal and the professional.

Collectively, our voices speak to the life experiences of women in twentieth-century North America, to experiences such as being the "trapped housewife,"[37] the "woman in the middle" who is responsible for both dependent children and aging parents,[38] those who are "off time" in critical life events,[39] women in their midlife prime,[40] women who have tasted of the "fountain of age."[41] Most of us followed conventional paths initially, then later in life, and often against daunting odds, made radical shifts in direction. These new directions challenged us, our sense of self-worth and competence, our personhood and identity. They also challenged our families and other relationships, and the institutions, individuals, and ideologies that supported or resisted our efforts. Our narratives are retellings and reinterpretations of our individual lives; simultaneously, they are commentaries, implicit and explicit, on our culture and society. In the broadest sense, our voices speak to the lives of late-blooming women who bring their maturity and creativity to many different enterprises. Our voices come from our need to speak about our lives, to make public the concerns that have previously been expressed only to close friends and family. But they also come from our sense of generativity, our desire to "preserve memories across intergenerational time."[42] We are creating legacies for the generations of women who will encounter both similar and presently unforeseen struggles.

Some call autobiographies fiction because of the unreliability of human memory and the fact that, to produce a comprehensible narrative, autobiographers impose coherence on the disorder of lived experience.[43] The word *fiction* is derived from the Latin *fictiō*, "a shaping." Autobiographies are shaped by selective remembering (and forgetting), the writer's goals and intended audience, and literary conventions. They represent "a complex interplay of language, memory, culture, and the conventions of storytelling. Autobiography is, above all, not experience written down but a *discourse* on original experience."[44]

All that does not necessarily make autobiographies any more factually inaccurate than other memories revealed in letters, journals, or ethnographies.[45] What matters is that autobiographies are about meaning and personal truths, "the truths of our experiences," "the truths of lived experience."[46] It is personal truths that matter here, the personal truths of our lives, and our discourse about them. At the same time, we are looking for shared patterns so we may see the ways our lives reflect the culture in which we grew up and find the shape (or shapes) of our experiences as women—as older women, as women from different class and ethnic backgrounds, as women who became anthropologists in midlife.[47]

~ Becoming Anthropologists ~

This section deals with our becoming anthropologists, including our experiences of growing up and coming of age in mid-twentieth-century Canada and the United States (from about 1920 to 1970) and discussion of what motivated us to pursue a PhD in anthropology in midlife—some of us at an age when many people are beginning to think of retirement. We examine the challenges and obstacles of the race we ran, the support we received along the way, and what becoming anthropologists has meant in our lives.

As noted earlier, for many years the modal PhD recipient in anthropology was young and male, but from about 1930 age began an upward climb and more women earned degrees. In 1973 the modal new PhD was thirty-four years old.[48] By 1988 the modal age had risen to thirty-eight, and the modal new PhD was a white male, married, with no children; in 1990 the mode shifted to a thirty-nine-year-old white female, married, with no children.[49] By the mid-1990s, the statistical composite was a forty-year-old white female in sociocultural anthropology who did her fieldwork in North America.[50] It is interesting to compare the seventeen women in this volume with this profile, though the majority of us earned our PhDs before 1990. Most of us are white (one is African American) and are sociocultural anthropologists (three are archaeologists). Most of us did our dissertation research in North America, though a few went to other parts of the world—Europe, Kenya, Samoa, Togo. Though all of us have been married, some currently are divorced or widowed. We were on the far side of the mode when we received our PhDs, anywhere from age forty-three to sixty. Our modal age was fifty-four. And our modal number of children was four.

Why did we wait so long to go to graduate school? Why did we bother getting a PhD so late in life? And what experiences did we have on that long journey?

~ *Before We Were Anthropologists: Multifaceted Lives*

Before we were anthropologists, we had other lives, multifaceted lives as daughters, wives and mothers, women in the workforce, community volunteers. We are not a representative sample, but many aspects of our lives reflect the sociocultural patterns detailed in the chapter on gender roles. Both cultural patterns and intracultural variation are amply illustrated by our lives.

Most of us were from middle-class backgrounds, with a few from working-class families. We grew up in a variety of religious traditions (Jewish, mainstream Christianity, Mennonite, fundamentalist evangelical, Christian Science, Jehovah's Witness), or in no religious tradition, which had varying impacts on our lives and worldviews. Though most of us more or less accepted and lived by the pervasive mid-twentieth-century gender ideology of the United States and Canada, Barbara

Olsen and Judy Rosenthal were sixties rebels whose lives embodied resistance to the patterns by which the rest of us had (more or less) lived our lives. As an African American, Jean Harris had to cope with racism as well.

Collectively, our childhoods and youth were framed by World War I and the tumultuous 1960s. Ruby Rohrlich and Eunice Boyer were born in 1913 and 1918, respectively, before American women got the vote. They reached young womanhood in the 1930s, during the Great Depression. Others came of age in the postwar 1940s and as part of the 1950s "Silent Generation." All these women married young (some at age eighteen, the rest in their twenties), had children, and became stay-at-home moms. The five women born in the early to mid-1940s experienced their coming-of-age on the cusp of radical changes in gender roles and family life. Three of them followed the old cultural model of marrying young and having children; the other two broke away from that model in 1960s hippie-and-flower-child style and, though they married, never gave birth to children. Barbara Olsen made the painful decision not to have children because she felt they would have interfered with her career (a thought, need it be said, that rarely if ever occurs to men), and Judy Rosenthal adopted three children during her preanthropology wanderings in France and Togo.

We were influenced by powerful role models and mentors within our families: grandparents, fathers, mothers, aunts. Though Jean Harris's "Mama" (her grandfather's sister who raised her) had completed only fifth grade, she made sure Jean completed her school assignments. Maria Cattell and Jane Day recall the father and grandfather who inspired in them a love of words and learning. Maria attended her mother's college graduation some years after Maria had received her own BA. Barbara Olsen's father's tales of Blackfoot Indians (along with the family's subscription to *National Geographic*) opened her mind to different worlds. Judy Rosenthal looks back on her growing-up years in a poor, working-class Jehovah's Witness family as akin to fieldwork; from her father she learned much about animals that came in handy when she was doing her dissertation research in West Africa. In Eunice Boyer's family, many women of the previous generation were college graduates, including her mother who graduated from Wellesley College in 1908 and made reading a central activity in her children's lives, and three aunts who became teachers and a librarian. Eunice was surprised to learn, later in life, that not all families thought women should be well educated.

For the majority of us from middle-class backgrounds, the idea of a woman going to college—at least long enough to find a husband—was acceptable. While a few married right out of high school, others finished a year or two of college or earned a degree before marrying. Eleven of us earned bachelor's degrees right out of high school (though Ruby Rohrlich was twenty-seven because her high school career was delayed). In those days, going to college was insurance in case something happened to your husband and you had to support yourself.

For most of us, anthropology was not part of the picture. Some of us had never even heard of it! We majored in humanities (English literature, history) and social sciences (economics, sociology), except for Marjorie Schweitzer, who majored in anthropology; and Marilyn Rose, who—in defiance of the expectations of her Mennonite community—wanted to have a career before she married and chose chemistry in order to become a medical technician. Marilyn's career was brief, however, and she spent twenty years in her next career as homemaker. Six women were in their thirties and forties when they earned their bachelor's degrees, four because they had decided to go for a PhD in anthropology and had to earn a BA first, the other two—with no notion of entering graduate study at the time—simply for the love of learning.

For those from working-class families, attitudes and expectations about going to college varied. Jean Harris's Mama encouraged Jean in her educational ambitions way past the point where Mama's own experience was helpful. Inspired by a high school teacher, Barbara Olsen defied her parents' expectation of her becoming a secretary and went to college instead. Judy Rosenthal took college courses out of love for learning, not with a career in mind. When she finally got to graduate school, she struggled with feelings of being out of place in what she perceived to be a privileged environment (in time she realized many other graduate students came from working-class families). Jacqueline Walden's parents, immigrants from Sicily, gave their children the dream of college but did not know how to help Jackie when she floundered as a Radcliffe freshman.

The mid-twentieth-century gender ideology in North America "allowed" middle-class women to be in the workforce until they married, or even after marriage until they had children. But with the arrival of a child, a middle-class woman was expected to retire from employment and devote herself to being mother, homemaker, and supporter of her husband in his work. Many of us did just that. Homemaking and childcare were not valued as work—though I doubt any of us who raised children and managed a home would agree with the idea that it was not work! Several of us explicitly state in our narratives that we regard homemaking and childrearing as our first *careers*—an attitude strengthened by our later anthropological understandings about the fundamental importance of childrearing in social reproduction.

Almost all of us feel that we spent too many years as stay-at-home moms, even if we were also taking college classes or doing volunteer or part-time work. We worked in a diversity of positions: archaeological consultant, bookstore owner, literary agent, mental health worker, medical technologist, office manager, personnel officer, propaganda analyst, secretary, social worker, speech pathologist, teacher. Eunice Boyer's "part-time" teaching job was actually full time; and Jean Harris, like many black women she knew, always combined motherhood with her career in social work, personnel, and office administration. For most of us, our ideas about what we wanted to do unfolded as our children went to school or a marriage ended, or in Cath Oberholtzer's case, when her husband lost his job. Louana Lackey tried her hand at a number of occupations in the restaurant and remodeling businesses and a few other things before settling into being a potter and elementary school art teacher. And Barbara Olsen, the only one of us without a child, owned a successful advertising agency.

~ *Why Did We Do It? We Came with Attitude*

Why did we shift from homemaking and assorted employment to the long, arduous journey to a PhD? And why did we choose anthropology over other possibilities?

Our attraction to anthropology and our motivations to pursue a PhD arose from many sources, some going back to our childhoods, others resulting from recent experiences and events. Some of us had a moment of enlightenment; others came more slowly to the realization that anthropology and graduate school were the way we wanted to go.

What we shared was attitude, an attitude commingled of curiosity and love of learning, tremendous determination, an optimistic outlook, a spirit of independence and adventurousness, a willingness to take risks and rebel against social and cultural expectations. We were dissatisfied with our lives as they were and wanted to do something for ourselves—for most of us, after many years of doing things for everyone else. We were (and are) hard workers and good managers. We had to be, or we couldn't have done it. Being older, which has in many ways worked against us, also gave us the advantages of experience and a strong sense of ourselves—though that sense of self was challenged and transformed by our pursuit of advanced degrees.

~ *Why Anthropology? The Ethnographic "I"*

When did the "ethnographic I" begin, asks Judy Rosenthal, "those anthropologizing eyes and ears and all the other ethnographic body parts and sites of desire and research in the mind?" Many of us were fascinated from a very early age by other people, times, and places. We were drawn to Others we met in books, in our local communities, through travel. We loved stories about children different from ourselves and experienced new worlds through *National Geographic* and books about exploration, geography, history, mythology, and travel. We did not label these interests as anthropological because we didn't know the word.

We also had our own experiences of being the Other. All of us know about the otherness of being female in a culture in which male is the norm.[51] As a girl longing to go to high school, Ruby Rohrlich felt herself acutely othered by gender discrimination when her brother (head of the family because their father was dead) did not allow her to complete high school. Ruby knew that had she been a boy, she would have finished high school. Like Ruby, we knew the cultural "rules" and most of us followed them—we got married, had children, and maintained the home base for our "working" husbands, though being "just a housewife" was not considered work and gained us neither money nor respect. Often we had little realization of the extent of the inequities we experienced because of our gender. Inequities were not necessarily perceived as inequities, just differences between girls and boys, women and men. The way things were. Such is the power of cultural ideologies.

All of us know, too, the otherness of being perceived as old, and thereby devalued, sometimes when we were only in our thirties or forties. The sixties slogan "Never trust anyone over 30" caught most of us on the far side of thirty. Even today the emphasis on youth and the denigration of age in American culture are strong, perhaps stronger than ever. Ageism is real, age discrimination in the workplace is real, and many of us experienced it both before and after receiving our PhDs.

Our experiences as the Other also came from other identities: Maria Cattell, from an urban, educated background, among barely literate Pennsylvania Dutch farmers; Barbara Olsen, a kid from a poor family among better-off neighbors and a white woman among Jamaicans; and Jean Harris, a black woman in a white world—all Others. Elizabeth Hoobler, Marilyn Rose, and Judy Rosenthal grew up in "outsider" Christian traditions: Christian Science, Mennonite, Jehovah's Witness. Being the Other can be a powerful motivation to study differences and otherness. Eventually, anthropology, and particularly feminist anthropology, opened us to a way of understanding these aspects of our own lives, so that our anthropology has been an exercise in self-understanding as well as a way of understanding others.

Some of us think we must have been born anthropologists, even though it took us a long time to discover anthropology as a formal discipline. Retrospectively, Maria Cattell and Judy Rosenthal see themselves as engaging in participant observation in childhood and youth. Esther Skirboll discovered anthropology and archaeology as a child in art classes at the Carnegie Museum. By the time she was eighteen, Cath Oberholtzer had strong interests in archaeology, other cultures, and the history of languages, though it was many years until a lecture enabled her to identify those interests as anthropological.

Only a few of us found anthropology as youthful undergraduates. Ruby Rohrlich and Marjorie Schweitzer "fell in love" midway through college, Ruby while studying with Adamson Hoebel, Marjorie in an instant from reading the description of anthropology in a college publication. Ruby, then a junior, completed her major in English literature and became an elementary school teacher and speech pathologist. But Marjorie majored in anthropology as an undergraduate and went on to a master's in the field, though marriage and motherhood then delayed further pursuit of anthropology. Barbara Olsen became fascinated with anthropology in an undergraduate course taught by Joan Campbell but was put off from a career in the field because it seemed a choice for wealthy dilettantes, not the daughter of factory workers. Judy Rosenthal took various anthropology courses in Paris but dismissed anthropology as an imperialist project in the system she spent so many years rejecting as a sixties rebel.

The rest of us came to anthropology later—or much later!—in various ways. Contacts with people from other cultures sparked interest in some of us. Dorothy Castille's interest in anthropology developed as a result of her contacts with Asian women who married American military men. When her husband's job took Elizabeth Hoobler to New Mexico, she began reading about Southwest Indian and Hispanic cultures in her new home region. A trip to Mexico when she was twenty inspired an abiding interest in Mayan archaeology and mythology in Molly Schuchat. Both Jane Day and Jacqueline Walden were strongly influenced by their work as museum volunteers. Her work as a potter led Louana Lackey to an interest in archaeology.

By various means and at different times of life we all came to anthropology. But why did we decide to go for a PhD in midlife?

~ *Why the PhD? Motivations and Triggering Events*

For some of us, the move toward entering doctoral programs was a long process; for others, there were triggering events in careers or family structures.

It took the urging of academic mentors for Maria Cattell and Ellen Holmes to enroll in a graduate program. For Barbara Olsen, a successful advertising agency owner, a nightmarish dream that she had reached age sixty-five without getting her doctorate inspired her to enroll in a doctoral program that same day. Judy Rosenthal, loving anthropology but ambivalent about getting a doctorate in it, was pushed into it by three Togolese Vodu women who demanded that she write a book about them. The sudden death of Molly Schuchat's father reminded her of her own mortality and opened a desire to establish herself in some field.

Some were spurred into entering PhD programs by the disdain of others or the need to expand their knowledge and get credentials to continue on their paths. Eunice Boyer was stung by the lack of respect from new faculty members with PhDs coming to the college where she had taught for many years. Louana Lackey made some comments about archaeologists' lack of knowledge about making pottery to an archaeologist, whose response was, "What do you know about it? You're not an archaeologist." True—but Louana was a potter. She knew what she was talking about. But in order to be heard, she had to get her PhD. Both women look upon their PhDs as "union cards." Dorothy Castille's determination to get a doctorate was reinforced by the derision of a Berkeley professor who laughed at her desire to enter graduate school and said, "You are a military wife with four children; what do you need with a PhD?"

For many, the timing was related to a woman's family situation, though ideas about where in the family cycle one might enter graduate school varied. For Molly Schuchat, the time came immediately after the birth of her fifth child. More commonly, the right time came when children were in school. For Jean Harris, who had long planned to go to graduate school, the time came when her older daughter left college and her younger daughter entered high school. Elizabeth Hoobler's MA in anthropology did not satisfy her sense of needing to be a "true" anthropologist, so with her children grown and her marriage ended by divorce, she enrolled in a PhD program.

~ *Challenges and Support along the Way*

Of course there were challenges and obstacles: the usual academic ones, and some resulting from our being older women with family responsibilities and from the ageism, racism, and sexism that were (and still are) manifested in attitudes and behavior in many places, even in our own families and among academics. The support we received from family members, mentors, and others was important to our ultimate success.

Just getting into graduate school was traumatic for a few of us. Some experienced dismissal as being "just a housewife" or were advised to be a volunteer and enjoy social life. Today such remarks would be actionable as gender discrimination. Then, you had to fight for yourself. Jane Day was initially refused admission into the PhD program at the University of Colorado because she was an older woman. It was only after she invoked the support of several prominent archaeologists that she was admitted. Elizabeth Hoobler and Ruby Rohrlich delayed even applying because of reluctant husbands who thought their own needs should come first.

Attending classes brought more challenges. Unwilling or unable to uproot our families, a number of us commuted (up to two hundred miles one way) on a daily or weekly basis. Financing our education—and sometimes our children's educations simultaneously—was a concern for most of us. Given our family needs, even generous fellowships or student loans, which were designed for the needs of a single person, were not sufficient. Some got financial help from husbands or other family members, and most of us were employed during our graduate school years.

Nearly all of us had dependent children at home—before daycare and after-school programs had become common. We struggled constantly to balance family responsibilities, the job requirements nearly all of us had, and the academic demands of studying and writing papers. Usually we juggled things pretty well, though often we felt rushed, distracted from everything, pulled in several directions at once. At times we felt we were doing nothing well. Papers were thought out amid household duties. First drafts often had to be final versions. Sometimes family responsibilities intervened more forcefully with academic responsibilities, as when Ellen Holmes had to withdraw midterm of one semester because of problems with her daughter.

Fortunately, most of us had family support from husbands, children, parents, and even in-laws, though Cath Oberholtzer's mother was so opposed to Cath's graduate studies that she never acknowledged her daughter's accomplishments. Over time, many husbands, whose ambitions had long been supported by their wives, grew into new roles as supporters of their wives' ambitions, though two never adjusted and even delayed their wives' efforts—and those marriages eventually failed. Cath Oberholtzer's husband, unemployable after losing his job, took over management of the home and children while Cath spent the week at her university in another city. Louana Lackey's husband (obviously an angel) typed all her papers and even her dissertation! Two ex-husbands helped relieve overextended student mothers of some responsibilities. Ellen Holmes, whose family was geographically distant, had a network of friends in her community who helped with childcare. Ellen also took a reduced course load in order to have more time for her daughters.

Our experiences in the graduate school environment varied widely. Most of us had supportive faculty who welcomed us into their programs, took us seriously, and were good advisors and mentors. Some professors were uncomfortable with students older than themselves; about half of us had to deal with faculty who were actively unsupportive, who made it clear that they regarded older women as "superannuated" or "retreads," "just housewives" who could not possibly be serious students and should not be in graduate school. Judy Rosenthal (who had many wonderful mentors) was treated with contempt by one professor who kicked her out of his class—though she was exceptionally well qualified to be in it. Unsurprisingly, this added to her doubts about whether a woman from a working-class family, whose parents had not even graduated from high school, belonged at Cornell. Esther Skirboll had little encouragement from faculty and found that women were not allowed to be teaching assistants in archaeology at her school; she had to settle for assisting in anthropology courses. Fellow students were hostile in some cases and friendly in others, but most of us were unable to participate much, if at all, in student social life since we had full—and more than full!—lives beyond academe.

When it came to fieldwork, in addition to the usual challenges, some of us had further challenges arising from our family situations. Dorothy Castille arranged for her ex-husband to take their sons while she went off alone to Chiapas, Mexico, shortly before the beginning of the Zapatista rebellion. Elizabeth Hoobler, longing to do research outside the United States, did it in New Mexico because she was caring for her mother, who had Alzheimer's disease. A few resolved their problems by taking family with them to the field, including Marjorie Schweitzer, who took her children to a field site thirty-three miles from home, and Jane Day, who took her husband and youngest daughter to Costa Rica as her field team. Cath Oberholtzer, her children grown, took her husband with her on visits to European museums. Molly Schuchat left her children in good hands to go alone to Hungary, but cut her research short by two weeks because she missed her family.

Though a number of us felt devalued by graduate school faculty, "older woman" turned out to be an advantageous fieldwork identity when age and experience were valued by those among whom we were working.[52] The most dramatic instance was that of Jane Day, who gained access to her site because she was a mature woman, while others (younger people, males) had been refused by the site's owner. Others found that "older woman" fit into a local cultural category that brought respect and facilitated rapport with either a broad range or a particular category of individuals, thus giving us easier access to desired information.

Somehow we all completed our dissertations! Successfully defending them gave us the last laugh over our detractors, if we wanted it. More important, though, the day of being hooded as new PhDs and being inducted into the "community of scholars" marked a commencement, a beginning. Where did we go from those beginnings?

~ Being Anthropologists ~

After overcoming all the obstacles and challenges to *becoming* anthropologists, how have we fared? What sort of careers have we had? What contributions have we made to our field?

This is not an attempt to put a comparative value on our careers. To do so would be problematic, since there are few objective measurements for that purpose, and such measures would scarcely capture the complexity and richness of an anthropological career. All of us have had active careers—much like the careers of other anthropologists—composed of teaching, ongoing research, publications, conference presentations, guest lectures, and organizational involvements. And like any random collection of anthropologists, some of us are well known in our fields while others are sturdy and equally important workers in the vineyard.

~ *Our Contributions to Anthropology*

Given the patriarchal origins of anthropology (and academia), it is not surprising that the academic ideology of success focuses on an objective indicator—publications.[53] Male anthropologists outpublish female anthropologists,[54] a gender difference replicated in the sciences regardless of family situation, professional status, and other factors.[55] Some of us have many publications, some few, but among us we have published twenty books and numerous articles and book chapters. Most of us have made many presentations at professional meetings. About a third of us have been active in professional organizations, serving as officers and on boards and in other ways. Several have been contributing editors to *Anthropology News* (*AN*), Molly Schuchat served a three-year term as *AN* editor-in-chief, and Maria Cattell has served for a number of years on the Program Committee of the American Anthropological Association.

All of us have taught, some for only a few years, others for fifteen or more years—and five achieved the rank of full professor. Only Eunice Boyer hit the thirty-year mark, though some who are still teaching may equal Eunice's record. Many of Judy Rosenthal's students have told her that her teaching has made a big difference in their lives.

As we were pioneers in undertaking graduate studies in midlife, so many of us have been pioneers in our research and teaching. Jean Harris and Judy Rosenthal were among the early researchers on Africans in the diaspora. Barbara Olsen has brought together two seemingly disparate careers in marketing and anthropology, teaching anthropology in a marketing department and continuing her research on American consumer culture and the symbolic dimensions of midlife women's brand relationships.

Perhaps not surprisingly, two-thirds of us have done research on age and/or gender. Ruby Rohrlich taught the first women's studies course in the United States and edited one of the first anthologies on the status and roles of women, *Women Cross-Culturally: Change and Challenge.*[56] Marilyn Rose and Marjorie Schweitzer were among the first to develop courses on women cross-culturally. About half of us turned to gerontological research in the early days of anthropological interest in aging, among them Eunice Boyer, who did her research on the residents of public housing for older persons in Milwaukee; and Ellen Holmes, who developed the gerontology program at Wichita State University and wrote (with her husband as coauthor) a major text, *Other Cultures, Elder Years.*[57] Research on retirement was cutting edge when Elizabeth Hoobler took that path. Maria Cattell was among the first anthropologists to do research on aging in sub-Saharan Africa. Dorothy Castille's life experiences have led her to advocate for "reentry women," and Esther Skirboll, an archaeologist, is carrying out ongoing research on women's retirement.

We have contributed in various ways to others' lives through education, advocacy, and political participation and by being role models. Jane Day's dissertation research led to the cataloging and photographing of two thousand ceramic vessels from Costa Rican prehistory and the creation of a small museum for archaeological artifacts on the farm in Costa Rica where she did her research. Esther Skirboll's experiences of gender discrimination led her to feminist activism at her school, Slippery Rock University, and in the entire Pennsylvania State System of Higher Education with its fourteen universities (of which Slippery Rock is one) and 106,000 students. Some have been active in their local communities, giving seminars on menopause (Jacqueline Walden) and aging (Marilyn Rose), doing counseling and educational consulting (Molly Schuchat), and serving as a county supervisor (Eunice Boyer). Reconstructing James Bay Cree social history from material objects led to Cath Oberholtzer's use of images of Cree artifacts to make a CD-ROM and a miniexhibition of one hundred objects on a Cree website. Louana Lackey participated in the Potomac River Archaeology Survey for nearly two decades, and Barbara Olsen uses her long-term research in Negril, Jamaica, to be an advocate for Jamaicans.

We are likely to have shorter careers—though not necessarily, if we follow Ruth Underhill's example. She received her PhD at the age of fifty-two—following a twenty-year career in social work—and went on to a fifty-year career in anthropology.[58] Staying active in retirement is a way to extend the career beyond formal employment. Some of us have retired from one thing or another—teaching or other positions, or just from the struggle to get a permanent position—but we continue to be active professionally. We seem to agree with Louana Lackey's sentiment: "I don't think I will ever have time to retire."

~ Being Role Models

From a feminist perspective, there is another value to our careers, a value less easily identifiable, and indeed, often not knowable: we can be role models within our families, for our daughters and granddaughters, students, and other women, sometimes women we barely know. Marilyn Rose's five daughters all became professionals—though surely without having to overcome the parental reluctance or cultural disapproval that Marilyn contended with! Jane Day considers the model our lives offer in the context of recent trends in American marital and family life. Could it be, Jane wonders, that a cultural pattern of a midlife career change is one viable option in a world where full-time mothers are becoming increasingly rare but are perhaps still needed? Jean Harris points out that, like many black women, she never had the luxury of being a stay-at-home mom but was always in paid employment. Most of us, however, as middle-class white women, had careers as full-time mothers for at least three or five years, even up to twenty years. Yet we were able to make the midlife switch to undergraduate or graduate school and, having acquired our PhDs, go on to anthropological careers.

Indeed, there are indications that Americans are in the process of experimenting with the notion of career changes and timing. Nontraditional students have been in the majority in postsecondary institutions for thirty years. Aging baby boomers are making radical career shifts in early midlife or retooling for new careers at retirement.[59] Questions arise. Is the competitive high-achiever professional career, modeled on the male pattern of "onward and upward" without deviation, the best thing for women—or indeed for anyone? Is it best for families and children? As Sylvia Ann Hewlett points out, there is no gender equity when the way is open for women to succeed in high-powered careers only by forgoing marriage and children in favor of career—choices men are rarely if ever faced with.[60] Is it perhaps not so bad, really, to start a career when you are in your forties or fifties? Is it perhaps even a good thing, especially for children and families—and even for the late-starting career aspirant, if our youth-crazy culture could shift its perceptions of aging and older persons?

~ Was It Worth It?

On the most personal level, was it worth it? Our collective response to this question is: YES! In American Anthropological Association surveys, about 85 percent of all respondents say yes, they would do it all again.[61] Two of us expressed some ambivalence, but even those with reservations do not regret their graduate studies, especially as the negative emotional aspects of their experiences have moved further into the past. As Jean Harris says, "Anthropology provides us with tools to understand ourselves and Others. Despite the pain, I have met both goals." Elizabeth Hoobler, angry and depressed about not being able to do the research she wanted to do (because she was caring for her mother) and frustrated by other aspects of her graduate program, did not even attend her graduation.

But later she came to appreciate the "priceless background" of knowledge and understanding she had acquired.

~ *The Personal Rewards: Identity and Meaning*

We all agree with Jane Day: "The years of a PhD experience change your life forever." The process of becoming anthropologists brought us the magic of new knowledge, widened our horizons, gave us new understandings, refocused our way of seeing, reshaped our worldview. We learned new tools for understanding others and ourselves, and for understanding the gender and age issues that have shaped our lives, even as societal attitudes have changed radically during our lifetimes. When we finished our dissertations and received our degrees, we felt a sense of accomplishment and fulfillment.

Since then, being anthropologists has brought us the pleasures of academic recognition and respect, new friends and colleagues, opportunities to travel. For many, there has also been an enriched family life as husbands pitched in and children got a new perspective on their mothers. Anthropology has brought new and wonderful meanings into our lives and has made our lives more interesting and exciting. We know the satisfaction of contributing to scholarly knowledge and our students' lives, our research communities, and our home communities. As Jackie Walden expresses it, "The wide lens of anthropology makes me feel at home"—at home in a world much wider and more complex than once we could have imagined.

In order to get a PhD, each of us gave up various things from our pre–graduate school days, such as aspects of our social life, time with our significant others (including children), a marriage. In a sense, we also gave up our old selves on the forge of change, as we were shaped into an expanded sense of personhood and a new identity, an identity melded into our inmost being. Before getting our PhDs, some of us had other careers, and some of us had felt the putdown of being regarded as "just housewives" or "housewives with hobbies." Whatever we were before, now we can all say with Cath Oberholtzer, we are "anthropologists with a passion." Becoming and being anthropologists has been transformative and empowering.

And there is no going back, no returning our anthropological identities. One of us, at the beginning of graduate school, said, "I can always go back to being a secretary, but I'll do anthropology as long as I enjoy it." Later she realized she hadn't got it right. She could give up doing anthropology (though she never has), but she cannot give up *being* an anthropologist. Being an anthropologist is in your blood and bones, in your breath and vision, in every fiber of your self. It is both a way of life and a way of being—no matter when you start.

~ Endnotes ~

1. See Babcock and Parezo (1988), Hare (1985), Lurie (1999), Parezo (1993a), Reyman (1992), Rohde (2004).
2. Of course, paying attention to gender has had profound impacts on theory and ethnography, e.g., di Leonardo (1991), Lugo and Maurer (2000), Moore (1988).

3. Lamphere (2004).
4. Bernstein (2002:557).
5. Givens and Jablonski (1995).
6. Traditional students are defined as earning a high school diploma, enrolling in the year of high school graduation as a full-time student in a postsecondary institution, depending on parents for financial support, and being employed part time or not at all during the school year. Nontraditional students are defined by any of these characteristics: does not have a high school diploma, delays postsecondary enrollment, attends a postsecondary institution part time, is employed full time, is financially independent, is a single parent, has dependents other than spouse. In 1999–2000, 28 percent of all undergraduates were "moderately nontraditional" (with two or three of these characteristics), 28 percent were "highly nontraditional" (had four or more of the characteristics), and 39 percent of all postsecondary students were age twenty-five or over (National Center for Education Statistics 2002).
7. Hales (1696), quoted in *The Compact Oxford English Dictionary* (1971).
8. Langness and Frank (1981:18) identify the publication in 1926 of Paul Radin's *Crashing Thunder* as marking the beginning of "truly rigorous work in the field of biography by professional anthropologists." In sociology, the landmark publication was Thomas and Znaniecki's five-volume *The Polish Peasant in Europe and America*. Historians have long relied on biography as a way to portray an era. Biography and autobiography are popular literary genres, and life-story narratives are used in gerontology for both research and clinical practice (e.g., Kenyon et al. 2001).
9. Shostak (1981).
10. Myerhoff (1974).
11. Myerhoff (1979).
12. Behar (2003:xv).
13. For example, Boris and Chaudhuri (1999), Freedman and Frey (2003a), Gornick (1990), Riley (1988), Warren (2000). Half a century ago June Helm (1996:ix) warned that anthropologists "cannot ignore the nature of the actors—his professional ancestors, his peers, and himself—who create his system of action [i.e., anthropology]." (Note that Helm, a woman, uses the male pronoun, the usual style in the 1960s—changed today in most writing.)
14. See Babcock and Parezo (1988), Claassen (1994), Cole (2003), Darnell (2001), Engelke (2004), Gacs et al. (1988), Handler (2000, 2004), Hare (1985), Harrison and Harrison (1999), Lamphere (2004), Lepowsky (2000), Lurie (1999), Parezo (1993a).
15. Behar (1995:8).
16. Parezo (1993b:30).
17. Behar (1995:6).
18. Gottlieb (1995).
19. Callaway (1992).
20. For example, Alverson (1987), Fernea (1965 inter alia), Myerson (1990), Turner (1987). Some wives eventually developed their own careers (e.g., Engelke 2004; Firth 1972; Tedlock 1995).
21. A few examples: Cassell (1987), Cesara (1982), de Laguna (1977), Golde (1970), Lewin and Leap (1996), Morris (1931, 1933), Nordstrom and Robben (1995), Raybeck (1996), Read (1965, 1986), Whitehead and Conaway (1986). Laura Bohannan (1964) published her fieldwork memoir as a novel (under the pseudonym Elenore Smith Bowen)

because she feared that a "popular" account would have earned her only demerits in the professional world.

22. For example, Dunham (1944), Hurston (1942), Laird (1975), Mead (1984), Powdermaker (1966), Schrire (1995). Bateson's (1984) story of the lives of her parents, Gregory Bateson and Margaret Mead, is as much autobiography as biography.
23. Parezo (1993b:4).
24. Dumont (1978:8) says women, who were needed to collect information on women and children, were "left with the task of conjuring the impurities of experience. They had to cope with the blood, sweat and tears aspect of fieldwork—feelings and sentiments included—while the men were exclusively doing 'the real thing.'" Cf. Lurie (1999) and Tedlock (1995).
25. Joyce (1994:53).
26. Lutz (1990).
27. An example of apparently self-chosen self-erasure is *In Sorcery's Shadow*, researched and written by a husband-wife team (Stoller and Olkes 1987), as acknowledged in their book, but the account is in the first-person masculine (see Tedlock 1995; cf. Gottlieb and Graham 1994).
28. For example, Behar (1993), Behar and Gordon (1995), Narayan (1995)—and many more!
29. Cameron and Dickin (1997:9), quoted in Cole (2003).
30. Bateson (1989), Jelinek (1980).
31. Conway (1998), Heilbrun (1988).
32. Conway (1992), Jelinek (1980).
33. Heilbrun (1988:39).
34. Tedlock (1995).
35. Jelinek (1986), Tedlock (1995).
36. Okely (1992:7).
37. Friedan (1963).
38. Brody (2004).
39. Nydegger (1986).
40. Kerns and Brown (1992).
41. Friedan (1993).
42. Schachter (1996:305).
43. For example, historian Jill Ker Conway (1992:vii) says that "autobiographies are fictions" in that they impose some degree of order on the unruliness of life—though they are not fictions in that they are accounts of real lives. Psychologist Michael Gazzaniga (1998:2) makes the dramatic claim that "[b]iography is fiction. (Auto)biography is hopelessly inventive"—a view on the far end of the spectrum of truth/fiction-in-autobiography, rising from considerations of how memory works and the ways individuals rethink and reinvent their lives as they remember them (cf. Cattell and Climo 2002:16–17; Schachter 1995, 1996). The postmodernist critique of cultural representation, kicked off by the publication of *Writing Culture* (Clifford and Marcus 1986), has raised the issue whether ethnographies are, in some sense, fictions. Such concerns do not mean that autobiographies and ethnographies have no truth value; rather, they are reminders to be sensitive to different kinds of truth and critically attentive to different ways of truth telling.
44. Ray (1998:118), emphasis in original.

45. Ethnographies are included in this list because anthropological fieldwork depends so heavily on memory, the memories of those among whom we do our research and our own memories as expressed in both field notes and "head notes," those notes written only in memory—because we could not possibly write everything on paper—that are invaluable in analyzing, organizing, and writing up our data (Ottenberg 1990). Okely (1992:16–17) expands this notion to include the totality of "embodied knowledge," the many things we learn in fieldwork through all our senses and through movement, as in dancing or doing manual labor. Indeed, says she, our written field notes may function primarily as a trigger for "bodily and hitherto subconscious memories."
46. Personal Narratives Group (1989:261) and Ward (1998:xiv).
47. Reed-Danahay (1997) calls an autobiography that places the self within a social context *autoethnography* in order to emphasize the connections between individual and society. The social context may include the self in relation to ethnicity, place, religion, academic discipline, gender, age, and other factors (cf. Freedman and Frey 2003b:18). Autoethnography has been variously defined, some definitions being fairly restricted, Reed-Danahay's offering a wide umbrella. Indeed, the abundance of labels and hairsplitting definitions for personal narratives (e.g., Denzin 1989) is astounding.
48. Givens and Jablonski (1995).
49. *Anthropology News* (1991)
50. Givens and Jablonski (1995). Why this dramatic shift, which is not mirrored in other disciplines? Because women were seen as necessary to anthropological research, anthropology was widely perceived as "the welcoming [to women and others] science" (Parezo 1993b; also Note 21). Many women became active but, as elsewhere in academe, were largely excluded from the formal recognition of jobs, especially higher-level jobs, and publications (cf. Hornig 2003; Martin 2000; Rossiter 1982, 1995). It is likely that, as views of women's roles changed, anthropology's "welcoming" reputation and the presence of so many active but hidden scholars contributed to this shift (Parezo 1993c).
51. Chafetz (1978:115).
52. Cf. Mead (1970), Wax (1986).
53. Roveland and Levine (1996).
54. Bradley and Dahl (1993).
55. Cole and Zuckerman (1987).
56. Rohrlich-Leavitt (1975).
57. Holmes and Holmes (1995).
58. Babcock and Parezo (1988:73).
59. Bauer-Maglin and Radosh (2003), Harkness (1999).
60. Hewlett (2002).
61. For example, Givens and Jablonski (1995), Evans et al. (1997).

~ References ~

Alverson, Marianne. 1987. *Under African Sun*. Chicago: Univ. of Chicago Press.

Anthropology News. 1991. 1990 PhD Survey Results. *Anthropology News* 32 (5): 1, 44.

Babcock, Barbara A., and Nancy J. Parezo. 1988. *Daughters of the Desert: Women Anthropologists and the Native American Southwest, 1880–1980: An Illustrated Catalogue*. Albuquerque: Univ. of New Mexico Press.

Bateson, Mary Catherine. 1984. *With a Daughter's Eye: A Memoir of Margaret Mead and Gregory Bateson.* New York: William Morrow.

———. 1989. *Composing a Life.* New York: Plume.

Bauer-Maglin, Nan, and Alice Radosh, eds. 2003. *Women Confronting Retirement: A Nontraditional Guide.* New Brunswick: Rutgers Univ. Press.

Behar, Ruth. 1993. *Translated Woman: Crossing the Border with Esperanza's Story.* Boston: Beacon.

———. 1995. Introduction: Out of Exile. In *Women Writing Culture,* ed. Ruth Behar and Deborah A. Gordon, 1–29. Berkeley: Univ. of California Press.

———. 2003. Foreword. In *Autobiographical Writing across the Disciplines: A Reader,* ed. Diane P. Freedman and Olivia Frey, xiii–xviii. Durham, NC: Duke Univ. Press.

Behar, Ruth, and Deborah A. Gordon. 1995. *Women Writing Culture.* Berkeley: Univ. of California Press.

Bernstein, Jay H. 2002. First Recipients of Anthropological Doctorates in the United States, 1891–1930. *American Anthropologist* 104 (2): 551–64.

Bohannan, Laura [Elenore Smith Bowen, pseud.]. [1954] 1964. *Return to Laughter.* New York: Doubleday.

Boris, Eileen, and Nupur Chaudhuri, eds. 1999. *Voices of Women Historians: The Personal, the Political, the Professional.* Bloomington: Univ. of Indiana Press.

Bradley, Candice, and Ulrika Dahl. 1993. Gender Differences in Careers. *Anthropology News* 34 (7): 35.

Brody, Elaine M. 2004. *Women in the Middle: Their Parent Care Years,* 2nd ed. New York: Springer.

Callaway, Helen. 1992. Ethnography and Experience: Gender Implications in Fieldwork and Texts. In *Anthropology and Autobiography,* ed. Judith Okely and Helen Callaway, 29–49. New York: Routledge.

Cameron, Elspeth, and Janice Dickin, eds. 1997. *Great Dames.* Toronto: Univ. of Toronto Press.

Cassell, Joan, ed. 1987. *Children in the Field: Anthropological Experiences.* Philadelphia: Temple Univ. Press.

Cattell, Maria G., and Jacob J. Climo. 2002. Meaning in Social Memory and History: Anthropological Perspectives. In *Social Memory and History: Anthropological Perspectives,* ed. Jacob J. Climo and Maria G. Cattell, 1–36. Walnut Creek, CA: AltaMira Press.

Cesara, Manda, pseud. [Karla Poewe]. 1982. *Reflections of a Woman Anthropologist: No Hiding Place.* New York: Academic.

Chafetz, Janet Saltzman. 1978. *Masculine, Feminine or Human? An Overview of the Sociology of Gender Roles,* 2nd ed. Itasca, IL: F. E. Peacock Publishers.

Claassen, Cheryl, ed. 1994. *Women in Archaeology.* Philadelphia: Univ. of Pennsylvania Press.

Clifford, James, and George Marcus, eds. 1986. *Writing Culture: The Poetics and Politics of Ethnography.* Berkeley: Univ. of California Press.

Cole, Jonathan R., and Harriet Zuckerman. 1987. Marriage, Motherhood and Research Performance in Science. *Scientific American,* February, 119–25.

Cole, Sally. 2003. *Ruth Landes: A Life in Anthropology.* Lincoln: Univ. of Nebraska Press.

Conway, Jill Ker. 1992. Introduction. In *Written by Herself: Autobiographies of American Women: An Anthology,* ed. Jill Ker Conway, vii–xiii. New York: Vintage.

———. 1998. *When Memory Speaks: Reflections on Autobiography*. New York: Knopf.

Darnell, Regna. 2001. *Invisible Genealogies: A History of Americanist Anthropology*. Lincoln: Univ. of Nebraska Press.

de Laguna, Frederica. 1977. *Voyage to Greenland: A Personal Initiation into Anthropology*. New York: W. W. Norton.

Denzin, Norman K. 1989. *Interpretive Biography*. Newbury Park, CA: Sage.

di Leonardo, Micaela, ed. 1991. *Gender at the Crossroads of Knowledge: Feminist Anthropology in the Postmodern Era*. Berkeley: Univ. of California Press.

Dumont, Jean-Paul. 1978. *The Headman and I*. Austin: Univ. of Texas Press

Dunham, Katherine. [1959] 1994. *A Touch of Innocence: Memoirs of Childhood*. Chicago: Univ. of Chicago Press.

Engelke, Matthew. 2004. "The Endless Conversation": Fieldwork, Writing, and the Marriage of Victor and Edith Turner. In *Significant Others: Interpersonal and Professional Commitments in Anthropology*, ed. Richard Handler, 6–50. Madison: Univ. of Wisconsin Press.

Evans, Patsy, Dave Givens, and Timothy Jablonski. 1997. 1995 Survey of Anthropology PhDs: Quantitative Summary. *Anthropology News* 38 (7): 17–18.

Fernea, Elizabeth Warnock. 1965. *Guests of the Sheik: An Ethnography of an Iraqi Village*. Garden City, NY: Doubleday.

Firth, Rosemary. 1992. From Wife to Anthropologist. In *Crossing Cultural Boundaries: The Anthropological Experience*, ed. Solon T. Kimball and James B. Watson, 10–32. San Francisco: Chandler.

Freedman, Diane P., and Olivia Frey, eds. 2003a. *Autobiographical Writing across the Disciplines: A Reader*. Durham, NC: Duke Univ. Press.

Freedman, Diane P., and Olivia Frey. 2003b. Self/Discipline: An Introduction. In *Autobiographical Writing across the Disciplines: A Reader*, ed. Diane P. Freedman and Olivia Frey, 1–37. Durham, NC: Duke Univ. Press.

Friedan, Betty. 1963. *The Feminine Mystique*. New York: Norton.

———. 1993. *The Fountain of Age*. New York: Simon & Schuster.

Gacs, Ute, Aisha Khan, Jerrie McIntyre, and Ruth Weinberg, eds. 1988. *Women Anthropologists: Selected Biographies*. Chicago: Univ. of Illinois Press.

Gazzaniga, Michael S. 1998. *The Mind's Past*. Berkeley: Univ. of California Press.

Givens, David B., and Timothy Jablonski. 1995. Survey of Anthropology PhDs. *Anthropology News* 36 (6): 11–12.

Golde, Peggy, ed. 1970. *Women in the Field: Anthropological Experiences*. Chicago: Aldine.

Gornick, Vivian. [1983] 1990. *Women in Science: 100 Journeys into the Territory*, revised ed. New York: Simon & Schuster.

Gottlieb, Alma. 1995. Beyond the Lonely Anthropologist: Collaboration in Research and Writing. *American Anthropologist* 97 (1): 21–26.

Gottlieb, Alma, and Philip Graham. 1994. *Parallel Worlds: An Anthropologist and a Writer Encounter Africa*. Chicago: Univ. of Chicago Press.

Handler, Richard, ed. 2000. *Excluded Ancestors, Inventible Traditions: Essays toward a More Inclusive History of Anthropology*. Madison: Univ. of Wisconsin Press.

———. 2004. *Significant Others: Interpersonal and Professional Commitments in Anthropology*. Madison: Univ. of Wisconsin Press.

Hare, Peter. 1985. *A Woman's Quest for Science: Portrait of Anthropologist Elsie Clews Parsons*. New York: Prometheus Books.

Harkness, Helen. 1999. *Don't Stop the Career Clock: Rejecting the Myths of Aging for a New Way to Work in the 21st Century.* Palo Alto, CA: Davies-Black.

Harrison, Ira E., and Faye W. Harrison, eds. 1999. *African-American Pioneers in Anthropology.* Urbana: Univ. of Illinois Press.

Heilbrun, Carolyn. 1988. *Writing a Woman's Life.* New York: Norton.

Helm, June, ed. 1996. *Pioneers of American Anthropology: The Uses of Biography.* Seattle: Univ. of Washington Press.

Hewlett, Sylvia Ann. 2002. *Creating a Life: Professional Women and the Quest for Children.* New York: Talk Miramax Books.

Holmes, Ellen Rhoads, and Lowell D. Holmes. 1995. *Other Cultures, Elder Years,* 2nd ed. Thousand Oaks, CA: Sage.

Hornig, Lilli S. 2003. *Equal Rites, Unequal Outcomes: Women in American Research Universities.* New York: Kluwer Academic/Plenum.

Hurston, Zora Neale. 1942. *Dust Tracks on a Road, an Autobiography.* Philadelphia: J. B. Lippincott.

Jelinek, Estelle C., ed. 1980. *Women's Autobiography: Essays in Criticism.* Bloomington: Indiana Univ. Press.

———. 1986. *The Tradition of Women's Autobiography: From Antiquity to the Present.* Boston: Twayne Publishers.

Joyce, Rosemary A. 1994. Dorothy Hughes Popenoe: Eve in an Archaeological Garden. In *Women in Archaeology,* ed. Cheryl Claassen, 51–66. Philadelphia: Univ. of Pennsylvania Press.

Kenyon, Gary, Phillip Clark, and Brian de Vries, eds. 2001. *Narrative Gerontology: Theory, Research, and Practice.* New York: Springer.

Kerns, Virginia, and Judith K. Brown, eds. 1992. *In Her Prime: New Views of Middle-aged Women,* 2nd ed. Urbana: Univ. of Illinois Press.

Laird, Carobeth. 1975. *Encounter with an Angry God: Recollections of My Life with John Peabody Harrington.* New York: Ballantine Books.

Lamphere, Louise. 2004. Unofficial Histories: A Vision of Anthropology from the Margins. *American Anthropologist* 106 (1): 126–39.

Langness, Lewis, and Gelya Frank. 1981. *Lives: An Anthropological Approach to Biography.* Novato, CA: Chandler & Sharp.

Lepowsky, Maria. 2000. Charlotte Gower and the Subterranean History of Anthropology. In *Excluded Ancestors, Inventible Traditions: Essays toward a More Inclusive History of Anthropology,* ed. Richard Handler, 123–70. Madison: Univ. of Wisconsin Press.

Lewin, Ellen, and William L. Leap, eds. 1996. *Out in the Field: Reflections of Lesbian and Gay Anthropologists.* Urbana: Univ. of Illinois Press.

Lewis, Oscar. 1959. *Five Families: Mexican Case Studies in the Culture of Poverty.* New York: Basic Books.

———. 1961. *The Children of Sanchez: Autobiography of a Mexican Family.* New York: Random House.

Lugo, Alejandro, and Bill Maurer, eds. 2000. *Gender Matters: Rereading Michelle Z. Rosaldo.* Ann Arbor: Univ. of Michigan Press.

Lurie, Nancy Oestreich. [1966] 1999. *Women and the Invention of American Anthropology.* Prospect Heights, IL: Waveland.

Lutz, Catherine. 1990. The Erasure of Women's Writing in Sociocultural Anthropology. *American Ethnologist* 17 (4): 611–27.

Martin, Jane Roland. 2000. *Coming of Age in Academe: Rekindling Women's Hopes and Reforming the Academy*. New York: Routledge.

Mead, Margaret. 1970. Field Work in the Pacific Islands. In *Women in the Field: Anthropological Experiences*, ed. Peggy Golde, 293–331. Chicago: Aldine.

———. 1984. *Blackberry Winter: My Earlier Years*. New York: William Morrow & Co.

Moore, Henrietta. 1988. *Feminism and Anthropology*. Cambridge, MA: Polity Press.

Morris, Ann Axtell. 1931. *Digging in Yucatan*. Garden City, NY: Doubleday.

———. 1933. *Digging in the Southwest*. Garden City, NY: Doubleday.

Myerhoff, Barbara. 1974. *Peyote Hunt: The Sacred Journey of the Huichol Indians*. New York: Cornell Univ. Press.

———. 1979. *Number Our Days*. New York: E. P. Dutton.

Myerson, Julia. 1990. *Tambo: Life in an Andean Village*. Austin: Univ. of Texas Press.

Narayan, Kirin. 1995. Participant Observation. In *Women Writing Culture*, ed. Ruth Behar and Deborah Gordon, 33–48. Berkeley: Univ. of California Press.

National Center for Education Statistics. 2002. *Findings from the Condition of Education 2002: Nontraditional Undergraduates*. http://nces.ed.gov/pubs2002/2002012.pdf (accessed August 28, 2005).

Nordstrom, Carolyn, and Antonius C. G. M. Robben, eds. 1995. *Fieldwork under Fire: Contemporary Studies of Violence and Survival*. Berkeley: Univ. of California Press.

Nydegger, Corinne. 1986. Age and Life-Course Transitions. In *New Methods for Old Age Research*, ed. Christine L. Fry and Jennie Keith, 131–61. South Hadley, MA: Bergin & Garvey.

Okely, Judith. 1992. Anthropology and Autobiography: Participatory Experience and Embodied Knowledge. In *Anthropology and Autobiography*, ed. Judith Okely and Helen Callaway, 1–28. New York: Routledge.

Ottenberg, Simon. 1990. Thirty Years of Fieldnotes: Changing Relationships to the Text. In *Fieldnotes: The Makings of Anthropology*, ed. Roger Sanjek, 139–60. Ithaca, NY: Cornell Univ. Press.

Papanek, Hanna. 1973. Men, Women, and Work: Reflections on the Two-Person Career. *American Journal of Sociology* 78 (4): 858–72.

Parezo, Nancy J., ed. 1993a. *Hidden Scholars: Women Anthropologists and the Native American Southwest*. Albuquerque: Univ. of New Mexico Press.

———. 1993b. Anthropology: The Welcoming Science. In Parezo 1993a: 3–37.

———. 1993c. Conclusion: The Beginning of the Quest. In Parezo 1993a: 334–67.

Personal Narratives Group. 1989. *Interpreting Women's Lives: Feminist Theory and Personal Narratives*. Bloomington: Indiana Univ. Press.

Powdermaker, Hortense. 1966. *Stranger and Friend: The Way of an Anthropologist*. New York: W. W. Norton & Co.

Radin, Paul, ed. 1926. *Crashing Thunder, The Autobiography of an American Indian*. New York: Appleton.

Ray, Ruth E. 1998. Feminist Readings of Older Women's Life Stories. *Journal of Aging Studies* 12 (2): 117–27.

Raybeck, Douglas. 1996. *Mad Dogs, Englishmen, and the Errant Anthropologist: Fieldwork in Malaysia*. Prospect Heights, IL: Waveland.

Read, Kenneth E. 1965. *The High Valley*. New York: Scribner.

———. 1986. *Return to the High Valley: Coming Full Circle*. Berkeley: Univ. of California Press.

Reed-Danahay, Deborah. 1997. Introduction. In *Auto/Ethnography: Rewriting the Self and the Social*, ed. Deborah Reed-Danahay, 1–17. Oxford: Berg.

Reyman, Jonathan E. 1992. Women in American Archaeology: Some Historical Notes and Comments. In *Rediscovering Our Past: Essays on the History of American Archaeology*, ed. Jonathan E. Reyman, 69–80. Aldershot, England: Avebury.

Riley, Matilda White, ed. 1988. *Sociological Lives*. Newbury Park, CA: Sage.

Rohde, Joy Elizabeth. 2004. It Was No "Pink Tea": Gender and American Anthropology, 1885–1903. In *Significant Others: Interpersonal and Professional Commitments in Anthropology*, ed. Richard Handler, 261–88. Madison: Univ. of Wisconsin Press.

Rohrlich-Leavitt, Ruby, ed. 1975. *Women Cross-Culturally: Change and Challenge*. The Hague: Mouton.

Rossiter, Margaret W. 1982. *Women Scientists in America: Struggles and Strategies to 1940*. Baltimore, MD: Johns Hopkins Univ. Press.

———. 1995. *Women Scientists in America: Before Affirmative Action, 1940–1972*. Baltimore, MD: Johns Hopkins Univ. Press.

Roveland, Blythe E., and Mary Ann Levine. 1996. Rites of Passage in a Feminist Archaeology: The Structure and Content of Graduate Education. *Anthropology News* 37 (1): 9.

Schachter, Daniel L., ed. 1995. *Memory Distortion: How Minds, Brains, and Societies Reconstruct the Past*. Cambridge, MA: Harvard Univ. Press.

———. 1996. *Searching for Memory: The Brain, the Mind, and the Past*. New York: Basic Books.

Schrire, Carmel. 1995. *Digging through Darkness: Chronicles of an Archaeologist*. Charlottesville: Univ. of Virginia Press.

Shostak, Marjorie. 1981. *Nisa: The Life and Words of a !Kung Woman*. Cambridge, MA: Harvard Univ. Press.

Stoller, Paul, and Cheryl Olkes. 1987. *In Sorcery's Shadow: A Memoir of Apprenticeship among the Songhay of Niger*. Chicago: Univ. of Chicago Press.

Tedlock, Barbara. 1995. Works and Wives: The Sexual Division of Textual Labor. In *Women Writing Culture*, ed. Ruth Behar and Deborah A. Gordon, 267–86. Berkeley: Univ. of California Press.

Thomas, William I., and Florian Znaniecki. 1918–1920. *The Polish Peasant in Europe and America*. Boston: Richard G. Badger.

Turner, Edith. 1987. *The Spirit and the Drum: A Memoir of Africa*. Tucson: Univ. of Arizona Press.

Ward, Martha C. 1998. *A Sounding of Women: Autobiographies from Unexpected Places*. Needham Heights, MA: Allyn & Bacon.

Warren, Wini. 2000. *Black Women Scientists in the United States*. Bloomington: Indiana Univ. Press.

Wax, Rosalie H. 1986. Gender and Age in Fieldwork and Fieldwork Education: "Not Any Good Thing Is Done by One Man Alone." In *Self, Sex, and Gender in Cross-Cultural Fieldwork*, ed. Tony Larry Whitehead and Mary Ellen Conaway, 129–50. Urbana: Univ. of Illinois Press.

Whitehead, Tony Larry, and Mary Ellen Conaway, eds. 1986. *Self, Sex, and Gender in Cross-Cultural Fieldwork*. Urbana: Univ. of Illinois Press.

Gender Roles in Sociocultural and Historical Context

Marjorie M. Schweitzer

THIS CHAPTER examines the sociocultural norms and historical context that existed in North America from the 1930s forward and some of the changes that occurred during that time. This summary background provides an essential framework for understanding the lives of the authors as they returned to school, did fieldwork, and became professional anthropologists. There are many excellent volumes that describe these years in greater detail.[1] We focus here on events we feel were particularly relevant to the lives narrated in this volume, as well as for women in general.

Historical Context: A Brief Review

The decade prior to World War II was marked overwhelmingly by the Great Depression. To help counteract some of the consequences of the Depression, President Franklin D. Roosevelt engineered several work programs to assist the vast numbers of unemployed, mostly men. In 1935 Congress passed the federal Social Security Act, which created insurance funds for survivors, the elderly, and the unemployed. Women were often the first to be let go as businesses failed. They did what they could to provide for their families, cobbling together various ways to make money: they opened beauty parlors in their homes, took in washing, cleaned houses, and boarded lodgers.[2]

With the official entry of the United States into World War II in December 1941, everything having to do with work changed. Men from all walks of life joined the military, creating an enormous vacuum in factories, particularly in the defense industry. Women on the home front did what they could to help the war effort: they turned in their scrap metal and kitchen grease to be used for war matériel, and they tried to live as frugally as possible.[3] But women did not stay at home. They responded in great numbers to the need for workers in the factories. The Office of War Information recruited women, and the National War Labor Board announced that they must be paid the same wages as men. They took jobs in munitions factories, they built airplanes, and Rosie the Riveter became the poster woman for the war effort. Even today she remains the symbol of women's active and essential contribution in the winning of the war.[4] By 1944 one of every three women defense workers had previously been full-time homemakers; many of them were also mothers.[5]

After many arguments against allowing women in the military, Congress passed a bill in 1942, a few months after Pearl Harbor, to establish the Women's Auxiliary Army Corps (WAAC; later Women's Army Corps, WAC), and soon every branch of the military had a women's unit. At the end of the war, records showed that WACs had served in every theater of operation,[6] and along with women in the other divisions of the military, had handled a wide range of jobs, including flying aircraft.[7] Although the armed forces were reluctant to accept women in their ranks, the manpower shortage changed their minds. Women had become essential to the military war effort.

Women may have been essential workers, but they were not yet equal workers. For example, the air force required women to achieve many more hours of flying time than men to qualify as pilots, women had to be high school graduates while men did not, and women were paid less than men with fewer qualifications and less experience.[8] Typically they could not achieve rank, and even after serving with skill and valor, were denied honors given to their male counterparts. For the thirty-eight women pilots killed in the war, there was no pay for the transport of their bodies, no money for burials, no flags to drape on their coffins, no Gold Star given to their parents.[9] In all branches of the military, women faced outright hostility from some officers and enlisted men. Outside the military, certain politicians and religious leaders also decried their participation.

Black women worked in war plants, in white-collar offices, as volunteers, in the USO, as WACs, and ultimately in the Army Nurse Corps. The segregation that black women endured in their communities continued in the military as they served in a segregated unit. Black women fought three concurrent wars: World War II, the war for the participation of women in the military, and the war against racism. Along with black men, they asked, "Are You for Hitler's Way (Race Supremacy), or the American Way (Equality)?"[10]

After the war, attitudes and conditions changed dramatically again. The men who were fortunate enough to come home from the war wanted and needed jobs. They also wanted to go to college.[11] As a result, women were suddenly and unceremoniously told to stay home. Many women who had worked during the war realized that they either wanted to work or needed to work in order to meet the rising cost of goods and the renewed emphasis on consumerism. However, instead of being asked to work in place of the men who had gone to war, they were told to leave the job for the veteran. They were encouraged to focus on being wives, mothers, and homemakers. Suddenly society frowned upon the notion of women working outside the home as a businessperson or as a professional. Social norms dictated that it was acceptable for young brides to become schoolteachers or nurses or secretaries—but just until the first child was born.[12]

The children born after World War II, between 1946 and 1964, are known as the Baby Boomer Generation. They were largely the children of stay-at-home moms. Particularly in middle-class families, "[m]other vest[ed] all of her pent-up energies and needs on her two or three children, dragging them from one organized activity to another, lavishing attention on their 'progress' like a horticulturist in a hothouse."[13]

No longer held back by the Depression and freed from the drain on production of household goods that occurred during the war, Americans now found themselves in a new era: increased wages accompanied a feeling that it was important to build houses and furnish them and to take advantage of the postwar good times. "Although the 'home of consumption' was firmly entrenched in American culture" by the 1930s, there was added emphasis on consumerism after the war.[14] Women were the focus of this consumer society,[15] and the print media supported the "happy housewife" syndrome.[16] It was her "duty" to be an integral part of a society recovering from war. If a housewife and mother found herself with small qualms of dissatisfaction or feelings of self-doubt with the roles she played, she was encouraged by advertisers to go to the store and buy: what better way to raise her spirits than to buy a new hat, new drapes for the dining room, or new clothes for the dinner she was hosting for her husband's boss.[17]

Of course, during and prior to the mid-twentieth century, many women defied the constraints on women's occupations and professions outside of the home and became writers, physicians, pilots, and even senators.[18] Clearly, though, this was the exception rather than the rule.

In the 1960s America witnessed wide-ranging transformations that affected the position of women and ultimately the lives of their male partners and children. This second wave of the women's movement tackled a host of issues, among them the right to fair treatment at work and at school.[19] These changes were part of a larger cultural upheaval in the 1960s that penetrated all levels and facets of society.

Young people coming of age in the 1960s engaged in a wide-ranging social and political rebellion against the consumer culture of their parents. "The very idea of preparing vigorously for a 60-year career in the suit-and-tie world followed by a few years' retirement, then a terminal illness caused by pollutants, did not appeal at all to quite a number of young Americans."[20] This counterculture movement effectively changed the cultural landscape of the United States.[21]

Against the backdrop of the 1960s cultural upheaval, several events directly affected women. Not the least of these was the approval in 1960 of a contraceptive known simply as the Pill. Although some argue that the Pill was (and is) yet another instance of women being forced to take sole responsibility for reproduction, it did allow women the option of timing their pregnancies or opting out of pregnancy entirely. "For women across the country, the contraceptive pill was liberating: it allowed them to pursue careers, fueled the feminist and pro-choice movements, and encouraged more open attitudes towards sex."[22]

In *The Feminine Mystique* Betty Friedan encouraged women to envision a life beyond the consumer, helpmate, and caregiver roles expected of them in the 1950s. In naming their unspoken and often-unarticulated feelings, Friedan's book awakened in women the possibility that perhaps there was another path they could follow. Women began to think that yes, perhaps they could do something more than worrying about tattletale gray laundry and peanut butter sandwiches.[23] Maybe they could go back to school, get a good job, and still raise a family and be a wife!

There were some feminists in this era of the 1960s who argued, on the other hand, that "the workplace offered women no escape from society's restrictive views,"[24] and it was certainly true that women would encounter sexism in professional life. In 1963 President Kennedy's Commission on the Status of Women called attention to discrimination in employment, unequal pay, continuing legal inequality, and a lack of social services for working mothers. The Equal Pay Act of 1963 became the first law prohibiting discrimination based on sex. This law has been effective in improving employment practices and attitudes, but women's earnings today still lag behind those earned by men.[25] Change in these areas was high on the agenda of the powerful National Organization for Women when it was founded in 1966.

During the same period, black women made critical contributions to the civil rights movement.[26] Racial and gender equality were now linked, and the unique experience of black women recognized. In fact, the word *sex* was added to Title VII of the Civil Rights Bill. When it was finally passed, the Civil Rights Act of 1964 prohibited "employment discrimination on the basis of sex."[27]

The 1970s brought further gains, both sweeping and incremental. The legalization of abortion through the ruling of *Roe v. Wade* in 1973 was perhaps the most radical and controversial of these.[28] It was a major turning point in reproductive rights that also had implications for women's professional lives.

Among the many professional gains women saw in this decade, the effort within universities to integrate women's voices and experiences into traditional—and traditionally male-dominated—academic disciplines is particularly relevant in this volume of narratives by women anthropologists. In 1970 the first women's studies program was established, and by the mid-1970s such programs were being offered at nearly forty universities. By the end of the decade, at least thirty thousand women's studies courses were offered annually at colleges and universities across the nation. *Women's Studies: An Interdisciplinary Journal* and *Feminist Studies*, both launched in 1972, and *Signs: Journal of Women in Culture and Society*, begun in 1975, provided much-needed outlets for the publication of research on women's issues. The new teaching styles and methods that emerged in university courses during this period have been recognized as the most revolutionary in educational innovation.[29]

Further gains were represented by Title IX of the Education Amendments of 1972, which prohibited discrimination on the basis of sex in federally funded education.[30] Although we may hear more in the media about Title IX and its far-reaching influence on sports (both women's and men's), it has had a profound effect on women's involvement in the academic side of higher education. The 1997 report *Title IX at 25: Report Card on Gender Equity* gave Title IX its highest marks for increasing women's access to higher education.[31]

Further gains appeared as black women scholars formed the Association of Black Women Historians in 1979 to encourage research on black women's history and push for the integration of that history into the main history texts. The association also provides important opportunities for black women historians to network and mentor other black women.[32]

The 1980s sent women into space, into corporate boardrooms, and into politics. Other legislative advances included the 1986 Supreme Court ruling against sexual harassment, though it is somewhat sobering to note that it was not until 1998, after a flood of sexual harassment cases in the 1990s, that the Supreme Court clarified contradictory case law concerning sexual harassment in the workplace.[33] It was a decade in which women felt that much had been accomplished, but much remained to be done.

While bias was less blatant in the 1980s, it was still widespread in various forms. For example, gender bias was apparent in the way girls were treated in school, how they were portrayed in textbooks, and whether or not they received the kind of encouragement that would have propelled them into science and math courses with confidence. Other analysts argued that the media—ads, movies, and TV—presented many images that were harmful to both sexes.[34]

While we have presented here a brief summary of the events of the twentieth century, there have been new challenges and rewards for young women in the 1990s and 2000s. We consider some of those issues in the final chapter of this volume.

~ Gender Roles: What Do They Mean? ~

This summary of events that took place in the twentieth century clearly demonstrates how much gender roles can change. In this section we first consider the complexity of culture as we address the nature-nurture debate—the question of biology versus culture in the creation of gender roles; we then describe the gender roles that were prescribed for women and men at mid-twentieth century; and, finally, we evaluate some of the forces that underlaid and supported those gender roles.

People everywhere categorize the many features of their world—material artifacts, ideas, and people. Categorizing is a shorthand that allows us to function in the social world; lumping items into categories makes it possible for us to handle all of the cultural clues that come at us each day in blinding complexity. But lumping also carries with it the danger of reacting to categories of events and/or people in a way that makes individuals invisible. We cannot see the trees for the forest. When we see groups of women or men, we make certain assumptions about them based in part on what we learned while growing up and on our experiences as adults. When we characterize, or stereotype, groups of people and assume that they will behave in a particular way, we are denying them their individuality and often their full potential. Such is the nature of the stereotypes associated with gender roles.

~ *Nature versus Nurture*

The age-old question of whether nature or nurture is the determinant of human behavior is still being evaluated and debated today. Some believe that biology (nature) determines role behavior, while others believe that socialization and enculturation (nurture) provide the more important foundation, overriding almost all of the sex-related characteristics of males and females.

From the nurture viewpoint, Ortner and Whitehead argue that "natural features of gender... [and] of sex and reproduction, furnish only a suggestive and ambiguous backdrop to the cultural organization of gender and sexuality."[35] Chafetz agrees that the more or less well-defined roles of men and women are socially prescribed and not inherent in the sex. They are not, in other words, innate.[36]

Those who attacked the feminist movement in the 1970s, as well as those who continue to argue against role changes today, assume that biology is the basis for gender roles and behavior and thus gender roles cannot and should not be changed. Often people are afraid of change: it threatens their current positions, or they find they are faced with rather fundamental assaults on their beliefs, or they do not have the skills or desire to adapt to new understandings of their world.[37]

Why does this question matter? It matters because when we weigh the evidence provided by anthropology, other social sciences, and the biological sciences, we find overwhelming evidence that behaviors are learned and changeable. We recognize that we are not bound by our gender roles and the stereotypes that have grown up around them. They are just that—stereotypes that have been promoted by and shored up by culture, society, and history.[38]

According to Jonathan Marks, "Ultimately, the fallacy is not a genetic but a cultural one—our reduction of the important things in life to genetics." He criticizes sociobiologists who study "the biological roots of human behavior, whether or not they exist" in the pursuit of an impossible goal, the discovery of something called "human nature." Marks argues that "[t]here is no human nature outside of culture.... Nature and culture act as a synergy. If the human is like a cake, culture is like the eggs, not like the icing—it is an inseparable part, not superficial glaze. Whatever humans do or look like is a product of both."[39]

Suffice it to say, the authors in this volume welcome changes towards a more egalitarian society, one that recognizes the full worth and potential of *all* of its members. We come down strongly on the side of enculturation and socialization as the defining factors in the creation of gender roles. As anthropologists we believe that human beings are malleable and cultures are immensely varied in their expectations for their members. Because there are so many different behavioral prescriptions, we argue that gender roles have more to do with the way people are socialized than with their respective sexes.

There are no easy answers. As we learn more about the brain and the differences that do exist between the sexes, we must conclude that we still do not know *exactly* how biology interacts with social factors and what these differences mean.

Although we cannot provide the final answer on the question of nature versus nurture, we do wish to point out how gender role stereotypes in North America have affected women's lives and to suggest that changes in behavior can be enlightening and rewarding for both females and males. Because of the restrictions inherent in gender role stereotypes, we assert that both men and women can benefit from a broad interpretation of gender roles.

Gender Role Stereotypes and Their Costs

Here we examine gender role stereotypes that existed at mid-twentieth century in order to explore the bases for their existence, the cost of limiting the gender roles of both men and women, and what they bode for present society and future generations.

Chafetz describes the gender role stereotypes for white middle-class and upper-middle-class females and males that were prevalent in the 1960s and 1970s. Adult women were characterized as weak and nonathletic homemakers associated with the domestic, private sphere of life. They were considered sexually inexperienced, but nevertheless were the ones responsible for birth control. They were described as emotional, scatterbrained, and passive followers.[40]

By contrast, adult males were described as virile, strong, and athletic. They were the breadwinners who worked at jobs in the public sphere. They were regarded as sexually aggressive and unemotional and as dominating leaders considered to be intellectual and aggressive in their dealings with others.[41]

Stereotypical expectations and behaviors are learned at an early age, beginning at birth. However, we focus here on the adult role stereotypes prevalent in the socialization of middle-class white men and women at midcentury.

A girl born in the mid-1960s was expected to become a wife eighteen or twenty years later, ensconced in her (hopefully) computerized kitchen, taking care of her children and husband. The socially accepted expectations and restrictions that characterized the late 1940s and the 1950s remained in place: a woman could work as a teacher, secretary, or nurse only until her first baby was born. A boy born in the mid-1960s was expected to become an active participant in the public sphere—building splendid objects, reading significant documents, or lecturing on important topics. They would become the doctors, lawyers, designers, and bosses, while the girls could aspire to being men's helpmates at work as well as at home.[42]

Gender role conformity carries with it costs for both men and women, to say nothing of the dysfunction experienced by members of ethnic and racial groups who may have more important issues than conforming to the dominant stereotypes. Men who conform to gender role stereotypes often have more obligations but fewer proscriptions on what they do. They complain about what they *have* to do. Women, on the other hand, have fewer obligations and more proscriptions. They complain about what they *can't* do. Sanctioning women to be passive and men to be active can create costs that clearly do not enhance the lives of either group.[43] The costs and rewards for both sexes depend in part on whether one abides by the roles that are expected or tries to adopt behavior that is contrary to what the stereotypes dictate.

Midcentury socialization may have prepared girls for the roles of homemaker and caretaker of her husband and children, but it did not prepare her for roles outside of the home. Some women left with an "empty nest" and no alternative role might develop psychological problems. With "no one to take care of" after the last child left home, they lost their primary role and their sense of worth.[44] Women who conformed to the domestic stereotype were handicapped if they were widowed or divorced since they were unprepared for a job or profession.

The Foundations of Midcentury Gender Role Stereotypes

It is not possible to include here all of the factors involved in mid-twentieth-century role stereotypes, but we want to note four important features of society and culture that have permeated the lives of both women and men: 1) religion and the role of the patriarchal church; 2) the legal system and women's rights; 3) the value assigned to domesticity; and 4) language and communication styles.

Patriarchy in the Church

The dominance of patriarchy in religious institutions in the prescription of gender roles is undeniable.[45] In many expressions of the Christian religion, for example, women have been measured against an unattainable model, that of the Virgin Mary and the Virgin Birth. In contrast, patriarchal interpretations of the Christian Bible have held that womankind is evil and the source of all disaster. Thus there have been only two extreme roles for women: the good woman or the bad woman.[46] Procreation within the bonds of marriage has been the only way a woman could avoid being regarded as "dangerous."[47] The "proper woman" was chaste and unassuming, not reckless or sensual.

The division of labor (and all societies have some sort of division of labor) in the United States and other Western societies is related to the patriarchal foundation of the Judeo-Christian religious heritage, and is sometimes characterized as the "public" sphere for men and the "domestic" or "private" sphere for women. According to patriarchal mores, womanly virtue meant silence or a passive expression (or no expression) of personality and behavior that acquiesced to every demand and desire of the men in her life, beginning with her father, and later her husband. Women had few or no roles in the church and were expected to be stay-at-home mothers and wives. The subordination of women as a basic tenet of the church has been slow to change.

Women's Rights

Since early federal documents did not expressly mention women, laws regulating women's lives were left to the states. The legal system in forty-two U.S. states is based on English common law; that of the remaining eight states is based on community property law that originated in continental Europe. In practice, these two systems operate similarly.[48] Common law held that "the legal existence of the woman is suspended during the marriage, or at least is incorporated into that of her husband."[49] Although the Fourteenth Amendment (1865) defined for the first time the terms *citizens* and *voters* as male, both the Fifth and Fourteenth Amendments were supposed to procure "equal protection of the law" to everyone. On more than one occasion, women were excluded.[50] For example, it was not until the second decade of the twentieth century that women, except in isolated cases, gained the right to vote after suffragists protested against the U.S. entry into World War I in 1917, proclaiming that "[d]emocracy should begin at home."[51] Congress finally passed a suffrage bill that went into effect in 1920.

During the first half of the twentieth century, women were denied credit in their own names, and work-related discrimination against women was permissible. Protective legislation regarding how long and when a woman could work was not covered under the due process clause of the Fifth Amendment. It was not until 1971 that gender-preference statutes were struck down by the Supreme Court.[52]

While it is not possible to detail here all of the different levels of law (federal, state, or local) or the different types of law (common law or case law) and their interpretations, it is worthwhile to note that many aspects of the legal system and public policy have reinforced the "separate and unequal" treatment of women over the decades, supporting stereotypical interpretations of gender roles in a patriarchal expression of the law. In fact, income tax laws and Social Security benefits still have unequal effects on women and men. And in many cases, positive changes have been piecemeal, as different states have changed different aspects of the law.[53]

The Value of Domesticity

In the 1970s U.S. homemakers were doing over $250 billion of unpaid work a year, but none of this production was included in calculations of the gross national product, and women were given no economic credit for these labors. Nor was homemaking highly valued in noneconomic ways, despite the fact that it was essential to the "good woman" role.[54] Because women's work is so vital on the one hand—after all, what is more important than raising the next generation to be caring, productive individuals?—and is so devalued on the other hand, women suffer from a conflicted sense of their own worth. We address this issue further in the last chapter, "Lessons for Today," as we assess the conditions for women in the 1990s and early twenty-first century.

~ *Language and Communication Styles*

The insights of feminist thought suggest that "concepts of gender structure the perception and the organization of all of social life."[55] This echoes the Sapir-Whorf hypothesis that language shapes and constrains thought.[56] Language, then, is a major factor in interactions between men and women.

Language has a persuasion all its own. It is "the fundamentally symbolic activity that permeates and suffuses all forms of human activity."[57] In essence, it is the thread that binds together the different parts of culture. Language and cultural norms begin to affect an individual's identity from the moment a baby is born.[58] Knowing whether it is a boy or a girl is fundamental in directing the parents' attitudes and reactions to their newborn, which will be modeled after cultural views they learned regarding males and females.[59] The descriptive terms used to talk about the newborn convey subtle but influential images. By using certain descriptive terms for each gender, we automatically characterize individuals as boys and girls and later as men and women.[60]

Changes are being made in how we raise our children today. Many people may choose to give a new baby a nonsexist blanket in green or yellow and toys that are nonsexist in their design. But our cultural heritage is strong and persistent. With the words that we still often use for boys, we have already started persuading a baby boy that he is expected to be strong, active, and even aggressive.[61] And one day we will expect him to be ambitious, dogmatic, practical, logical, experienced, and adventuresome. On the other hand, if we describe a baby girl as dainty and petite, we are encouraging her that she is expected to be "feminine" in her demeanor. It may seem as though there is nothing wrong with this on the surface, but it is what such language implies about expected roles in the future that creates the problem.

The effort to make language gender neutral and more inclusive introduced the use of *she/he* and *him/her*. Although a difficult and sometimes awkward task, the use of gender-neutral language has been important in lessening gender role bias. After the introduction, for example, of *Ms.* as a term for women comparable to *Mr.* for men, its use has become standard practice.[62] In the 1970s other changes in language use occurred. Signs for public restrooms changed from "Ladies" to "Women." Advocates for change wanted females to be recognized as normal people, not as a stereotype.

How we communicate with each other is not a trivial matter and often is at the root of misunderstanding. Women's and men's styles of talking tend to be different, including the (sometimes) more subtle nonverbal aspects that are always a part of communication. According to Deborah Tannen, men prefer "report-talk," a public type of speaking through which they attempt to maintain status in a social hierarchy. Women, on the other hand, are more comfortable with "rapport-talk," a more private type of speaking. Women tend to interweave the sentences in their conversation, taking note of what the other person is saying[63]; they express a desire to take turns in talking with others while men tend to center on what they want to say.[64]

Nonverbal aspects of communication also affect the interaction between males and females. While men frequently don't look directly at a person with whom they are conversing, women will usually be tuned into what the other person is saying. As such, she is probably more observant of the nuances of gestures, attitudes, and feelings of the other person. This is often referred to as "a woman's intuition."

Understanding aggressive, passive, and assertive behavior and conversation is fundamental to understanding some of the differences that occur when men and women interact with each other. Aggressive behavior is standing up for your own rights while trying to dominate or ignore the rights of others. Passive or nonassertive behavior means not expressing your own opinions, needs, or ideas and ignoring your own rights. Assertive behavior simply means acknowledging that you have rights and standing up for yourself without violating the rights of others.

Women at midcentury were traditionally raised to be passive. When women acted or talked in an assertive way, they were often perceived as being aggressive. This misunderstanding of the different kinds of behavior and conversation styles still exists and has made it more difficult for women (and for passive men) to be assertive on their own behalf. Men, on the other hand, were socialized to express independence and achievement with restriction and suppression of emotion; to avoid femininity and homosexuality; and to be socialized toward physical aggressiveness, toughness, and status seeking, often including an aggressive style of speaking.[65]

We can translate these aspects of communication to the business world or—as in the case of the authors in this volume—to the academic world of graduate school and the classroom, PhD committees, and faculty meetings. A man's style of speaking may mean that a woman's more intimate style inhibits her participation in the discussion. When she succeeds in stating her point, she may find herself either not well understood or not credited for an idea for which someone more dynamic and forceful instead is given credit.[66] If she tries to interject her ideas and opinions, she may be seen as aggressive rather than assertive, or she may back down and revert to a passive stance if someone challenges her in an aggressive way.

~ Women with Multifaceted Lives ~

The women whose narratives compose this volume are women with multifaceted lives who defied the constraints placed on them by the social, cultural, and legal realities of North America in the mid-1900s to achieve their goals. They wanted to become bona fide, full-fledged anthropologists, even though all of them but one had spent several years raising their families. They were well educated and intelligent, and all of them knew that their jobs as mothers and homemakers were important. But they also felt that they were capable of expanding their lives to include more education, fieldwork, a dissertation, and maybe even a job.

The paths they followed to their PhDs were different, as their narratives point out, and not everyone found the job that she might have wanted. But there are many ways to make use of education and experience, and these women provide proof of that. How they achieved success in various guises reflects their persistence and faith in something larger than themselves and their abilities to juggle many roles and to create new ones.

Some women's families gave them unquestioning support; the families of others very little. The women who managed duties at home while also going to school settled on a variety of solutions—making sure the household ran efficiently and someone was there for the children while they attended classes, catching up on the housework on the weekend after several days away at school, planning and preparing meals for the week ahead, juggling kids' activities with the need to study or attend classes, doing laundry, shopping—all of the many and varied household chores that help make a home run efficiently.

Even when spouses were supportive and took over some of the household chores, they usually held down full-time jobs and their time was limited. Some husbands and fathers took charge of household chores, such as the shopping or the cooking. In other cases, husbands and fathers supported their wives' pursuit of an educational dream only if their wives would continue to fulfill all of their wifely and motherly duties. It was a big job to succeed at school without neglecting children and husbands at home.

Almost all of the narrators dealt with some sort of bias on the part of the professors and academic administrators they met. Returning to school to finish an undergraduate degree or take on the more rigorous studies required by graduate degrees meant that they were competing with younger students who were presumably more up to date, and they needed to show that they were up to the task.

Women who stepped outside of the more traditional roles were often greeted with disdain or just plain misunderstanding. They were sometimes looked upon as if something must be wrong with them. Why else would one of the women be rebuffed when trying to enroll in a graduate program? Why else were some looked upon as not serious about their schooling? Both men *and* women were uncomfortable with women who attempted to occupy roles that were not prescribed for them and in many ways were proscribed from their participation.

In general, if a woman wanted to go to college, she needed a higher grade point average than a male applicant. Once there, prejudice against women on the part of faculty and administration was rampant and can be illustrated by one choice comment made at an educational institution in the 1960s: "I know you're competent and your thesis advisor knows you're competent. The question in our minds is are you *really serious* about what you're doing."[67] The authors have their own stories to tell.

Frequently responsible for caring for both their parents and their children, many of the women were bona fide members of the "sandwich" generation. Sometimes these duties coincided with their schedules at school, and they responded in the only way they could—they carried out their family duties and picked up their school duties later. Often untimely events—such as a serious illness or death of a family member—interjected an alarming dimension to their career paths.

For some women in this volume, divorce and the loss of a familiar family setting added other difficult dimensions—either husbands did not grow and change along with their wives, or there were incompatibilities that occurred. Financial issues were important factors for some. For others, however, the support of their husbands and families, both moral and financial, was integral to their success.

This introductory chapter has demonstrated the fact that the ideology behind gender role stereotypes is complex and slow to change. But this chapter has also shown that behavior, events, actions, and laws can gradually effect change for the better. We believe that even while there are strong forces striving to maintain the status quo, society will continue to work for the equality of *all* of its citizens.

~ Endnotes ~

1. See especially Felder (1999), Rowland (2004), Stetson (1997); Howard and Kavenik (2000).
2. Rowland (2004:69, 71).
3. During the war, many items were rationed, including sugar, butter, and meat. Bacon grease and scrap metal were recycled and used in producing war matériel. See Truman Presidential Museum & Library (2005).
4. Felder (1999:170), Rowland (2004:70).
5. Rowland (2004:75, 83).
6. Yellin (2004: 109–34, 133).
7. Ackmann (2003:31).
8. Yellin (2004:151).
9. Ackmann (2003:31–32), Yellin (2004:157–59).
10. Yellin (2004:202, 208–15).
11. Many veterans returning from World War II went to school on the GI Bill, which paid for their education.
12. Harvey (1993:69–73, 88–91).
13. Chafetz (1978:195).
14. Matthews (1987:172).
15. Harvey (1993:xv).
16. Chafetz (1978:44–46).
17. Friedan (1974:197–223).
18. Harvey (1993:147). For detailed accounts, see especially Felder (2001), Matthews (2000), Ackmann (2003).
19. Meadows (1998:5).
20. Sanders (2000:14).
21. Keltz (2000), Kopecky (2004).

22. Gazit (2003).
23. Friedan (1974:1, 11).
24. Meadows (1998:5).
25. Felder (1999:240–43), Meadows (1998:6); http://www.infoplease.com/spot/equalpayact1.html (accessed June 7, 2006); Kleiman (2005).
26. Hine and Thompson (1998:272–73).
27. Felder (1999:245, 247).
28. The Supreme Court ruled that "through the end of the first trimester only a woman and her doctor have the legal right to decide on an abortion" (Felder 1999:286). It was not long thereafter that antiabortionists attacked the ruling, beginning with the Hyde Amendment of 1976 that barred use of federal funds for abortions except where the life of the mother is endangered (Felder 1999:287). These attacks on women's rights continue nonstop today as the impact of this enormously important and contentious ruling is gradually and continually eroded.
29. Felder (1999:261–64).
30. Felder (1999:274–79).
31. As reported in Meadows (1998:5–6). *Title IX at 25: Report Card on Gender Equality* was published by the AAUW and more than 50 other groups in the National Coalition for Women and Girls in Education in 1997. This report marked the progress made by women in the 25 years since Title IX had been enacted in 1972.
32. Fisher (2004b).
33. The Court's ruling further affirmed and extended the prohibition of sexual harassment as defined under Title VII of the Civil Rights Act of 1964 (Felder 1999:305–8).
34. Felder (1999:315–18).
35. Ortner and Whitehead (1981:1).
36. Chafetz (1978); see also Epstein (1999:45–48) and Teitelbaum (1976).
37. Chafetz (1978:2, 4–5, 10–12, 21).
38. Chafetz (1978:21).
39. Marks (2002:103, 159–79).
40. Chafetz (1978:38–40).
41. Chafetz (1978:38–40).
42. Chafetz (1978:1).
43. Chafetz (1978:51).
44. Chafetz (1978:57).
45. Chafetz (1978:99–100); see also Sered (1999).
46. Feree et al. (1999:194).
47. Harvey (1993:41, 75, 78).
48. Chafetz (1978:149).
49. National Women's History Project (2005:1).
50. Chafetz (1978:149).
51. The long battle for women's right to vote, led by women such as Susan B. Anthony and Carrie Chapman Catt, was finally won when members of the National Woman's Party picketed the White House on an around-the-clock basis, taunting the president of the United States that to deny democratic rights to women at home was, to say the very least, hypocritical. This and ensuing demonstrations finally led to a favorable climate for passage of the Nineteenth Amendment (Felder 1999:97–105).
52. Rowland (2004:59–60, 100–2).

53. Chafetz (1978:153); see also McCaffery (1999).
54. Chafetz (1978:117, 164).
55. McElhinny (2003:848).
56. Whorf (1987:212–14).
57. Marks (2002:182).
58. Young (1980).
59. Young (1980), Chafetz (1978:68).
60. Bloom et al. (1975:23).
61. Chafetz (1978:41–42, 53–54, 75–79).
62. Crawford (2001:239).
63. Tannen (1990:76–77).
64. DeFrancisco (1991).
65. Good and Sherrod (2001:203).
66. Bloom et al. (1975:16–18).
67. Chafetz (1978:144–45).

~ References ~

Ackmann, Martha. 2003. *The Mercury 13: The Untold Story of Thirteen American Women and the Dream of Space Flight.* New York: Random House.

Bloom, Lynn Z., Karen Coburn, and Joan Pearlman. 1975. *The New Assertive Woman.* New York: Dell.

Chafetz, Janet Saltzman. 1978. *Masculine/Feminine or Human: An Overview of the Sociology of the Gender Roles*, 2nd ed. Itasca, IL: F. E. Peacock.

———, ed. 1999. *Handbook of the Sociology of Gender.* New York: Kluwer Academic/Plenum.

Crawford, Mary. 2001. Gender and Language. In Unger 2001, 228–44.

Crittenden, Ann. 2001. *The Price of Motherhood: Why the Most Important Job in the World Is Still the Least Valued.* New York: Henry Holt & Co.

DeFrancisco, Victoria. 1991. The Sound of Silence: How Men Silence Women in Marital Relationships. *Discourse and Society* 2 (4): 413–24.

Epstein, Cynthia Fuchs. 1999. Similarity and Difference: The Sociology of Gender Distinctions. In Chafetz 1999, 45–61.

Felder, Deborah G. 1999. *A Century of Women: The Most Influential Events in Twentieth-Century Women's History.* Secaucus, NJ: Carol.

———. 2001. *The 100 Most Influential Women of All Time: A Ranking Past and Present.* New York: Kensington.

Ferree, Myra Marx, Judith Lorber, and Beth B. Hess, eds. 1999. *Revisioning Gender.* Thousand Oaks, CA: Sage.

Fisher, Luchina. 2004. Black Women's History Gaining Ascendancy. *Women's eNews*, February 27, 2004. http://www.womensenews.org/article.cfm/dvn/aid/1730/context/archive (accessed March 24, 2004).

Friedan, Betty. [1963] 1974. *The Feminine Mystique.* New York: Dell.

Gazit, Chana. 2003. *The Pill: Sex. Religion. Politics. It Changed Everything.* Video recording. WGBH Educational Foundation. Alexandria, VA: PBS The American Experience.

Good, Glenn E., and Nancy B. Sherrod. 2001. The Psychology of Men and Masculinity: Research Status and Future Directions. In Unger 2001, 201–14.

Harvey, Brett. 1993. *The Fifties: A Women's Oral History*. New York: Harper Collins.

Hine, Darlene Clark, and Kathleen Thompson. 1998. *A Shining Thread of Hope: The History of Black Women in America*. New York: Broadway Books.

Howard, Angela M., and Frances M. Kavenik, eds. 2000. *Handbook of American Women's History*, 2nd ed. Thousand Oaks, CA: Sage.

Keltz, Iris. 2000. *Scrapbook of a Taos Hippie: Tribal Tales from the Heart of a Cultural Revolution*. El Paso, TX: Cinco Puntos Press.

Kleiman, Carol. 2005. The Mommy Wage Gap. *Daily Camera*, August 29.

Kopecky, Arthur. 2004. *New Buffalo: Journals from a Taos Commune*. Albuquerque: Univ. of New Mexico Press.

Marks, Jonathan. 2002. *What It Means to Be 98% Chimpanzee: Apes, People, and Their Genes*. Berkeley: Univ. of California Press.

Matthews, Glenna. 1987. *"Just a Housewife": The Rise & Fall of Domesticity in America*. New York: Oxford Press.

———. 2000. *American Women's History: A Student Companion*. New York: Oxford.

Meadows, Michelle. 1998. Measuring the Distance. In *150 Years of Women's Activism. AAUW Outlook. American Association of University Women*. 92 (2): 4–8.

McCaffery, Edward J. 1999. *Taxing Women: How the Marriage Penalty Affects Your Taxes*. Chicago: Univ. of Chicago Press.

McElhinny, Bonnie. 2003. Three Approaches to the Study of Language and Gender. *AA* Linguistic Review Essays. December:848–52.

National Women's History Project. 2005. Timeline of Legal History of Women in the United States. http://www.legacy98.org/timeline.html (accessed July 7, 2005).

Ortner, Sherry B., and Harriet Whitehead, eds. 1981. *Sexual Meanings: The Cultural Construction of Gender and Sexuality*. New York: Cambridge Univ. Press.

Rowland, Debran. 2004. *The Boundaries of Her Body: The Troubling History of Women's Rights in America*. Naperville, IL: Sphinx.

Sanders, Edward. 2000. Introduction. In Keltz 2000, 14.

Sered, Susan Starr. 1999. "Woman" as Symbol and Women as Agents. In Ferree, et al. 2000, 193–221.

Stetson, Dorothy McBride. 1997. *Women's Rights in the U.S.A.: Policy Debates and Gender Roles*. 2nd ed. New York: Garland.

Tannen, Deborah. 1990. *You Just Don't Understand: Women and Men in Conversation*. New York: William Morrow.

Teitelbaum, Michael S., ed. 1976. *Sex Differences: Social and Biological Perspectives*. Garden City, NY: Anchor Books.

Truman Presidential Museum & Library. 2005. Mobilizing for War: Poster Art of World War II. http://www.trumanlibrary.org/museum/posters/conserve.htm (accessed July 20, 2005).

Unger, Rhoda K., ed. 2001. *Handbook of the Psychology of Women and Gender*. New York: John Wiley.

Whorf, Benjamin. 1987. *Language, Thought, and Reality: Selected Writings of Benjamin Lee Whorf*, ed. John B. Carroll. Cambridge, MA: MIT Press.

Yellin, Emily. 2004. *Our Mothers' War: American Women at Home and at the Front during World War II*. New York: The Free Press.

Young, Veronica L. 1980. *The Pinks & the Blues*. Video recording. WGBH Educational Foundation. Paramus, NJ: Time Life Video.

Section 1

Possessed by Anthropology

POSSESSION HAS been part of Judy Rosenthal's life since childhood. Held first by her religious faith, then by 1960s political activism in Paris, she carried that passionately involved emotional style into her discovery of anthropology—or her discovery that in a sense, she had always been an anthropologist. Anthropology became Judy's religion, though a different sort from her earlier fundamentalist Christian faith. Anthropology, she says, has been for her a "pagan religion, never a totalizing one." In addition, in the small African nation of Togo, she has carried out field research on—what else?—Gorovodu possession. It was there, in Togo, that anthropology finally caught her.

We put Judy's story first because many of our contributors (and many other anthropologists we know) also feel some sense of being possessed—or called or grabbed—by anthropology. Some have a sense of having been born an anthropologist or having always been an anthropologist. Some speak of being in love with anthropology. Others recognize in anthropology, when they finally discover it, a focus for lifelong interests and passions. As in the children's song, "you put your whole self in, you put your whole self out," we put our whole self into anthropology; we made anthropology our passion and our way of life. And in return, we got our whole self back, transformed from everything we had been to someone who was also an anthropologist.

Possessed by Anthropology

Judy Rosenthal

The Challenge

The three Vodu women and I drank our beer with relish, enjoying a temporary victory over heat and dust. Conversation darted back and forth, and my friend Sylvio translated now and then. There seemed to be an agenda that didn't belong to any one of us. Our banal respite from weather and work was happening on the porch of a little bar in Togo, West Africa, on the beach road that stretched from the border with Ghana to the border with Benin. It was 1985. I was in the country for a year to teach English at the American Cultural Center in the capital, and was living with Sylvio in a little house near the bar, about twenty minutes from Lomé.

A month earlier I had seen one of the three women in trance during a Gorovodu ceremony.[1] It was held in a nearby village with no plumbing or electricity, but with breathtaking dancing and all-night drumming that I still heard in my head weeks afterwards. Antou was beautiful in and out of trance. That first time I saw her, she moved with abandon and sang at the top of her astonishing voice, shouting vibrato instructions to the drummers. In a state of sheer grace, she stamped first one foot and then the other, over and over, into the sand of

Judy Rosenthal: PhD 1993, Cornell University. Dissertation: "The Dancing Gods: Personhood, Possession and the Law in Ewe Gorovodu." Judy, who has done extensive research in West Africa, is associate professor of anthropology and women's studies at the University of Michigan–Flint. Her publications include a book, *Possession, Ecstasy, and Law in Ewe Voodoo.*

the ceremonial ground. While in trance, she embodied Nana Wango, a fierce grandmother spirit "from the north," who was also a crocodile and a *piroguier*, the ferryman who took people to the other side of dangerous rivers and other crossings. One of the other Vodu women in our little beer party had asked me to let her clean our house, as she badly needed financial support. Akoko's husband was favoring his other wives and children, and one of her children was "a child of the Vodu," in need of rituals that required her to spend money she didn't have.

Afi, the third woman, lived five minutes away from the beer bar, on the other side of the road, on the way to Dogbeda, where I had first seen Antou possessed by her spirit. I often passed by her compound while walking to the village, and she would wave for me to come visit. Soon I would meet Comfort and Kponsi, two other spirit hosts in Dogbeda that took center stage in my life several years later. I don't know whether I took center stage in their lives—perhaps the stage I am imagining is after all a shared one, giving us all access to each other's performance.

At a certain moment that day when we sat drinking together, I turned to Sylvio to make sure I had understood what Antou was telling me. "Did she just ask me to write a book about Gorovodu?" He nodded. "The women are saying that they're very interesting people and white folks know nothing about them. They want you to write about them." "But I'm not an anthropologist," I protested. "I wouldn't do a good job." "Then go learn whatever you must learn to write about Gorovodu," they commanded, "and afterwards come back here." I was stunned.

⁓ Growing Up as Other ⁓

My earliest memory is of cold sand on my bare bottom. It was the early 1940s. I was two years old and we were living on a tiny farm in Uvalde, Texas. My eighteen-year-old mother had been arrested for selling *The Watchtower* on the street corner and accused of un-American activities by the American Legion.[2] Daddy had to walk three miles into town with me on his shoulders to get her out of jail. It was there in Uvalde that my father plowed under, by accident, our last forty dollars. That was the straw that broke the camel's back. Our family moved back to Corpus Christi. "I am simply not a farmer," Daddy insisted. So he became a bread-truck driver. My mother was still a teenager who liked dancing jitterbug. Daddy danced the Charleston.

When I was five and six, my family lived on Harvard Street in Corpus Christi, where my brother Danny was born. My father sold insurance door-to-door, became a welder and then a construction worker. We moved almost every year, from town to town, state to state—wherever there was work. I went to twelve different schools in as many years, and in every school, because I was a Jehovah's Witness, I could not salute the flag in class every morning, for that would have been an act idolatrous of the state. Everywhere we went, my mother and I and both my grandmothers worked door-to-door, insisting to everyone who would listen that a paradise earth would someday be our home, that the wicked would no longer be here to disturb us, and that they—the householders, we called them—should join us.

In Corpus Christi, at the age of six, I wrote my first poetry. It was about dogs, rabbits, and snakes, all of which would be in God's new world with us, the righteous people, after the battle of Armageddon. I had asthma almost constantly, so I often stayed inside. I spent entire afternoons fantasizing about God's earthly paradise that would be our home. I would roam around the entire earth on the head of a lion, his mane tickling my bare skin. And that lion would lie down with lambs without hurting them, and we would eat dust, like the serpent, so that no animals would be killed, not even for food. (I had a close reading of the prophet Isaiah.)

One night when my mother and I came home from the Watchtower meeting, we found an enormous, entirely black wildcat lying dead on the kitchen floor. My father liked to poach deer on the nearby King Ranch, but that night he had not found any deer, so he set his sights on the magnificent puma and brought it home as a trophy. I was not happy about the demise of the black cat, but its head made a statement on our walls from Texas to South Carolina and Colorado and back to Texas, from project houses to little caravans, from edges of towns to giant trailer parks for construction workers in the brush of pine forests. Sometimes when we were traveling, my father took his rifle from the trunk of the car and shot wild turkey, quail, anything we could eat, right from the side of the road. We ate almost everything except the Old Testament serpent's diet of dust (my fantasy of eating dust notwithstanding).

My father could smell snakes nearby, even from inside our dwellings. He would say, "Come on, Judy, let's go find out what kind of snake is out there." If it was a rattler, he would kill it. If it were a constrictor, he would toss it to me and I would play with it for a while before letting it go. He wanted me to feel at home with snakes and other crawling creatures. On Harvard Street and later in Brownsville there were horned toads and tarantulas, black widows and praying mantises. I learned to handle granddaddy longlegs without crushing any of their legs, learned to grab lizards darting up the side of the house quickly enough to prevent their "popping off" the wall (and thus landing on my face, a fate worse than death), yet gently enough to avoid injuring any lizard guts, or so I hoped. Catching and controlling minimally without killing or maiming was my constant project in all of our home sites throughout the years. This close knowledge of crawling things enabled me years later to live in intimate quarters with West African creatures like geckos and insects, some very big (but no bigger than cockroaches and scorpions in southern Texas), with little fear or discomfort. Indeed, I was eager to hold the sacred pythons of the Vodu.

In Corpus Christi I played at being Jesus, "the little girl Jesus," with my hands nailed to the side of the house and my mouth open in pain. My friend Darlene said that if we died we would go to heaven, so we went and lay in Harvard Street, hoping to be killed by a car and thereby gain immediate access to paradise. At night read Bible stories to me about sex and violence and the wiping out of tribe of Benjamin because of the rape and murder of the Levite's concu- orah cut off the head of the Syrian captain after having seduced him and th him. King David was a handsome adulterer; Christ loved prostitutes; osalom died tragically (but justly), lifted right off his horse by the branch of a thanks to his very long and beautiful hair. I also had long and beautiful hair.

When I was seven, we moved to Brownsville to a big two-story house with my other's sister and her husband and two other single construction workers. We almost always lived in an extended family. The vast badlands beyond the houses were inhabited by many sorts of cactus. We children loved to roam that wild place, a place I believed was another world across all known borders. In third grade I began to learn Spanish. The Spanish language became part of my imagination and my reasoning, and I fell in love with Chuy, a Mexican boy my age.

Several years later I could see my father working on a construction site as I sat in my fifth-grade classroom. I saw him walk across beams three or four stories up in the air, with no support. I held my breath, terrified he would fall, and eventually I told him I was afraid for him. He said he was part Indian, and Indians could do that, it was a well-known fact, that's why so many Indians worked in construction. My grandmother, with long braids and salient cheekbones, was truly Native American, as everyone knew. But she would never tell me what kind of Indian she was, nor would anyone else. Even now I am not sure. I used to say she was Apache (I loved the story of Geronimo), but I suspect she was Cherokee.

In South Carolina, when I was eleven, I was infatuated with a boy I would see briefly every morning as we waited for the school bus. His parents knew we were Jehovah's Witnesses who did not believing in "fighting wars that only God should fight." One day he shouted to me, "Go home and kiss Stalin, you filthy Communist!" (That was the McCarthy era, and the FBI had put Jehovah's Witnesses on a long list with other groups suspected of seditious Redness.) That boy's parents held my family in contempt—much as my "fellow Communists" were held in contempt in court for being un-American, much as Jesus was held in contempt, I reasoned. We were poor. They lived in an expensive mobile home that only management could afford. They had a purebred English setter that impregnated my own lovely mongrel, and they blamed my dog for the scandalous miscegenation. Misplaced semen was apparently never the male's fault. I learned something then about class, race, and gender that I have never forgotten, and a tiny bit about an international Left that made me feel close to it before I had any actual knowledge of it.

Political Activism and Intellectual Lust

I didn't leave the Jehovah's Witness fold until I was twenty-five years old and about to divorce my Jehovah's Witness husband, a construction worker like my father, whom I married when I was barely twenty and he was only nineteen. The emotional security of close community was hard to give up. I was finally able to cut the cord thanks to the particular nature of the sixties. I began my period of sex-and-drugs-and-rock-and-roll at a later age than most hippies, but more importantly I began several years of apprenticeship in political activism. I studied alongside Angela Davis with Herbert Marcuse at the University of California, San Diego. I joined in civil rights, antiwar, antiracism, and feminist demonstrations and went to jail once because of having helped lead a campus sit-in against the U.S. invasion of Cambodia. I worked some with Students for a Democratic Society (a leftist campus organization), helped begin a women's liberation group, supported the Black Panthers, and attended their big 1969 meeting in Oakland. I went to Cuba with the Venceremos Brigade.[3] By 1971 I was being watched by the FBI. They tapped the phone lines of even very small game at that time. But I was no longer sure what could be done politically to bring about lasting structural change. I was fruitfully lost.

A dear friend of mine, a woman who had been a member of the Black Panthers, put me on the plane to France, where I taught English for fourteen years. I also took marginal part in numerous political movements there and joined more street demonstrations than I can now remember. For twelve years I raised Clara, my French daughter, the child of a man I lived with. Then I was seduced to Africa. Had I not spent all those years involved in political movements, thinking through problems of inequality, racism, colonialism, and state violence in the world, I don't think I would have been ready to know West Africa up close—its colonial past, its difficult present, and its uncertain future.

As my parents had never graduated from high school, and no one in my mother's or father's families had a university education, and given the fact that I spent numerous years not wanting to be "part of the system," I was very long in imagining a PhD for myself. I loved university life in San Diego and Paris, where I also had to work to earn a living and was already older compared to most of the students I knew in those places. But my degrees—a French *license* and *maîtrise*[4]—were not career driven. I just wanted to be in school for the rest of my life. I never thought of myself as a "real" intellectual, certainly not on the path to becoming a professional academic. I was ever a novice in book learning for the pure enjoyment, and sometimes terrible sadness, of getting to know the world as deeply and broadly as possible. I studied Foucault, Derrida, and Lacan with women from the group called Politique et Psychoanalyse. We also worked with Julia Kristeva and the writings of Michele Montrelay, Luce Irigaray, and Hélène Cixous.

I took courses in political economy for a year and a half, and then studied Chinese, music, comparative literature, sociology, and anthropology at Paris VIII, the Vincennes campus founded in 1968 through the political events that united so many students and workers. Thousands of students in Paris were from unprivileged origins, and many were immigrants, fleeing prison or worse in Latin America, North and West Africa, Iran, and other parts of the globe. I thought we were a dazzling crew in Paris, motley in our origins and experience;

and we all were somehow amazed to be alive and on the move, still engaging in huge street demonstrations for various African and Latin American revolutionary struggles, against neocolonialism, against Franco, against racism, for women's and workers' and immigrants' rights, and so on. From so many different countries, we were used to tapping into each other's "otherness," and the cultural differences between us were fundamental to our enjoyment of life.

Later I went to Hautes Etudes for a course on the political writings of Max Weber and another on the sociology of religion. It was all for love, not for a degree. But all those Marxist, feminist, poststructuralist, and deconstructionist theorists played a strong role in my ethnographic thinking and in my teaching years later.

~ The Lure of the Other ~

I had been attracted to African and Latino cultures since my youth in south Texas, when my aunts taught me to dance mambo and cha-cha to the music coming from Mexican radio stations. I began to speak Spanish around the age of eight. I always went to the local movie houses to see the "native films," those half-ethnographic, half-sensationalist black-and-white reportages of African villages. Years later I was aware of the problematic romanticism and exoticism in my attraction to these other cultures—a romanticism and exoticism that remain in my anthropology, a serious flaw that I criticize but also mine for energy.

As a teenager in the 1950s, while attending international conventions of Jehovah's Witnesses in Yankee Stadium in New York, I went religiously to all of the sessions that showcased "our African and South American brothers and sisters." I felt that if I were in sufficient contact with them, I would finally come to know people really different from me, that something of their wondrous strangeness would infect my sameness, and I would be new.

In 1970 I was a member of the Venceremos Brigade, doing agricultural work in Cuba. After long days in the fields, I spent some memorable evenings with an Afro-Cuban farmer from Oriente Province. Night after night he talked about his life, about Santeria, a New World offshoot of African Vodu and Orisha religions, about love and death and trouble. I also spent many hours in the company of Latin American guerrilla fighters, men fresh out of prison who told me about their experiences and their hopes. Those six weeks of working and dancing, singing and shouting, listening and learning in Cuban Spanish marked me indelibly.

During my fourteen years in France, I often went to African and Caribbean nightclubs on weekends with my dear friend Mathilde, from the south of France, and with Rachel, a remarkable woman from Chile who had been given political asylum following the Pinochet coup. We prided ourselves on our expertise of *son montuno*, *guaracha*, soukous, merengue, and zouk.[5] We loved the famous Cuban orchestras that played jazz as well as salsa. We craved the music of the latest soukous stars from Kinshasa, accompanied by more instrumentalists, singers, and dancers than could fit on the stage at the Chapelle des Lombards (the best nightclub in Paris). Paris could be an intensely African and Afro-Latin city for those who knew where to work and where to dance. Mathilde, Rachel, and I had working-class origins and lived in relatively modest circumstances in France, but we were experts in where to listen to music and where to dance. This knowledge of African and Caribbean music and my dancing experience turned out to be my "ticket to ride" in West African villages years later. It was because I could perform the Vodu dances reasonably well that the women decided I should be the one to write about them.

~ Encounters with Anthropology ~

I had begun to read anthropology when I was working in Paris during the seventies and early eighties. In 1974 I completed several courses with Pierrette Desy, a protégé of Lévi-Strauss, at the University of Paris VIII. But I didn't feel that I myself could do anthropology because I thought of it, especially its Africanist wing, as an imperialist project full of the arrogance of trying to know more about Others than they themselves could possibly know, including deciding how to classify "them." I didn't take seriously the advice of several West African government trainees in my English classes who used to tell me I should be an anthropologist. I figured they were teasing me, however affectionately, perhaps signifying on me,[6] the clueless white woman who liked to learn their dances and hear about their lives.

In 1984 I read Marc Augé's ethnographic meditation on religions with many gods, *Le Génie du Paganisme*,[7] which drew on field research carried out in Togo. It made me long to know more about West African women—and write about them. I went to Hautes Etudes (a place for graduate teaching and research in France) to speak about Togo and Vodu with Augé, then director of African Studies at Hautes Etudes. He was very kind, advising me on how to write about the religion I knew best, Jehovah's Witnesses. I had in fact already written a *mémoire de maîtrise* about the Watchtower Movement in an effort to lay to rest that part of my past.

In April of 1985, I went to visit friends working in Togo. Upon landing for the first time in Lomé, I was taken unawares and disoriented, almost disturbed, by the redness of the earth, the redness of the light, the apparent redness of the air, the redness of the royal poinciana blossoms, the glowing greenness of the leaves, the starkness of the contrast between the yellow and gray patches of the bark collage on the baobab trunks. I had to warn myself that life on the ground in West Africa was not a version of magical realism. *Lo real maravilloso* was indeed marvelous for novels,[8] but not for respecting real people trapped in the real predicaments of neocolonialism and development gone awry. I met numerous Togolese, including Sylvio, a high school teacher who invited me to come back and stay for a while in his country.

I took up Sylvio's offer, pulled up stakes in Paris, and accepted a yearlong teaching position with the English Language Program at the American Cultural

Center in Lomé.[9] That led me to my first Gorovodu ceremony and the subsequent conversation with the three Vodu women at the beer bar. I accepted their challenge to go and learn how to write about them. In January of 1986, I applied to Cornell University and miraculously was accepted with a tuition fellowship.

~ Becoming a "Real" Intellectual—at Last ~

Graduate school at Cornell was daunting, for I still wore my working-class Texan origins on my face and often felt out of place in such a privileged setting. Actually, few of my fellow graduate students in anthropology came from wealthy or highly privileged families. Even so, I was the only one from a truly blue-collar family with parents who hadn't even graduated from high school. I had also been entirely out of my element at the University of California, San Diego, during the late 1960s, but the urgency of political action and the stunning nature of cultural change during those years relativized everything else.

Curiously, I felt less foreign at the University of Paris in the early 1970s than I did at Cornell a dozen years and a technological revolution later. At Cornell there was organized campus activism against apartheid, and that was significant, but it was the only fight I saw happening there. Times were different. I also was different—my activist self was muted. I was at Cornell to become an anthropologist. This time I was in it for the degree, a complex commitment. And I was carrying out the orders of the three Vodu women. I had a contract to honor.

During the second week of class at Cornell the very professor I had thought would become my dissertation advisor treated me with positive contempt. He told me I was out of place in his course on Marx and French poststructuralism. Although I had studied Marx with Marcuse and had read Lévi-Strauss, Foucault, Barthes, Althusser, and Lacan in the original, I did not know how to talk to him about all that, how to convince him that I knew more than he imagined. I hadn't read those books in order to write papers or dissertations or defend myself from the assumptions of professors who apparently despised older working-class women (or who just despised me, which I preferred to think for the sake of other women students; yet that made me feel even worse about myself). I had read those books for pleasure and also because of the urgency of finding out what theorists had to say about the world and human nature.

The day that professor told me I couldn't stay in his class, I left his office feeling ignorant, old, and frightfully ugly. There were several beautiful young women in the class and he clearly enjoyed having them there. I was more than depressed, for, like many women and students of working-class origins, I felt at times that I was an imposter at the university. This was one of those times, and it was as though that professor had found me out. I must have been trying to fake it. I could never sharpen my mind sufficiently to think as a real intellectual. How could anyone with my background and of my age possibly deserve to become a real anthropologist!

I mustered the courage to speak to Carol Greenhouse, the graduate representative, about what I had experienced as terminal rejection. Her immediate and utter support pulled me back from a certain abyss. She assured me that I would find someone else to advise me, someone worthier of being my mentor. I finally asked her to be the one. In spite of her frightfully busy schedule, Carol accepted with what looked like delight, and she made my years in graduate school the period of transformation I was desperately hoping for. All of her classes were models of and for thinking and teaching anthropology. Although she is younger than I am, she has continued to be a mentor and an unbelievably giving colleague right up to the present. I could never do as much for her as she has done for me, but I try to do for other women students, young and old, and working-class men, too, at least some of what she did for me.

I also asked Jim Boon, who was and is astonishing in his scholarliness as well as mordantly funny, and ever so specialized in French anthropology and social theory, to be on my committee. He still surprises me and makes me happy when I read him and hear him speak at anthropology meetings. Jim wrote and spoke anthropology not only as deadly serious business but also as excess, as madly creative fun, as expenditure in the sense of Bataille.[10] I could never have done without that component of the discipline.

Henry Louis ("Skip") Gates Jr. also accepted to join my committee, in spite of the fact that he was already on dozens and very rightly had students of color on his priority list. Skip helped me with my apprenticeship in the materials from and about Africa and introduced me to Wole Soyinka, Ngugi Wa Thiongo, Toni Morrison, and other stars who came to visit Cornell at his invitation. When Skip couldn't come to a dissertation committee meeting, he was replaced grandly by Kwame Anthony Appiah, for whom I had immense respect and liking. He was charismatic as a theorizing bridge from splendid West African texts to splendid European ones.

I thus had four mentors whom I could fully admire and who seemed to think I was a worthwhile person and a promising intellectual.

Other anthropologists at Cornell supported and energized me. David Holmberg, in particular, saw to it that I received full financial support when I returned to Cornell after nearly three years in West Africa.

I did not leave Cornell for field research before having one more damaging experience, this time with a professor who oversaw my work in the collections room, and who insisted that I raise very heavy windows daily. When I asked for help, he told me he would replace me if I couldn't do the work. I badly needed the job so I kept lifting. One day I heard something snap in my spine. A couple of weeks later, the pain began, but the on-campus clinic did not take it seriously. By the time I arrived in Paris for ten days before going to West Africa for fieldwork, I suffered constantly. One night I had a frightening pain crisis and came out of it with a noticeable limp. A scan indicated that without an operation the damage would be permanent. I underwent neurosurgery in Paris, which made me five weeks late arriving in Togo for research in villages with no plumbing or electricity and a dearth of straight-backed chairs so necessary for people having just undergone removal of the L5-S1 disk. Had I told my faculty friends at Cornell about my difficulties with the offending professor, they would have helped me, but I tried foolishly to muddle on without too much complaining.

Except for those two men who had little respect for me and for my age, my experience at Cornell was excellent, and I made many friends. It is an annual feast for me when I see these friends at professional meetings—they have more than made up for the close community of Jehovah's Witnesses that I gave up so many years ago. Once in Togo, when I went for a consultation at a Baptist missionary hospital upcountry, the receptionist asked me which religion I practiced. I answered "anthropology." She wrote that down without batting an eyelash (she knew how to spell it, too). When I think of the peasant or rustic remains in the word *pagan*, I think of anthropology as a pagan religion, though never a totalizing one, and neither very doctrinal nor admitting of numerous clashing doctrines. And, in memory of the etymology of the word *religion*, we must admit that anthropology is also an adherence, a "sticking to," both ethical and intellectual, but not an adherence to orthodoxy. Anthropology sticks to change that happens on the side of life, and on the side of as many common, unprivileged, and unwritten particular lives as possible. It sticks to heterodoxies and heterologies, even to the interpretation of heteronormativity as the melancholy residue of a sacrificed homoerotic love![11] (Thank you, Judith Butler, faithful friend of so many anthropologists.)

In 1993, as I was finishing my dissertation at Cornell, I began applying for teaching positions at various universities. When I saw an advertisement for a position at the University of Michigan–Flint, I remembered the famous sit-down strike of 1937, which I had emphasized as one of the high points of U.S. labor history when I was teaching English in Paris. I had been told about the movie *Roger and Me* (by Flint native Michael Moore) that came out when I was still in West Africa. I watched it and decided I wanted the University of Michigan job. I would surely have a certain immediacy with the working-class students who were the majority at the Flint campus. I realized during my first interview in Flint that some members of the search committee had originally believed I was too old for the position, but after they saw me they changed their minds.

I have absolutely loved teaching at UM–Flint. I have taught too much and would rather have had more time for writing, but I have taught happily and have had the privilege of turning the heads of many, many students. They still come back, years later, to tell me that such-and-such a class changed their lives. Once again, I have to say how grateful I am to Carol Greenhouse and others for passing that practice and that immense satisfaction on to me. I also have to thank a number of Flint colleagues who have become yet another family. Sociologist and feminist scholar Linda Carty, who is now chair of Africana Studies at Syracuse University, was particularly influential; much younger than I am, she guided me through tenure and into politically engaged teaching.

~ The Ethnographic "I" ~

I thought it would be easy to write an account of how and why at the age of forty-five I went back to school for a doctorate in anthropology, eventually carried out ethnographic research in West Africa, and at the age of fifty-two became a university professor. In fact, it wasn't all that easy. This sort of narrative presents the same predicaments that go with the territory of ethnography, of writing about Others. The Other I become when writing about the last twenty years of my life is a familiar foreigner to me, either merrily self-centered and narcissistic with the narration recklessly unguarded, or strangely dignified and idealized beyond recognition after removal of the most offensive warts.

When did that "I" really begin, those anthropologizing eyes and ears and all the other ethnographic body parts and sites of desire and research in the mind? Was tiny Judy already a baby anthropologist back in southern Texas in 1941? Has she always been writing culture, starting with the awkward poetry of childhood and adolescence scribbled in one place after another as her family followed the jobs in construction? Was going from door to door as a little Jehovah's Witness already a form of fieldwork? Was the political activism of the sixties and seventies, including jail and a trip to Cuba, a form of participant observation?

I never knew what I wanted to be when I grew up, because I grew up thinking I might not have a chance to grow up in the "wicked old world" (a Jehovah's Witness concept). The end of the world would sweep away all reality as we then knew it. I would certainly never bring children into such a frightening world. And the new world of the paradise earth would become after the battle of Armageddon—could such a thing (magical realism?) really be believed? No, not in the long run.

Even now in my sixties, I still feel not-grown-up, notice myself green in my field, find myself remiss in my discipline and a maverick in my work. I also am deeply happy to have found myself in anthropology and especially to have found astonishing others in anthropology. I am thankful to be suffering as a university professor suffers and not as a JCPenney salesclerk suffers. (I once did that job among many others.) I am relieved to get paid for reading mind-altering books and talking about them. After fifteen years of university teaching, I am still glad to be inviting discussion about the perilous yet inescapable traveling between cultural relativism on the one hand and universalist ethical accountability on the other (the dizzying aporia of it all), instead of warning people about the battle of Armageddon from door to door in English and Spanish.

I still find the world unbearably violent. Field research in West Africa has only increased the worry and sadness that I already felt as a child being taught about the wickedness of the world. I know that most victims of violence in our time are innocent; that is, they do not deserve what has happened to them. I still wonder whether some mad U.S. president is about to ignite a Third World War that will signal the end of humanity as we know it, a secular Armageddon.

My colleagues tell me that I do not lecture; I preach. My dreams are still in brilliant Old Testament and Revelation of John technicolor, sometimes in apocalypse, sometimes in millennium. The fact that I have been an atheist for many more years than I was a fundamentalist Christian has not taken away the psychic primacy of a Biblical Imaginary[12] and the thrill of the expectation of cosmic change that I knew so intimately during childhood. I wonder today whether this embodied religious life that was my person so many years ago, the indelible traces of which scar and decorate my psyche and my memory even now, has been a help or a hindrance as I have studied Vodu possession trance in West Africa these past years.

Certainly the dry positivist notions of absolute scientific and godly truth that came from the Watchtower Society had me poring over the texts as soon as I could read, trying to find the absolute proof that "real science" validated every detail of the Biblical master narrative. On the other hand, I honed a practice of hermeneutics—all Jehovah's Witnesses do—as I preached from door to door, looking each person in the eye while flipping from scripture to scripture to argue the Watchtower interpretation of Armageddon and the "paradise earth to come" and God's will as we knew it. It was perhaps not an altogether unworthy beginning for an anthropologist, although it was bereft of cultural relativism. It was a most American beginning, in any case: the American cultural moorings of Jehovah's Witnesses and many other fundamentalist Christian movements originating in the United States appear in the form of a particular hubris, a belief that they alone possess The Truth, and in truly heroic efforts to convert the rest of the world.

Recently a friend told me he found it a shame that my adopted daughters from West Africa would probably not return "home" to Togo to live and thus "give back" to the people who originally produced them. Instead, they will no doubt remain in the United States and/or Europe, attending university and then working in jobs that will enable them to earn sufficient money to send some to their birth mother and other close family across the Atlantic from time to time. At the same time, I notice that my teaching and mentorship has produced, quite against my will, about a student a year in the past six or seven, who will somehow follow my lead and work "in the field" in Ghana, Togo, or Benin, especially among Ewe and Mina Vodu adepts, or among Flint African Americans who still remember the sit-down strike of 1937, or researching the history of the Ku Klux Klan in Michigan. One of them just wrote me something to the effect that he had finally found home in West Africa. These Michigan "children" of mine are variously more or less Native American, African American, Asian American, Arab American, and European American, all of them already thoroughly "mixed."

Fifteen years ago, when my adopted daughter Dede was eight and we were in an Ewe village in Togo, I asked her whether she considered the United States or Togo to be her home. She answered in French, "Tu sais, Maman, ou qu'on soit, c'est l'autre endroit qui va nous manquer. C'est comme ça." ("You know, Mom, wherever we are, we're going to miss the other place. That's the way it is.") I remembered my own childhood and how everywhere was tentatively home, and perhaps nowhere. We never stopped moving. In our family culture and in our practice with others in the communities into which we settled, we were always different from everyone else. Our interpretations of others were different from their interpretations of themselves. And our interpretations of ourselves were certainly different from others' interpretations of us. My Mina-speaking and French-speaking daughters from Togo, who are now very African American and especially Michigan American, also have peculiar emic and etic qualities to their interpretations of life and others. They are anthropologists whether they intend to be or not. Their sensory memories join a more literary remembrance of different lives on different continents among different peoples.

~ Ethnography and Beyond in West Africa ~

I did what the Vodu women told me to do. I learned how to do anthropology and went back to them many times. When I returned to West Africa in January of 1990, my husband and children were waiting for me. We left at the end of July 1992, pushed out of Togo by the alarming political events that provided a pretext for the police to threaten our family. I cannot say that I was a very professional ethnographer. I was tired much of the time, although never in the middle of Vodu spirit possession ceremonies, which always brought me back to life with almost alarming efficacy and made me focus on the cultural discourse of transformation. I was sometimes depressed. I never did manage to speak (or more precisely, to understand) Ewe and Mina truly fluently. I was short on the energy necessary to do many things at the same time: to be mother and wife, to observe and participate and write, to learn West African tonal languages, to teach English in town (research fellowships were never sufficient), to dodge Togolese police and soldiers and the social control of American Embassy watchdogs, and especially, to be accountable to and protective of the numerous persons helping me learn Vodu culture.

I was fifty years old while doing dissertation research, and I was still trying to stay out of jail and also trying to keep a husband out of jail. I was angry and heartbroken at the same time when our young daughters and their caretaker were followed—virtually chased—by soldiers with machine guns looking for my husband and me. While I hated the brutality of a police force and army gone mad, I bore even more intense anger against the French government and its military trainers who had facilitated the dictatorship and its corruption. I was also furious with the Americans for not being vigorous in their denunciation of state terrorism and for not understanding what was happening. Almost all outsiders decried the "tribalism" in Togo, the south against the north, the "traditional hatreds." That was utter hogwash.[13]

The Vodu people of coastal (southern) Togo and Benin keep on honoring the "people of the North," some of whom were "bought persons" (slaves) in southern lineages. Vodu spirits have names from the north. In possession trance, spirit hosts speak a glossolalia of northern and southern languages that remembers their common history. In trance they embody north/south relationships and the reciprocity of their exchange. Northern gods keep on healing and celebrating the southerners, who in turn keep on re-creating northern gods, singing and drumming them back into life, re-creating the collage fetishes over and over again. These practices and this discourse about regions, genders, history, and change, and the multiplicity of personhood and of all sorts of identities, individual and collective, inform my personal and professional life in the United States, my teaching anthropology against racism, my feminist work, and my social theory.

All of this—the tragedy of the political situations in West Africa and the fabulous nature of Vodu culture—has fascinated me, worn me out, resurrected me, and transformed me into an anthropologist, a problematic anthropologist, but a real one.

Gorovodu and Mama Tchamba priests and spirit hosts, the latter mostly women, have given my life surplus meaning and made my motherhood something different from the other motherhood that I had already experienced. They have made writing something new although I have been writing all my life; and they quite literally made me publish a book, an ethnography that is not bad at all, if somewhat unorthodox. It is theirs. I kept my promise to them. And they have changed me.

In 1999 I spent four months in Lomé, receiving Comfort and Antou and other women in my rented house. We told each other everything. Everything was too much, but I am attempting to write it anyway. We also went to ceremonies together. One day in a dusty street in the Tokoin neighborhood of the capital, Comfort and Antou and I walked along happily hand in hand, about to join a large Gorovodu festival. We saw a Vodu priest coming in the other direction. Passing up the ceremonial ground in order to greet the priest, I bowed and saluted him in the Gorovodu fashion. Antou suddenly entered trance, began swirling and crying out in the street, making demands of me and others. I did my best to "cool" her, as I had learned to do years before, but she grabbed my arm and propelled me into the dancing throng on the ceremonial ground. The drummers noticed and began to play for Antou and her spirit. Antou/Nana Wango was ravishing. We danced as never before. I died with pleasure and with the uncanny recognition of the incredibility of life. The anthropological life has given me that rapture over and over again. It continues to give me pleasure as well as anxiety. It continues to make me think and teach and write. Thank you for that, Antou and Nana Wango, Comfort and Sunia Komfo, Da Adjo and Banguele Ketetse, Ablosi and Mama Tchamba, Gbetsogbe man-woman and Papa Kunde, Maimouna and Nana Ablewa, Fo Komla and Togbui Kadzanka. (Here I have named spirit hosts along with their spirits.)

And thank you, Sylvio, for leading me to all of that in the first place. Thank you, Dede and Koko, for being my beautiful and wise daughters. Thank you, Delphine (my African daughters' birth mother), for the supreme gift of making me the mother to raise the children you bore. And thank you, Clara, my French daughter, for continuing to call me back to France every year and for making me French, too, and for making Lola and Sacha, and thus making me a grandmother. And on and on... no end to the making... no end to the thanking...

~ Endnotes ~

1. Gorovodu and Mama Tchamba are two forms of Vodu (spirit, divinity) religions that appeared in coastal villages of Ghana, Togo, and Benin during the colonial period. Vodu cultures provide the same kinds of meaning, protection, community, and links to the past that most other religions in the world provide. Gorovodu and Mama Tchamba involve possession trance and the worship of spirits of enslaved people who were captured upcountry from the coast during the period of the Atlantic slave trade. Vodu communities invite these spirits to come into the bodies and minds of their hosts so as to enjoy life once more, and also to heal and protect their worshippers.
2. Jehovah's Witnesses (or the Watchtower Society) distribute their publication, *The Watchtower*, during their door-to-door work intended to warn all people about the impending battle of Armageddon mentioned in the New Testament book of Revelation (the Apocalypse of John). They hold that this war, brought by God, will destroy the present world and wipe the earth clean of wickedness. Only the faithful will survive and live forever on earth, which will become a paradise, a Garden of Eden. Jehovah's Witnesses refuse to engage in political activity, even voting. They consider all wars and political activism to be part of the "wickedness of this world." Thus, many of them spent time in prison as conscientious objectors during World War II. During the McCarthy anti-Communist witch hunt of the late 1940s and early 1950s, Jehovah's Witnesses were suspected of un-American activities. Their refusal of all "earthly politics" looked like seditious antipatriotism to those charged with rooting out Communist sympathizers in the United States. Little did Senator McCarthy and his crew realize that Jehovah's Witnesses were perhaps even more anti-Communist than the McCarthyites and the FBI, if that was possible.
3. The Venceremos ("we shall overcome") Brigade took individuals to Cuba to work there as a way of showing solidarity with Cuban workers and challenging U.S. policies toward Cuba.
4. A *license* is a three-year university degree, similar to a BA in the United States. A *maîtrise* is roughly the equivalent of a master's degree in the United States.
5. These are rhythms and dance steps from Cuba, Mexico, Zaire, and elsewhere. Zouk is a preferred rhythm everywhere in "Black Paris" and is familiar to virtually everyone in France.
6. "Signifying on someone" is an African American category of cultural games that include elaborate forms of teasing, as well as competitive performances such as "yo mama" jokes, "the dozens," and "loud-talking." It also involves tongue-in-cheek insults that may not register as such in the mind of the target because they are carried out in cloaked or insider language. See Gates (1988) for a scholarly treatment of these practices that originate in West Africa (although forms of "signifying" probably exist in all cultures) and Rosenthal (1995).
7. Augé (1982).

8. The concept of "magical realism" has been employed for the interpretation of literary works such as Gabriel García Márquez's *One Hundred Years of Solitude* (1995), in which surreal fantasy and realism intertwine.
9. A few months later, Sylvio and I married, and in 1989 I adopted Sylvio's daughters, Dede and Koko.
10. Georges Bataille (1985:120–26) wrote, for example, about "unproductive expenditure," a "constitution of a positive property of loss," the opposite of accumulation or "functional bourgeois expenditure."
11. Here, I refer especially to Judith Butler's *The Psychic Life of Power* (1997). Butler's work during the past twenty years has been central to theorizing gender and sexual orientation. It has been dubbed "queer theory," although she herself did not coin this term. It is also appreciated as a rereading or reworking of Hegel, Lacan, Foucault, and Althusser on questions of power and the construction of subjectivity.
12. I employ the Lacanian *Imaginaire* here to stand in for the imagery in dreams and the unconscious, for the imagination in all its guises, and for the dual and "duel" oppositional thinking and either/or logic of the ego.
13. While it is true that the army and police force are at least 80 percent "northern," especially Kabre, the same as the longtime dictator, the villages and lineages that produced these men are not themselves violent or dictatorial—quite the contrary. Northerners and southerners have often intermarried, worked together, and learned each other's languages. There was and is no tribalism. The north/south predicament began during the colonial epoch and continues to the present, thanks to neocolonialism. The Togolese people, northerners and southerners and people in between, tried many times to transform that situation, but to no avail (see Piot 1999).

~ References ~

Augé, Marc. 1982. *Le Génie du Paganisme.* Paris: Gallimard.

Bataille, Georges. 1985. *Visions of Excess: Selected Writings, 1927–1939*, ed. Allan Stoekl and tr. Allan Stoekl with Carl R. Lovitt and Donald M. Leslie Jr. Minneapolis: Univ. of Minnesota Press.

Butler, Judith. 1997. *The Psychic Life of Power: Theories of Subjection.* Stanford, CA: Stanford Univ. Press.

García Márquez, Gabriel. 1995. *One Hundred Years of Solitude.* New York: Alfred A. Knopf.

Gates, Henry Louis, Jr. 1988. *The Signifyin' Monkey: A Theory of Afro-American Literary Criticism.* New York: Oxford Univ. Press.

Piot, Charles. 1999. *Remotely Global: Village Modernity in West Africa.* Chicago: Univ. of Chicago Press.

Rosenthal, Judy. 1995. The Signifying Crab. *Cultural Anthropology* 10 (4): 581–86.

Section 2

Changing Roles, Challenging Stereotypes

Women's Roles in Twentieth-Century North America

WE WERE born between 1913 and 1947 and reached young womanhood in the years of the Great Depression, during World War II, with the "Silent Generation" of the 1950s, in the 1960s. For today's young people, these times are ancient history. For us, they are personal memories.

It was a different world then. Most of us grew up before the days of TV, suburbia, shopping malls, jet planes, and fast food (yes, there was no McDonald's!). We grew up before the age of instant communication, before computers, e-mail, cell phones, videos, DVDs. We came of age in cultures of much more restricted life choices for women than our daughters and granddaughters have known, before "women's lib" and the second wave of feminism, before reforms like Title IX and the Equal Credit Opportunity Act opened doors in areas such as athletics and economic opportunity, before we realized there was a "glass ceiling."

Gender ideologies and women's roles changed throughout these different eras. From the 1920s until 1945, when World War II ended, women's options for education and employment were expanding. After the war the U.S. government and policy and opinion makers, including social scientists and the media, tried to reverse the trend and return women to the home. For a while they succeeded. The social and cultural pressures for women to conform, to be "homemakers" dependent on husbands and devoted to children, were enormous, deep, ubiquitous. Many of us—like the great majority of middle-class American women—conformed. We stayed home and produced the baby boomers. To do something different required imagination, courage, and either defiance of or indifference to the cultural norms. These stories reveal women, enmeshed in marriage, motherhood, and family, struggling to find different paths as they challenged cultural stereotypes of women's roles and created new roles for themselves.

From Academe to County Politics

Anthropologist as Activist

Eunice Felter Boyer

When traveling with a group of women educators to visit women's colleges in the Middle East, I remarked casually that my mother had graduated from Wellesley in 1908. The reaction of my traveling companions amazed me—they teased me as though this were a source of pride and hubris! To me, this was just the way my family was.

I was born in Eureka, Illinois, in 1918—the older of two daughters. My parents both came from old families—my father's grandparents had been among pioneers who moved from Kentucky to Eureka as members of the Disciples of Christ; they were moving out of slave territory. The town still retains some of the pietistic flavor of the revivalist founders, with no liquor stores or taverns in town. Eureka College was founded to educate the sons and daughters of these pioneers. My father's family was very education oriented. He had five younger sisters, all but one born before 1900, and they all graduated from Eureka College.

My mother came from Quaker stock; her ancestors had lived in southern Ohio, the *Friendly Persuasions* territory. Her father was a strongly Republican newspaper editor in Streator, Illinois, and as a loved only child she was sent to Wellesley College. Not very good training for a farmwife! But she stuck it out and maintained reading as a major activity in the household.

Eunice Felter Boyer: PhD 1975, University of Wisconsin–Milwaukee. Dissertation: "Health Perception among the Elderly in Public Housing." Eunice also earned an MA in sociology of religion. She taught sociology and anthropology for many years at Carthage College and was politically active in her community, serving as county supervisor for twenty-four years. She was a feminist long before the term became fashionable.

I suppose a strong influence on my career plans came from my three unmarried aunts. One was a high school teacher in a steel town near St. Louis, one was a librarian, and the third followed the pattern of an earlier generation—after her mother's death she gave up her role as a kindergarten teacher and kept house for her father. When he died, she moved to Chicago, started a daycare center, and kept house for her librarian sister. The career pattern was there.

When I finished college in 1939, almost no small college offered courses in anthropology. At Eureka I had majored in sociology, working closely with a professor from England who was at the same time a doctoral candidate at the University of Chicago. He was very liberal and took full advantage of the growing political influence of the New Deal. So my thinking on the role of government in social and economic matters was shaped by the times, just before World War II, and by an instructor who was influenced by the Labor model in England. After graduation, at his recommendation, I went to the University of Chicago on a Divinity School fellowship to study sociology of religion. From a strictly career standpoint, this was a mistake—my interests were not deeply involved in religion and I should have taken the available scholarship to the University of Illinois. Nevertheless, the university was an exciting place and the use of the city of Chicago as an urban laboratory was in full cry. I was employed as student assistant on projects involving churches in changing neighborhoods and worked with Dr. Samuel Kincheloe, who was an authority on this subject. He advised me to attend the Chicago Theological Seminary (Congregational affiliation); take courses in the sociology of religion at the Divinity School of the University of Chicago; take as many courses in the Sociology Department as possible; and in short, focus on the study of sociology.

At the time, the Congregational Church (United Church of Christ) maintained a survey research department where students were employed as research assistants. Dr. Kincheloe was the director. As a research assistant, my first assignment was a survey of possibilities for further mission work on the Near West Side of Chicago, an area in transition to a Hispanic population. I didn't have enough sense to be afraid and consumed countless five-cent hamburgers without dying of food poisoning. Dr. Kincheloe finally pointed out that the animals went into the ark two by two—visits to the Near West Side were perhaps better made by young women who went two by two.

~ Teaching Sociology: My First Career ~

I finished my master's in 1941 and married. After two years my husband, Merle, was given an appointment at Carthage College in Carthage, Illinois, where he taught philosophy until 1982. I had grown up in a small town and felt quite at home in Carthage. It was, however, too remote for me to commute to a doctoral program in a nearby university—there was no such thing! My daughter was born in 1945, and the next year, as postwar enrollment of GIs began, I was tapped to teach two or three courses in sociology. My most successful course was probably the one in rural sociology because students could actively work on surveys of small communities in the area. We all had a lot of fun and did what I still believe was good research in rural sociology.

I continued to teach part time, had two more children, and found that I was teaching four or five courses a semester under the rubric of "part time" with no pension fund payments, no secretarial help, no tenure. When my youngest child was in third grade, I decided it was time to give up the part-time fiction, which involved teaching as many as fourteen hours under the part-time banner. I announced that I was ready for full time. My department had no problem with this, so I at least gained a certain security.

In the meantime it was increasingly difficult to recruit students for a small college in a small town in rural west-central Illinois. Dr. Lentz, Carthage's president, with a real leap of faith decided to move the college to Kenosha, Wisconsin, almost three hundred miles away. My friends in small-town Carthage regarded Kenosha as Sodom or Gomorrah: "You mean you are going to take your adolescent boys into *that city*?" Kenosha was indeed a contrast to Carthage. In Kenosha economic and industrial life centered around American Motors. When the Motors was hiring, high school dropouts could get very good jobs. When the Motors laid off, a ripple effect extended through the community—even bakeries sold fewer decorated birthday cakes. Another fascinating view for a social scientist was the ethnic diversity. Italian Americans were the most visible ethnic group, although the German Americans were more numerous. The African American population was very small and almost invisible. Other groups were Lithuanian, Slovak, Polish, Serbian—a fascinating mélange. Lest this sound patronizing, you must realize that I had spent much of my life in towns where WASP (white Anglo-Saxon Protestant) was the predominant ethnic group. "Late" arrivals were German families whose immigration dated back to the mid-nineteenth century, immediately after the Civil War.

The move was made in 1964. I shortly found that the demands were different in a large school and town. After the move to Kenosha, Carthage College attracted a larger student body, which resulted in the rapid hiring of bright young PhDs who were very scornful of those with lesser degrees. My dissatisfaction with my inferior status soon surfaced—I have a lot of academic ego that doesn't like being put down. The "union card" of academia, the PhD, began to loom larger and larger in my mind. At the same time that these pressures were developing, family pressures were lessening. I also realized that much of my professional reading was in anthropology rather than sociology. At that time sociology was almost exclusively statistical. Anthropology (which was not statistically oriented) was more interesting to read, especially since I was not familiar with it. I decided to explore graduate study in anthropology or sociology at the University of Wisconsin–Milwaukee, which was within easy commuting distance.

Getting My Union Card: The PhD

At UW–Milwaukee I talked with people in both sociology and anthropology, but the anthropologists were more welcoming. I was fortunate enough to meet Nancy Lurie, then chair of the Department of Anthropology. She was very encouraging and suggested classes that I could take as refresher courses (I'm not certain what I was refreshing!). Nancy Lurie, Ed Wellin, and Alvin Wolfe were senior members of the department who were not far from my age; the reading and studying I had done for the previous twenty-five years was appreciated, not scorned. My wide and miscellaneous reading in anthropology began to have some purpose. So I decided on anthropology.

In retrospect, I believe that returning to graduate school was easier than the shift from being "that nice little Mrs. Boyer who has three small children and insists on teaching a few courses—how peculiar of her!" to being a full-time faculty member. When I became full time, I no longer had the privilege of lunch at home or with a friend—I was in my office during my free time. That change in roles was probably more difficult than the later shift to graduate student, albeit as an "older" student. My young colleagues in graduate school were incredibly kind and accepting.

I had changed disciplines, from sociology to anthropology, so in a way I was starting over from the beginning. I was fortunate that Ed Wellin, with whom I had my first graduate courses, liked to teach evening courses, so I could teach at Carthage during the day and drive to Milwaukee to be a student at night. My first test made Ed a friend and backer. He and I had, over the years, read many of the same authors and he did not despise my years of reading as not up-to-date. This meant that in his courses I was able to use my experience rather than discard it, though eventually I developed a more current reading list. In many ways Ed's encouragement contributed to my attaining the PhD.

My family situation made a big difference, too. When we still lived in Carthage, there was some juggling with childcare when my children were little because I was taking an evening class in another city, but my husband was always more than cooperative. My kids were not tiny when we moved to Kenosha—my daughter was a freshman in college and my sons were in high school and upper grade school. They got to be pretty self-sufficient over the years.

Altogether, graduate school was a new and exciting world. I had always been a good student and I enjoyed every minute of my courses, though I struggled with statistics. You have to realize that my first experience as a graduate student happened in precomputer days. In the 1940s we were lucky if we could use a very primitive calculator instead of a slide rule! Graduate studies in the 1970s involved a whole new world of computers. Fortunately I had a good background in statistics and was able, with difficulty, to cope. In 1970 computer work at UW–Milwaukee involving large databases was done by phone connection with UW–Madison, where the mainframe was located. Our data were stored on magnetic tapes; sometimes they wore out and destroyed data. I was fortunate that the new state university in Kenosha let me use their link to Madison.

The Urban Observatory at UW–Milwaukee had given Dr. Wellin a grant to investigate the health and social well-being of residents of public housing for the elderly in Milwaukee. This research was not typical of traditional anthropology because it was not in some exotic locale and not in a community with families and people of different ages. Most of the residents were in their sixties. The research was a lot of fun as well as significant for the new area of anthropological gerontology. I found that I was rather good at interviewing and creating rapport with interviewees. Furthermore, this research gave me the basis for a dissertation. A sabbatical enabled me to complete my residency requirement of one year of full-time coursework at UW–Milwaukee and to complete my dissertation. It was in many ways a more data-based and less theoretical dissertation than I had wanted to write—but it was completed. Ed Wellin was particularly helpful as my dissertation advisor, and I cannot give too much credit to my husband for his support and patience. As most of us know, living with a dissertation is not easy!

My degree was awarded in 1975, and I had earned the desired union card of a PhD. I was fifty-seven years old.

~ Teaching Anthropology: My Second Career ~

Was it worth it, getting a doctorate when I was only eleven years from retirement? In terms of personal satisfaction, absolutely! Did it change my teaching? Greatly, in many ways, especially in that I then taught only one lower-level sociology course a semester with most of my teaching in anthropology. Did it change my role in the academic community? Yes, I had earned respect, and the younger faculty began treating me as an equal. Perhaps the most difficult adjustment was with the administrators, who somehow felt the sums I earned, when considered in conjunction with what my husband earned, need not be commensurate with my qualifications. Perhaps my former role as "that nice Mrs. Boyer who has three children and is helping us out" was a hard vision to lose. When equal pay for women with equal training and experience became a federal cause, a friend at Carthage and I received very good raises.

~ Community Activism: My Third Career ~

When I was a student at the University of Chicago, sociologists were encouraged to become community activists, not to hide in an ivory tower. When I lived in Carthage after my marriage, I had no political aspirations. Indeed, no one from the college had ever gained an elective office. I think there was a fear that we might take over the entire town. But in Kenosha I was persuaded to run for the school board—my first political venture. I was elected and served one three-year term but was about to start my dissertation when it came time to run again, so I opted out of running for a second term. Then I was appointed to the Library Board.

In 1980, PhD firmly in hand and promotion to full professor also secured, I ran for the county board of supervisors. (Ironically, the friend and longtime colleague who urged me to run was defeated in the same election.) Wisconsin has rather large county boards. Today there are a fair number of women supervisors, but in 1980 I was only the second woman to run on her own rather than taking a husband's seat after his death. Because the roots of Kenosha politics are in labor politics, I never stressed my PhD, but what I gained from it was the understanding of cultural differences and class and age differences that change and distort local issues. Over the twenty-four years of my service as a county supervisor, I got the nickname of "Supervisor Welfare" of Kenosha County. I served as chair of the board of the county nursing home, chair of the Human Services Committee, and member of the Mental Health Board. These matched my interests and training well. I also served on statewide committees and boards.

In 1986 I retired from teaching but continued on the County Board until 2004. This service provided an excellent retirement activity, kept my hand in, gave me a voice on the Commission on Aging and indeed on many projects that the county has developed. When I announced that I would not seek reelection in 2004, the *Kenosha News* interviewed me. I told them: "I've been in county politics a long time and I love it. I will miss it. I guess I'm just getting older. Funny, people do."[1] I was eighty-six. However, I didn't completely retire, as I continue to serve on several committees.

I don't want to paint too rosy a picture of my transformation from university liberal to practicing politician. I am reminded of a speech Paul Douglas gave after he had served on the Chicago City Council as alderman. He said that he had spent his years at the University of Chicago fighting with PhDs, and that when he went on the city council he found that the aldermen—many educated in the college of hard knocks—were smarter, more determined, and better at the infighting. Labor politics is rough, and I have earned my scars honorably—by fighting for what I wanted to do and what I believed was right. On one occasion the unions wanted the city and county to sue Chrysler for planning to close the assembly plant. We voted against suing, which seemed to have had a dubious legal basis. On my way home that night, I stopped for a red light and somehow the pickup truck behind me managed to ram my car, inflicting forty-five dollars' worth of damage to my taillight. It was *not* an accident!

On another occasion I dared to challenge a member of the "old boys' network" for chairmanship of the County Board. I lost—and spent the easiest two years of my tenure as a supervisor: I was chair of no committee and was asked to do nothing. I was in exile!

In spite of all this, my third career in local politics has been rewarding and I find that I still believe that social scientists should have some public involvement—theory alone is not satisfying. I have never lost the belief, learned at the University of Chicago so long ago, and before that as an undergraduate studying under a Chicago-trained professor, that knowledge in social science is not something abstruse, to be treasured for its own sake, but is to be applied for the common good in the community. In short, I remain an unreconstructed activist.

Perhaps I should end with an appreciation for my husband, who encouraged me throughout my somewhat on-and-off career. He does show a touch of resignation when he asks, "And where are you going tonight?" But he remains supportive and patient.

~ Endnote ~

1. Patrick Marley, "Supervisor Plans to Step Down." *Kenosha News,* December 5, 2003:C1.

An Anthropological Odyssey

A Midlife Beginning

Marilyn Preheim Rose

THE YEAR was 1971. The place was Iowa City, Iowa. Our sixth child was in fourth grade. I had come to think that life had to hold more surprises than dust bunnies under the bed or a washing machine that ate socks. So I resolved not to spend the rest of my life devoted to a house and housekeeping. A return to school became an attractive alternative to a life of domesticity, a life that conformed to my family's and my community's expectations, a life that had become mind-numbing.

Rebellion and Conformity

My earlier degrees, obtained before marriage and children, were a BA in chemistry, an MA in biochemistry, and certification as a medical technologist. Going to college and earning advanced degrees were not the norm for females in the late 1940s and 1950s. High school, perhaps teaching elementary school or nurse's training, then marriage and children were the "right" and "natural" course for a woman from a close-knit rural midwestern Mennonite community. A farm girl was supposed to marry a farmer, or if she was lucky she might marry a preacher,

Marilyn Preheim Rose: PhD 1982, University of Iowa. Dissertation: "On the Move: A Study of Migration and Ethnic Persistence among Mennonites from East Freeman, South Dakota." Marilyn has taught at the University of Iowa, where in 1976 she developed one of the early courses on women cross-culturally. Marilyn is one of a small group of anthropologists who has studied the cultural aspects of her own ethnic group.

which meant less money but more status! Against my parents' better judgment and wishes, I refused to follow the community norm.

My parents promoted my taking the one-year course offered at Freeman Junior College that prepared one for teaching in the local country schools. This is what my sister had done, and to my folks this seemed a fine and logical path to follow. My sister lived at home and taught at the country school three miles east. What more could I possibly want? I agreed to attend Freeman Junior College, but I enrolled for every noneducation course offered. I had no noneducation courses to take in a second year at Freeman, so I lobbied my parents to let me attend Bethel College, a four-year Mennonite college in North Newton, Kansas. With reluctance they agreed to let me attend and to pay my room, board, and tuition. I earned spending money by working a few nights a week at the campus soda fountain.

Bethel's course offerings were more extensive than those of the junior college and gave me the opportunity to take much-desired courses in natural science. In 1947, at the age of twenty, I graduated with a chemistry major and a biology minor. These opened doors to further education and career possibilities: certification as a Medical Technologist—American Society of Clinical Pathology (MT ASCP) and a Master of Science in biochemistry from the University of South Dakota. Jobs as a medical technologist in polio research and early experiments in cardiac catheterization proved to me and to my parents that I could support myself in a nontraditional, skilled profession based in an urban setting.

My vow not to marry a farmer did not deter me from falling in love with a World War II veteran who had a dream of forsaking ranch life to become a physician. Again, my parents were less than enthusiastic about my choice. He was not a Mennonite but a young man from South Dakota West River ranch country who had served in the military—anathema to Mennonite beliefs and practice. They would have been much more approving of Mennonite theology students and preachers, but I was not interested in them. Reluctantly my parents gave their blessings, and with time came to love and appreciate my husband. We were married after his second year of medical school.

Tradition then dictated that a woman could work until the birth of a child. After that, the role of full-time wife and mother was to be accepted. Though I had rebelled against my parents' attempts to make me into a rural schoolteacher, it never occurred to me to question these conventional mores. My job skills helped support us, and I worked until the birth of our first child. Then I stayed home. I was pleased to be the primary caretaker of our six children—five daughters and one son born within eight years. There was little time for reflection and no time for regret. It was during these years that my husband completed his medical training; spent two years in general practice; took residencies in clinical, anatomic, and forensic pathology; earned his law degree; and worked as a forensic pathologist–medical examiner.

As the laboratory-technologist working wife of a medical student, I did just fine. As the mother of an infant and wife of a hard-working low-paid intern, I did fine. As the mother of six children and wife of a hard-working moderately paid resident, I did fine. My adaptive skills, however, were less adequate for the culture of doctors' wives in Dallas, Texas, in the 1960s. I refused to learn to play bridge after the mother of a doctor's wife told me bluntly she didn't see how I could be a successful doctor's wife if I didn't play bridge! Neiman Marcus shopping, suntans, pink teas, white gloves, flower arranging, big houses with servants (also called nannies, cleaning ladies, gardeners, and cooks) were never part of my upbringing or aspirations. Social pressures, well-defined boundaries of membership, and leveling mechanisms kept this culture intact. Periodically I put on my Sunday best with mink stole and participated in the afternoon teas or soirees, but never enthusiastically. In retrospect, some anthropological insights have helped me understand that culture and my rebellion against it.

~ A New Beginning ~

Thoughts of once again becoming employable were never far from my mind during the years I was a full-time mother. Precisely what I wanted to do was not clear, and as long as we were living in Dallas, distances, children, and commitments allowed neither time nor opportunity to take any specific action toward a job or further education. Our move to Iowa City in 1968 made the logistics of returning to school a manageable possibility. Iowa City, with a population of about sixty thousand, is home to the University of Iowa. Our home is within walking distance of the campus, an important consideration when juggling schedules for my classes and for my children's and family needs.

During my twenty years of childbearing and childrearing, enormous informational and technological advances occurred in medical technology and biochemistry. Reentering these areas would have meant complete retooling in order to incorporate the new knowledge and new techniques. Such a repeat of earlier training held little interest for me. Rather, this was a great time for a new beginning in a different area of interest. I thought initially about child psychology and counseling, but since I was doing that on a daily basis with our own six children, to do it formally held little appeal. Looking through the university's summer course catalog, my attention was drawn to the social sciences. In college I had enjoyed the one sociology course that I had taken. Other than reading about Margaret Mead, I had little knowledge of anthropology. The class schedules fit, the hours were manageable, and so my first foray back into school included two summer courses, one in anthropology, the other in sociology.

Because of its emphasis on people, culture, history, and behavior—topics that were of special interest to me as a Mennonite in a non-Mennonite world—anthropology was the clear winner. That fall I applied and was accepted into the master's program in anthropology at the University of Iowa. It was a world of new concepts, information, and vocabulary, a new world of fascination and interest. With the enthusiastic support and encouragement of my husband and children, I embarked on my academic adventure. The children thought it "cool" to have a graduate student mother. My thoughts were much more pragmatic and defensive: "I'll give it a try, but I can stop any time." "My livelihood does not depend on another degree." "If family needs overwhelm, I can stop." But I did not stop, family needs were manageable, and eventually I earned a PhD in anthropology.

The first several semesters were a tremendous challenge as I worked through what seemed like endless reading assignments and term papers in every class. In the natural sciences, term papers were rare, so my writing skills had never been honed. Consequently, each term paper was an exercise in organization, analysis, and clarity.

In addition, just because I was back in school did not mean family responsibilities suddenly disappeared. I soon realized that graduate school could not be my single purpose and focus. The Friday-afternoon social gathering of graduate students at a local bar was an event I had to forgo. Children would be home from school and had lessons, sports, rehearsals, or any of a hundred activities that needed my attention or chauffeuring. Consequently the close-knit relationships often developed among graduate students were limited for me. Since our six children were spread over elementary, junior high, and high school, my husband would attend one event, I another, and once in a while an event did not get covered. There were times I felt I did nothing well—not studies, not parenting, not husband, not self-maintenance. In fact, I concluded there was a big conspiracy "up there" that made sure every school program, concert, play, or back-to-school night was scheduled the evening before a major exam or term paper was due. Every deadline seemed to coincide with a family event. The ultimate "conspiratorial" event was the funeral of my mother-in-law on the day on which my dissertation defense had been scheduled. She died unexpectedly, so the need for a contingency plan had not been anticipated. We kept our priorities straight and attended the funeral. It was too late to reschedule the defense for that semester, so I enrolled for yet another semester. At my age, what did a few more months matter?

Professors were friendly and helpful for the most part, but were a bit uncomfortable with a student who appeared old enough in some cases to be their mother. Terms of address were problematic. "Mrs. Rose" seemed too formal and "Marilyn" seemed too familiar for a gray-haired matronly type. As time went on and rapport was established, everyone became comfortable with Marilyn. Faculty, though generally encouraging, never involved themselves with me or my research. Perhaps because of my age, they felt I needed no mentoring or perhaps I failed to adequately express my needs. This lack of faculty interest and support also may have been due to my unique research focus—ethnic persistence and migrations.

The lack of professorial interest was forcefully demonstrated at the time of my dissertation defense. My dissertation was titled "On the Move: A Study of Migrations and Ethnic Persistence among Mennonites from East Freeman,

South Dakota." After the defense, my advisor and another faculty person took me to lunch. In the course of conversation, my advisor stated that he never believed in the concept of ethnicity at all. I was stunned. Never in the time I worked on my dissertation had he mentioned his lack of belief in ethnicity as a viable anthropological concept. Perhaps this explained why his focus was always on my grammar and sentence structure but almost never on the substance of what I had written. Needless to say, I have felt vindicated since then by all the attention to ethnic groups and ethnic conflicts discussed in the media as well as subsequent literature in anthropology.

Whatever the reasons, there was little sense of collegiality with my advisor or committee members or among faculty in general. They seldom had time for an exchange of ideas or discussion of theories related to my research interests. The result was a feeling of isolation, of working in a vacuum, of not knowing what the expectations were. Many times I suffered crises of confidence about classes, papers, and dissertation research and writing. A counterbalance to these negatives were my budding abilities to synthesize and analyze materials and see the world in new and more interesting ways—through the eyes of an anthropologist. In particular, anthropology gave me a lens through which to view my own ethnicity and to better understand my background and ancestry.

With three children in college, graduate, or professional school at the same time for many of the years in which I was a student, I felt it necessary to earn enough for my tuition and books. Fortunately for me, the Department of Anthropology was generous in awarding teaching assistantships that meant both work and income for a graduate student. However, the policy of the department is not to fund graduate students after completion of comprehensive exams, so a new source of income for me was teaching in the Division of Credit Programs at the university. This teaching also introduced me to the women's liberation movement that was gaining momentum in the mid-1970s.

My return to school and movement away from a purely housewife and mother role had created in me an intense interest in feminist and gender issues. To someone who for twenty years had focused mainly on children and family, the world now assumed wonderfully intriguing and mind-stretching dimensions. In 1976 the first classes in women's studies were initiated at the University of Iowa, and I was asked to teach a course titled Women's Roles: A Cross-Cultural Perspective. Like most early feminists in academia, I had to become self-educated. Ours were the first courses offered. There was some anthropological literature on women, but for the most part, it had to be gleaned from within other topics, such as ethnographies and family and childrearing studies. My first class had fifty-two students. What an introduction to teaching! With time, practice, and enthusiasm for the subject, teaching became a pleasure and a forum in which lives could be influenced and ethnocentric biases transformed into tolerance and understanding.

~ Researching My Own Community ~

With an emerging grasp of the tools of the trade and spurred by interest in my ancestry and ethnic background, I embarked on my dissertation research, the focus of which became present-day migration and ethnic persistence among a group of Mennonites who had lived in Russia for one hundred years before migrating to North America in the 1870s. To do research on one's own culture was not quite what a "real" anthropologist did; however, it was where my interests lay and was something I could feasibly accomplish. The group I selected was economically and politically assimilated but culturally, socially, and religiously unique.

One church congregation of 449 members became the focus of my research. I identified the persons who had moved away in the previous fifteen years, where they went, and their next of kin (usually their parents) who remained in the community of origin. I then interviewed those migrants who were within a reasonable distance from Iowa and sent questionnaires to those more distant. I also interviewed the next of kin in the community of origin. My purpose was to determine the push and pull factors behind the migrations: who left, where did they go, why did they go, what occupations did they have, who did they marry? Did they still identify as Mennonites in formal or informal ways? How important was their Mennonite identity? Was it theological, ethnic/cultural, kinship based, some combination of the above, or irrelevant? Because the community of origin is almost exclusively agricultural and land is a limited resource, I researched inheritance patterns such as who got the farm.

Anthropological concepts provided the means through which to understand and interpret the social organization and culture of this relatively close-knit community. Concepts of kinship provided the framework that explained patterns of mutual aid, inheritance, care of the elderly, work groups, visiting, and the "Mennonite Name Game" of determining the region of origin and possible kinship links of any two Mennonites based on their surname. Concepts of social organization and related boundary markers and maintenance provided a paradigm through which to understand the church structures, religious beliefs and practices, marriage patterns, food preferences, and residence patterns that tried to duplicate and expand the early settlement pattern of contiguous farms. Economic concepts helped to explain the successful farming practices, whether individuals were risk takers or conservative in their approach, and their general prosperity. Attitudes toward land tied in with the religious beliefs of stewardship of all resources. Directly bearing on the study were the anthropological concepts of migration, the push and pull factors that caused people to move, which helped me understand their choices of time, place, mode of movement, and occupation. Related to this was their sense of who they were and who they are: in other words, their self-identification and ethnic identity.

This was a study of my home community that I had left thirty years earlier. As with many migrants, I maintained ties of kinship and friendship through the years. Returning to my home community as an anthropologist interested in studying migration and ethnic persistence placed me in a new and expanded role vis-à-vis community members. My role now was that of interviewer and observer as well as that of daughter, sister, niece, cousin, and friend. I was received not as a privileged stranger, as one might be in a foreign society, but as an ordinary person who, it was assumed, knew the norms of the society. At the same time, because of the many years of living away from the community, I was an uninvolved and unobtrusive observer interested in and able to record the views of the people, their families, and activities. My personal knowledge of the people and the community made it easier to comprehend the social system and to place component parts into their proper configuration. This background made it easier to understand the dynamics and appreciate the humor, nuance, and occasional conflicting explanations.

~ After the PhD ~

I earned my MA in 1976 and finally, in the summer of 1982, at age fifty-five, I was awarded the PhD. Because six to nine hours per semester was all I could manage, this educational adventure extended over eleven years. When I graduated, our youngest was in college and our eldest was married. I experienced some "postpartum blues" as I struggled with what to do next. The Department of Anthropology does not hire its own graduates—a philosophy with which I agree—but this limited my options. The road upon which I had embarked in graduate school became my major option. The department conferred adjunct assistant professor status, and I continued teaching in the Division of Credit Programs. In addition to the Women's Roles course, I taught Anthropology and Contemporary World Problems and Aging in Cross-Cultural Perspective, as well as a telecourse titled Faces of Culture. This teaching satisfied my professional needs and desires and provided a great deal of student contact and monetary reward. The downside of such a position is that the wages are low and there are no benefits and no academic stature.

It was gratifying to have AMS Press solicit and publish my dissertation in 1989 as part of a series on ethnic groups in the United States. In addition, I have published articles in the *Journal of the Steward Anthropological Society* and *The Mennonite Quarterly Review*. The Army Corps of Engineers solicited me to do a study analyzing the effect of the Missouri River Gavins Point Dam on the Bon Homme Hutterite Colony. I visited the colony, did interviews, and wrote a detailed report for the corps that became part of their records. I have also conducted seminars on aging in a number of communities.

In thinking of my life as a graduate student for eleven years and now as a person with an advanced degree, some serendipitous benefits have accrued. Perhaps the most important is that of role model to students, especially older women returning to school and students who became excited by anthropology, and—most importantly—to my own children. All five of our daughters are professionals. Three are lawyers, one is a physician, and the fifth is an art historian/

gallery director. Our son is a writer-columnist and assumed the role of primary-care parent for his son for five years—a role I applaud. Our relationships with our children are now those of friend, professional confidant, and hub of an ever-expanding kindred for celebrating, sharing, and mutual aid. To my roles of wife, mother, and teacher, I have added grandmother, senior citizen, court-based mediator, and volunteer. Anthropology continues to broaden my horizons, stir my imagination, augment my understanding, and intensify the joy of living.

Born an Anthropologist

From a Housewife with Hobbies to an Anthropologist with a Passion

Cath Oberholtzer

"You Are So Good with Children"

In the 1950s in a small Canadian town, an esteemed physician advised a young teenager that her aspirations for a career in the medical field necessitated a decision: one could be a doctor or one could be a wife and mother, but never both. And, he added, "You are *so* good with children." While young women in the twenty-first century would take umbrage at such advice, in the post–World War II era with its burgeoning economy and its constant but subtle pressures to both "rebuild" populations and put Rosie the Riveter back into the kitchen, this advice was not uncommon.

Certainly, as impressionable youngsters in Canadian elementary schools, we were fed the cozy ambience of the Dick and Jane reading books in which the nuclear family was highlighted. Every morning Father went to work in a suit while Mother, perpetually attired in dress and apron, lovingly cared for the family. When we reached the senior levels of high school in the later 1950s, guidance classes continued to reinforce these gender roles. While the boys were encouraged to explore a variety of careers, we girls were left with the option to become a nurse or a teacher or a secretary—at least until we married, at which

Cath Oberholtzer: PhD 1994, McMaster University. Dissertation: "Together We Survive: East Cree Material Culture." Cath has made important contributions to public understanding of the social history and contemporary culture and language of Cree Indians. She works with the Cree to make available CD- and Web-based images of their artifacts and linguistic materials.

time we took on the joint roles of wife and mother with the expectation that we were to stay at home.

Responding to these explicit and implicit attitudes, and to the implied advice of my male mentor, I—like many women of that period—married young and started a family. No one suggested that I was too young to marry at eighteen, nor that I should develop my budding interests in medicine, archaeology, exotic cultures, and the history of languages through university study. Rather, I was encouraged to marry and to raise a family. Within ten years of marriage, we had produced four children and acquired the requisite cat, dog, and mortgage. But while I enjoyed this role of mother and homemaker, there always remained a persistent yearning for "me."

~ The Beginning of a Hobby ~

In the late 1960s and early 1970s, Ontario universities began to offer part-time courses, partially in response to the Ministry of Education's newly enforced requirements that all elementary teachers must possess a Bachelor of Arts degree. Evening courses were offered both on and off campus to enable certified teachers to acquire the necessary accreditation. As the accessibility of a university degree through part-time studies gained in popularity, people other than teachers took advantage of the situation. A university-sponsored promotional lecture given by university professors at our local high school introduced me to the world of anthropology, a world I had long been interested in, but which, until that time, had not had a name. Thus, in the early 1970s, I, too, became a part-time student.

At that time, the prevailing attitude expressed within family, community, and academic circles made me feel that I was a "housewife with a hobby." Nevertheless, with the completion of that first course and the piece of paper officially acknowledging that I, hobby or no hobby, had accomplished something just for me—not as someone's wife, daughter, or mother, but as "me"—I was hooked.

And so as Super Mom, I began the first stage of my academic work.

~ Getting My Undergraduate Degree ~

Philosophically, my husband had no objection to my going to school. After all, he was still hoping that I might become a doctor and support him in a manner to which he would like to become accustomed! However, his career as a professional engineer was paramount (or should I say sacred?). As long as meals were prepared and served on time, the children looked after, the laundry done, the grass cut, and so on, whatever I chose to do in my spare time was acceptable. At first, the children were not quite as agreeable until they realized that I would be taking care of them as before, that I would still bake cookies and go on school outings. Friends and other family members expressed an ambivalence ranging from "Why do something that requires thinking and/or work?" to "How exciting; I wish I had the guts to do that, too."

Professors also voiced an ambivalent acceptance; some considered part-time students as second class. One male professor insisted upon denying me my own identity by always referring to me as *Mrs.* Oberholtzer, emphasizing my status as a married woman, as not really belonging in his class. Another made continual sneering comments about my neglect of domestic duties, although he had no knowledge of what was or was not being accomplished on the home front. Nor would a male department chair allow me, as a part-time student taking day courses, to take corresponding daytime tutorials as priority was given to full-time students. Offsetting this negativity, other professors openly expressed their respect for the dedication of mature students.

Fellow part-time students (remember, the majority of them at that time were teachers) were often openly hostile in their concern that I might be competing for their precious teaching jobs. For the most part, full-time students accepted me as one of them and many lasting friendships were formed. At this time during the 1970s, however, there was still some latent sexism evident. After I attained a fairly decent result on an exam, a male full-time student commented that it was "not bad for a woman."

My own reactions during those years ranged from anger at a husband who had "forgotten" to turn on the oven to cook the meal prepared before I left for class, to exhaustion from balancing the demands of family, school, housework, volunteer work, and paid work as a research assistant, to frustration with a system that was not accommodating to housewives' schedules and needs, and yes, to euphoria upon receiving scholarships in recognition of academic success *and* character.

~ The Hobby Intensifies ~

By the time I had completed an undergraduate degree in 1981 while managing the demands of house, garden, family, part-time employment, and community service and had applied for graduate school, I began to detect certain attitudinal changes. By then, most of my family and friends recognized the sincerity of my academic interests, but my mother was so against my decision to continue that she would never admit any knowledge of it. Fortunately in the academic community, professors were very willing to accept me as a serious student and not just as a housewife with a hobby. Fellow students, suffering from the usual grad-student paranoia, offered varying degrees of friendship and support. In the wider perspective of the community, however, there was a general lack of understanding. Since I had finished my degree, why was I not working? And if I wasn't working, why did I have to give up some commitments (that is, "hobbies" of greater social value), as well as reduce the number of volunteer hours I worked? But many men in the community, who had openly scoffed or politely nodded at my comments, now reacted to those very same comments and ideas as though my word now had validity.

Graduate school was also a period of personal growth and a period in which a wonderful young man made a positive impact in our household. Our future son-in-law, then working on his PhD in pharmacology and molecular biology, arrived with an "attitude." His attitude was premised on the equality of men and women, and on the complementary nature of men's and women's roles, a concept espoused by many ethnologists, native societies, and less militant feminists. According to his principles, it is not demeaning to do housework or laundry, to cook or shop for groceries. As these chores constantly need to be done, whoever is free should attend to them. The ensuing change in attitude that developed through my family's acceptance of this ideal was a critical first step towards the pursuit of full-time doctoral studies.

And then the axe fell: my husband's job became redundant in the wave of corporate downsizing in the 1980s. With two children in university, one still in high school, a mortgage, and no income, it was a difficult time. Despite this stress, compounded by my husband's clinical depression, it proved to be a year of positive changes. Accustomed to working six days a week and many evenings, my husband now had ample opportunity to learn to shop, cook, and do laundry. He acquired banking skills and took over the routine of bill paying. Along with these practical aspects of daily living, he began to enjoy socializing as he went about his errands or walking the dog. With these new skills and a positive attitude change, plus the realization that there were no jobs for him, he wholeheartedly endorsed my decision to pursue a doctoral degree in anthropology at a university in another community.

Other factors also influenced my decision to return to school. I had a small archaeological consulting firm with two others (a woman and a man), but with little income coming in, we all decided that to get anywhere we would have to obtain PhDs. I decided at that time to switch from archaeology to social anthropology. The second factor in deciding to pursue graduate work again was financial. Since my husband no longer had a job, it was important for me to acquire a stronger, more marketable academic background. Further reinforcement came from a discernible change in social attitude: the idea of women with careers was beginning to supplant the one of housewives with hobbies.

From Hobby to Profession: In Pursuit of a Career

On a personal level, the first two years (1987–1989) of living in the university city during the week and coming home on weekends had elements of being the best of both worlds. When I arrived home, my husband would have the housework and shopping done, leaving me free to catch up on other chores and to enjoy our time together. On Mondays I went back to an apartment that had been cleaned by my roommate (who happened to be our younger son), leaving me free to pursue my studies. For someone driven to avoid housework at all costs, this was indeed heaven.

But this was real life and not the heavenly hereafter. On my way home from school every weekend, I made a detour to visit my mother, who was in the process of establishing yet another long-term and frustrating pattern of power and control. She continually made herself ill by refusing to eat while continuing to smoke and consume alcohol. The only time she was "well" was the day I visited. Once I had done her laundry, shopped, prepared some food for the coming week, and played cards with her, I was free to catch the train home. Subsequently she moved to our community but continued to require hospitalization every time I went off to do research, go to a conference, or spend any time away. Her initial disapproval of my participation in the master's program of study became manifest in this recognizable form of hysteria.

The attitudes of others were, and continue to be, more positive. Other than the voiced disapproval of an older male professor who strongly eschewed older women as students, and a department chair who assumed that as I was married, I did not need adequate funding, the academic community demonstrated equitable and positive attitudes. Friends and family continued being supportive. And as a doctoral student, I was viewed as having a certain cachet that had not been apparent earlier. On each level, however, there continued to be implicit expectations towards the fulfillment of my various roles as wife, mother, daughter, friend, student, volunteer, and employee.

From another perspective, the position and privilege of being a mature female student was brought home to me a number of times while doing fieldwork in numerous museums in Europe. My husband's unemployable status fortunately allowed him to accompany me for this step of the anthropological process. As we moved from area to area, we invariably met couples and single women who were running bed-and-breakfast accommodations. Virtually every woman expressed a latent desire to go back to school, but their husbands refused to allow them to do so. These women felt very constrained by European patriarchal social attitudes towards women and their roles as wage earners and housewives. It wasn't just that they perceived the traveling I was doing as glamorous. What they saw was the freedom to pursue their interests on their terms, to have a career, and to be accepted as an equal partner in their marriages.

As a barometer of North American social attitudes, television programming of the 1990s and beyond features "female heroes" (not heroines) in the "super she shows." Actresses portray women as captains of spaceships, police officers, lawyers, doctors, and in other positions of authority. On the downside, all the women are young and beautiful, chosen to appeal to a male audience. Most significantly, these progressively modern roles, as cutting-edge models for gender equality, implicitly and visually document that career and motherhood still cannot be combined. The only programming in which a woman can fulfill both aspects of her life are those that surround the leading woman with a support team of family and/or hired help. This raises questions—at least to me—whether attitudes have actually changed, or are merely reiterated in another form.

Being an Anthropologist

Surprisingly, receiving my PhD in 1994, when I was in my fifties, seemed somewhat anticlimactic. No longer a student with the pressures (and, let's face it, the stimulation) of deadlines for essays, oral examinations, and the ever-present anxiety of "the thesis," the end was merely a piece of paper acknowledging that I was now a full-fledged anthropologist. Smitten with the allure of research, I was ecstatic when I received a two-year postdoctoral fellowship to explore the Cree collections held in North American museums. My "hobby" had become serious. It was taking shape as a means for fruitful employment as an occasional lecturer and part-time researcher.

I had directed my initial research towards an attempt to reconstruct the social history of the James Bay Cree by considering the items of Cree material culture that had been acquired and sent back to Britain and Europe by traders, missionaries, and travelers. After compiling a list of museums containing material that might be Cree (not all museums have detailed cataloguing for those early pieces), my husband and I spent four months traveling from museum to museum, examining and photographing these collections. Once home, a selection of these photographs was enlarged into an eight-by-ten-inch format prior to our going into the Cree communities on the west coast of James Bay. I recorded Cree responses to these images during informal interviews. I then carried out similar procedures on the east coast of James Bay the following summer. The information from these two periods of fieldwork became the foundation of my dissertation.

During the two-year tenure of the postdoctoral fellowship, I focused my research on the Cree collections of several North American museums and was able to broaden my knowledge and to increase the amount of data with which to work. A recent three-year grant has provided the means to access historical documents pertaining to the European presence in the James Bay area, in particular the practices and influences of the traders and missionaries. A fascinating history is unfolding that highlights the enormous role Cree artifacts have played. Through the study of these material items, the Cree symbol system and the Cree perspective of artistic expression and aesthetics have been disclosed—for example, the embedding of Cree symbols within European-looking beadwork. The use of these processes as "negotiators" in native and nonnative relations was established, and now, with the addition of archival evidence, the documentation of a longstanding tourist trade has been revealed.

Looking Back: Women in Academe

Social attitudes appear to have changed for the better in support of women in academe in the more than thirty years since I took that initial anthropology course. Academically and professionally, women anthropologists have come a long way since British scholar Beatrice Blackwood, choosing career over marriage because she was "too plain," received her degrees retroactively once the male bastion of Oxford University began granting degrees to women in 1920.[1] Or even two decades later when graduate student Regina Flannery was told that a woman's place was in the home and that there was no place for women in anthropology.[2]

Although social attitudes appear to have changed for the better in support of women academics, there still remains a certain undercurrent at the community level and, to some extent, at the familial level. I sense that mature women graduates are still viewed to some degree as housewives with hobbies. On reflecting about the path my life has taken, perhaps the mentor of my teen years had a well-intentioned and valid concern that women shouldn't combine marriage and children with a career, but I would do it all again. Accordingly, I tend to encourage female students to be flexible about what comes their way and to be comfortable with who they are, rather than rigidly scheduling stages of their lives.

Feeling that I was "born an anthropologist," it is satisfying to have achieved academic recognition as such. Certainly, sharing my enthusiasm for the four-field discipline of anthropology with students is regularly rewarded by comments that anthropology is so exciting and by fervent requests to supply letters of reference for graduate programs in anthropology. On another level, having juggled all the aspects of being a wife, mother, grandmother, daughter, and volunteer while pursuing my hobby of learning, these life experiences have produced an empathy with, and respect for, my mature students and their same struggles. Their evident appreciation is gratifying and their dedication inspiring.

Now that my husband and I have become the senior members of the family with the deaths of our parents and aged dog, and having only one adult child at home, I now have the time to pursue a career full time. Ironically, hampered now by a reduced income due to lack of teaching positions and my husband's limited pension, my research can truly be labeled a hobby! This concept of hobby, nonetheless, is tempered to a great degree by the recognition that I am just now attaining for my results in reconstructing James Bay Cree social history from extant historical material culture of museum collections. Without doubt, the pleasure and satisfaction I derive from research and piecing together tidbits of information extend beyond the parameters commonly referred to as "work." And certainly the opportunity to travel to "exotic" places for museum and archival research, fieldwork, and conferences happily exposes us to new friends and experiences. Additional fulfillment comes from sharing the results of my research with the descendants of the Cree artisans who created the beautiful items that are now housed in various museums and private collections.

Recent advancements in technology now permit the Cree to access images of the creative expressions of their ancestors in their own homes and schools. In 2001, in collaboration with the Cree and based on my own research, we produced a CD-ROM with the images of one hundred objects housed in museums along with the database for the objects. In 2005 I began the process of preparing a virtual miniexhibition of these objects for a Cree website. I am also working with a linguist to provide the images for an online Cree dictionary. It is rewarding to be able to share my research results with descendants of the Cree women and men who created the objects.

No longer do I think of myself as a housewife with hobbies. Now I like to think of myself as a professional anthropologist with a passion!

Endnotes

1. Gacs et al. (1989:17).
2. Gardner (1990:87–88).

References

Gacs, Ute, Aisha Khan, Jerrie McIntyre, and Ruth Weinberg, eds. 1989. *Women Anthropologists: Selected Biographies.* Urbana: Univ. of Illinois Press.

Gardner, William M. 1990. Regina Flannery Herzfeld: Anthropologist and First Full-Time Woman Faculty Member. In *Pioneering Women at the Catholic University of America*, ed. E. Catherine Dunn and Dorothy A. Mohler, 85–100. Privately printed.

Changing Roles, Challenging Irrelevance

My Story as a Reentry Woman

Dorothy M. Castille

"What Do You Need with a PhD?"

On a brilliant Northern California July day in 1983, I left my children with a neighbor and drove to Berkeley for an appointment with the graduate advisor at the University of California. Naively, I felt secure in the knowledge that my life experiences were unusual and potentially interesting. Sitting across the desk from me, a distinguished, silver-haired senior male professor listened tolerantly as I introduced myself as a military wife and mother of four boys. I explained my interest in research and my observations of Asian women married to U.S. military men. I told him I had developed observational skills, the ability to communicate effectively across cultural boundaries, and sensitivity for other cultures. In response to the customary battery of "why" questions—why anthropology? why here? why now?—I clearly articulated my reasons for seeking graduate training. Nevertheless, he laughed in response. "You are a military wife with four children, what do you need with a PhD? Go to Cal State Hayward and get a master's degree. That's all you need." I can recount this incident now because I met that professor's challenge. I received my MA from California State University, Hayward, in 1986 and, at the age of forty-nine, my PhD from Berkeley in 1996.

Dorothy M. Castille: PhD 1996, University of California, Berkeley. Dissertation: "Psychological Affliction and Traditional Treatment of Mental Illness among Maya Indians of Highland Chiapas, Mexico." Dorothy received postdoctoral training in psychiatric epidemiology. Currently, she is a research scientist at the New York State Psychiatric Institute in New York City. She has written a number of articles about her research.

How could I make sense of that brief interchange? What did it tell me about the value of life experience, self-disclosure, and the rules for success in a highly competitive environment? Where does "having a life" fit into the gestalt of being a graduate student? This encounter was the first of many lessons on appropriate behavior in a male-dominated work environment. It is instructive to examine more closely what was implied by the professor's response:

~ *Life experience—it does not count.*

Although life experience for both men and women frequently guides our choice of discipline, the direction our research takes, the questions we identify as important to pursue, the information we determine to be significant, and our analysis of that data, it is often not assigned value.

~ *Self-disclosure—don't do it.*

Self-disclosure is a process women use to establish links with other women.[1] In daily life and in fieldwork, men and women form connections with others by sharing pictures of one's children or talking about a personal experience, but women use this intimacy-building behavior far more than men. Since there are times and places when self-disclosure is or is not appropriate, one of the important lessons in professionalism is the timely use of self-disclosure.

~ *A life outside of school hours with physical, emotional, and financial responsibilities for other lives—don't mention it.*

That other independent existence, the personal life of a graduate student, provides the concrete experience on which the anthropological training builds. A valuable and essential characteristic is the ability to compartmentalize. It is a skill needed especially in the social sciences, where researcher and research participant are so intimately influenced by each other.

~ Military Wife: Expectations of Conformity ~

Understanding the response of the distinguished professor implies understanding the context that brought me to that point. Women of my generation entering college in southwest Louisiana in the mid-1960s were encouraged to get an education as insurance should something happen to their husbands. The expectation was that once children arrived, a woman was to be "all wife and mother." She was to live out dreams and desires through her husband and children.[2]

For the wife of a man in the military, those expectations exist within an even more rigid set of demands. The military is one of the most conservative segments of American society. A woman who marries a military man is literally married to the military culture, in which she is expected to be willing to be dependent on and deferential to her husband. She must be solicitous of his needs when he is home, yet independent and capable of assuming all responsibilities for home, family, and frequently her own career when he is away. She must be flexible, able to entertain guests without prior warning, and never forget the part she plays in shoring up his masculinity and by extension that of the military establishment and the American government by her traditional femininity.

The mobility of the military family (we moved eleven times in thirteen years, and were not exceptional among military families) means the military wife lives without the support of family and must quickly form alliances with other women upon whom she can rely. If she has career aspirations, she must develop them in areas amenable to short-term involvement and frequent change. She must also consider the impact of her career on that of her husband's. She may find herself simultaneously overprotected and underprotected. In sum, except in that she shows commitment in long-term projects, the "successful" military wife does not exhibit characteristics that express independence and assertion of personal priorities—characteristics, incidentally, that are essential to being a successful graduate student or anthropologist.[3]

~ New Roles: Single Mother, Graduate Student ~

From the age of seventeen, I had dreamed of a career conducting research, writing, and teaching at the university level, a dream postponed by marriage and family but never abandoned. Prior to my first course in anthropology in the fall of 1983, I had to my credit a number of accomplishments normally viewed as milestones of adulthood. They included an undergraduate degree (1969) and some graduate training in English; thirteen years as a military wife on bases in the United States, the Philippines, and Iceland; and birthing and parenting four boys whose ages then ranged from four to thirteen years. I also had taught grammar, composition, public speaking, and adult education courses at a variety of levels at a number of duty stations.

I developed a specific interest in anthropology through my contacts with Asian women—Taiwanese, Japanese, Korean, Filipina—who were married to American military men. Experiences at each duty station raised new questions for me. I did not have the anthropological skills that would have helped me to organize my observations into more satisfying answers. However, in 1982 my family transferred to a naval base in Northern California, and I began to investigate the feasibility of graduate study in anthropology to productively fill my time—my husband was usually out on a ship—while meeting longstanding goals.

When I returned to school in the fall of 1983 to take one course in cross-cultural childrearing, it had been thirteen years since I had seriously dedicated myself to study. That course was a snap, but the ones that followed were not. The complete works of Dr. Seuss did little to prepare me for the wonders of kinship algebra. With my brain the consistency of watery oatmeal, I attended class while the boys were in school; cooked, cleaned, met needs, and ran errands in the afternoons and evenings; and studied when they finally slept. I read with two anthropological dictionaries at my side and wrote in my head while driving, doing dishes, and folding laundry.

My first interviewees were other military wives. In a small study designed to understand the impact of frequent moves on military mothers and children, I learned that flexibility and awareness of a range of options available to solve any problem characterized women who adapted well, in contrast to those needing psychological support.[4]

My husband went to his next duty station in 1985. I remained in California with the children to provide the rest of us with geographic stability and to continue my education. By that time, I had been single-parenting through a number of his six-month cruises and enjoyed the feeling of autonomy that came from successfully setting and achieving my own goals. However, in that same year, we filed for a divorce (not as a consequence of my continued education) and lost not only the myth of an intact family but also the familiar network of military families and their practiced support.

Members of my family were concerned when I chose graduate school over return to the bosom of the extended family. They asked, "Don't you think you're overachieving?" and "Why don't you move back home where we can take care of you?" Others commented: "You're just a perpetual student." "You should have finished school before you got married." "You can't take the kids to the field." "You'll never finish your degree." The decision to stay in California was the most rebellious act of my life and ultimately the most affirming.

My return to graduate school coincided with major issues of the loneliness of living without a spouse and of no one to help with the children, even for a few hours. Necessary identity shifts occurred regularly each day as I went from competent adult to lowly graduate student—a shift one professor referred to as a "return to latency"—and then back to functioning adult. It evoked for me and for other older women of my cohort the impotence of feeling small and powerless in interactions with powerful, self-absorbed faculty members. My best preparation for entering the academic environment was the flexibility, developed as a military wife, to respond rapidly to changing demands on my time and inner resources.

Financial concerns pushed me to seek employment as a research assistant, reader, graduate student instructor, and bookkeeper for a psychologist in private practice, combining as many as three part-time jobs with single parenting and full-time graduate study. There was never enough time to think before writing a critical essay, never enough time to deal adequately with the quantity of reading. Nor was there recognition by professors or other graduate students of the completely independent and much more tangible life going on at home. Mention of these extracurricular activities was inappropriate and would be met only with scorn at school. I grew to meet the demands of the job.

~ Anthropologist in the Field ~

For family members who did not understand the need for, or the process of, graduate study, the requirement of field research was even less comprehensible. In the summer of 1993, I left California for the field, alone and responsible only for myself for the first time in my life. After months of soul-searching and discussion, it was mutually decided that the three younger boys (the oldest now being on his own) would go to live with their father at his next duty station in Italy while I did my research in Chiapas, Mexico. Among the many perceptions thrown in relief by this process, the most significant for me was yet another aspect of changing identity.

Functioning as neither wife nor mother nor student but as independent researcher, I recognized fear as my constant companion. Fear of what? Fear of making mistakes, of not keeping commitments in the field, of hurting collaborators and informants. Fear of not collecting enough data or data of the right kind to answer the questions I proposed to investigate. Practical fears included falling and serious injury on the mountain trail, intestinal parasites, terminal diarrhea, and flying bullets. My fieldwork coincided with the Zapatista rebellion, which began in Chiapas in January 1994, and the subsequent crash of the Mexican economy. In spite of generous funding from the National Science Foundation and campus-based sources, I feared not having enough money to finish my work and return home. One advisor suggested that feeling afraid was a normal sign of being alive. Most of all, I felt fear to leave behind my familiar roles and take on the new role of professional anthropologist. After all, I was then in my late forties, alone, with no gainful employment or other means of support and no encouraging prospects on the horizon.

I finished my fieldwork in spite of my fears, and in 1995 was hired as a tenure-track assistant professor in an anthropology department in Idaho. Women who do not complete their doctorates frequently stumble at the dissertation stage.[5] But, motivated by personal, professional, and economic forces, I finished writing my dissertation during my first year of teaching and filed it in the spring of 1996. My boys attended the graduation ceremony with me that year, videotaped the event, and loudly cheered my hooding.

~ Assistant Professor: Working with Reentry Women ~

Even in the most homogeneous environment (Idaho apparently being extreme in that sense), there is tremendous diversity and much to be learned. Working with reentry women at the university who also had lives outside of school (my two younger sons had joined me in Idaho), I confronted my own ambivalence. There was a harshness in me that came from my belief that reentry women could be successful only if they were able to perform at the same level as young uncommitted students. On the other hand, I recognized that their many other responsibilities not only competed with but also interfered with their ability to perform. How can we faculty recognize the complexity of older students' lives, evaluate their work fairly with respect to the work of younger students, and still adequately prepare them to be competitive performers in a tight job market?

In part the answer is to capitalize on the richness of experience older students bring to the classroom. No one had to sternly warn those women of the tight job market or the highly competitive nature of the discipline. They learned that lesson through the experience of applying to graduate programs and not getting accepted, through reevaluating their own goals and priorities, and through dealing with the limits of their own abilities. My job was to be available to provide an insider's perspective that included a range of options.

~ Research Scientist ~

The most secure and possibly the only path to a research career is through postdoctoral training. In March 1998 I applied for and received a National Institute of Mental Health research training fellowship in psychiatric epidemiology (PET) in the Mailman School of Public Health at Columbia University. Research and writing were the specific goals of the fellowship. My PET fellowship terminated a couple of months early, in April 2001, to enable me to accept a full-time position as a research scientist at the New York State Psychiatric Institute. In this position I direct research on the outcomes in the community for people under court orders to remain in treatment after discharge from a psychiatric hospitalization, a contracted study funded by the New York State Office of Mental Health. This final transition has been as exhilarating and challenging as each step that preceded it; however, no feat has been as difficult or meant as much as realizing my dream over the admonitions of my first encounter with that senior male anthropologist in July of 1983. Now, with tools at hand, the real learning begins. The journey has been worth every ounce of energy it took to complete.

~ The Anthropology of Reentry: Older Women as Resources ~

My experience resembles that of other women who went back to school in the 1980s and 1990s, the modal anthropology PhD graduate of 1994–1995 being a forty-year-old white female with a focus in sociocultural anthropology who conducted her fieldwork in North America.[6] This characterization of the age and sex of graduating anthropologists of the 1990s suggests several possible life-course patterns, including that of the woman who enters graduate study after having followed a more traditional life pattern. The sequence of events in women's lives commonly includes marriage and parenthood in one's early or middle twenties and subsequent attainment of other markers of adult status in our society. Helson et al. refer to this pattern as the "feminine social clock."[7] One alternative of this pattern occurs when a woman changes her life structure through divorce. For that woman, divorce may mark a time of rapid change in social roles, loss of approval from family and friends, loss of an appropriate model for meeting current and future challenges, and an increased sense of personal failure.[8] While divorce is a life-changing event that is often associated with entry into graduate school, the period of graduate study itself marks similar changes for many women.

While the roles I combined may be unique to me—military wife, mother of four boys, single parent, graduate student, fieldworker, tenure-track professor, and research scientist—occupying multiple roles is common to many reentry women.[9] An anthropological perspective gave me the ability to be more thoughtful in choosing the roles I wanted to undertake and how I wanted to fulfill them. Anthropology made me aware of the plasticity of culture and the active role of the individual in shaping participation in a culture as no other discipline could.

For me, graduate school in midlife was a complex experience bridging roles that, while apparently contrasting, transformed old skills to new purposes.[10] Rather than satisfying achievement needs through contributing to my husband's career, I turned my attention to remodeling my own talents and resurrecting dusty career plans to support my family in a less traditional way. I redirected personal goals toward professional markers of success. A perspective tuned to subjective and frequently emotional responses to experiences was rigorously reworked toward objectivity and grounded intellectual analysis. In the process, I went from adult expert status to that of novice in an arena in which life experience and family responsibilities directly counted for little. I competed with young men and women whose lives were exclusively devoted to graduate study.

Reentry women have lived full lives before returning to school; many enter college for the first time on the heels of divorce or during that process. However, they frequently return to gain an education with neither financial resources nor the understanding or support of family or community in the process. Their identities as wives, mothers, and students are devalued by American culture. Their personal experiences, while eventually relevant in terms of awareness gained from the process of living, are perceived as useless and are regarded as more of a hindrance by professors accustomed to eager-to-be-shaped young minds. Graduation means facing not only the vagaries of the job market, in which there is an average two-year wait for employment after receiving the PhD,[11] but also the worry of paying the student-loan piper.

As experienced older women, we can challenge established programs of graduate study to consider the complexity and richness of the resources reentry women bring to the learning process with support programs specifically aimed at this population. For example, grant and fellowship programs earmarked for women over thirty-five with dependent children would be a starting point, as would graduate student instructor and research assistant slots expressly designated to be filled from this group. Cooperative childcare groups for children of all ages might be designed to enhance parenting skills, as well as to provide respite to overtaxed mothers. Support groups, too, can be pivotal in spelling success for women entering a process apparently particularly designed to enhance one's insecurities. It would also help to extend student-loan forgiveness programs, such as exist for physicians, other medical practitioners, HIV/AIDS researchers, and some researchers at the National Institutes of Health. These programs permit the proportional cancellation of debt based on a broad range of specified community service options.

As anthropologists, we must consider how we might use the forge of our own lives to create relevant programs for our students and to suggest much-needed change in the institutions in which we work. There is a growing literature on women in midlife in psychology and psychiatric epidemiology. Narratives such as those in this volume complement that literature with an anthropology of reentry, filling out the statistical picture with meaning, emotion, and experience. Older women represent for the nation a resource too valuable to ignore.

Endnotes

1. Gilligan (1986).
2. Helson et al. (1984), Baruch and Barnett (1986).
3. Helson et al. (1984).
4. Castille and Berlin (1996), Ritsher et al. (2002).
5. Givens and Jablonski (1995).
6. Givens and Jablonski (1995:11).
7. Helson et al. (1984).
8. Helson et al. (1984:1086).
9. Baruch and Barnett (1986).
10. Cf. Helson et al. (1984).
11. Givens and Jablonski (1995).

References

Baruch, Grace, and Rosalind Barnett. 1986. Role Quality, Multiple Role Involvement, and Psychological Well-Being in Midlife Women. *Journal of Personality and Social Psychology* 51 (3): 578–85.

Castille, D. M., and E. A. Berlin. 1996. Ethnomedical Explanatory Models and Indigenous Classification of Mental Illness. In *Ethnobiology in Human Welfare*, ed. S. K. Jain. New Delhi: Deep Publications.

Gilligan, Carol. 1982. *In a Different Voice: Psychological Theory and Women's Development.* Cambridge, MA: Harvard Univ. Press.

Givens, David B., and Timothy Jablonski. 1995. Survey of Anthropology PhDs. *Anthropology News* 36 (6): 11–12.

Helson, Ravenna, Valory Mitchell, and Geraldine Moane. 1984. Personality and Patterns of Adherence and Nonadherence to the Social Clock. *Journal of Personality and Social Psychology* 46 (5): 1079–96.

Ritsher, J. B., A. G. Ryder, A. Karasz, and D. M. Castille. 2002. Methodological Issues in the Study of Psychopathology Across Cultures. In *New Directions in Cross-Cultural Psychology*, ed. P. Boski, J. R. van de Vijver, and A. M. Chodynicka, 129–45. Warsaw: Polish Psychological Association.

Section 3

The Web of Lives

Family Involvements, Career Interactions

MOST OF us entered graduate school after a period of being stay-at-home moms. All but one of us have children, and that one—deliberately and regretfully—rejected motherhood in favor of career. Nine of us have four or more children. Eight have had lifelong marriages (one recently ended, after fifty-three years, by her husband's death). The other nine have experienced divorce, widowhood, remarriage, and/or living together, and about half of us had periods of being single mothers of dependent children.

While doing our graduate studies, we were deeply involved in our personal web of lives, more or less encumbered by husbands, children, aging parents, community involvements, and other careers. Our daily concerns included much more than studying for the next day's exam, finishing a term paper, doing well on our prelims, or doing the research for our dissertations. We were managing homes, raising children, caring for parents, working in paid jobs, and generally coping with the fullness of life as mature adults.

In our roles as students, though, we found ourselves "demoted" to novice or apprentice. The stories in this section (and many others in this volume) reveal the ways we dealt with daily identity shifts from adult to novice, as we struggled with the complexities of balancing the responsibilities of our adult lives with our responsibilities as students working toward our passionately desired PhDs. They show how families—husbands, children, parents—can be supportive or, sometimes, a hindrance. They also reveal our determination and persistence—and it took a lot of that to push through to our PhDs!

On Becoming an Anthropologist[1]

Louana M. Lackey

As a member of the Association of Senior Anthropologists, I have been asked for any advice I might give to young anthropologists. I do not know if I am competent to do so, as I have never been a young anthropologist. During my misspent youth, after becoming the world's first college dropout, I was an art student, an artist's model, a waitress, a cook, a bartender, a house painter, a plumber's helper, a remodeling contractor, a dressmaker, and a seller of toys, among other occupations. I also married, settled down, and had children as was then the fashion.

By the time I decided to become an archeologist, I was an elementary school art teacher and a potter. The most compelling reason for this midlife career change was that archeologists seemed to be writing such stupid things about how people made pottery. I complained about this stupidity to one archeologist. "What do you know about it?" I was asked. "You're not an archeologist." Since I evidently couldn't say that one scholar or another was ill informed, wrong, or worse without my "union card," a PhD, I resolved to go back to school to get one.

After the youngest of my five children began kindergarten, I applied for admission to the American University in Washington, D.C. The university

Louana M. Lackey: PhD 1978, American University. Dissertation: "Materials, Methods, and Techniques of Modern Pottery Making in Acatlán, Puebla, Mexico." Louana was associate director of the Potomac River Archaeology Survey, 1982–1987. Her many publications include three books, one of which is based on her long-term field research among contemporary ceramic artists in the United States. She died in December 2005.

accepted me conditionally, both due to my less-than-outstanding record in my earlier academic career and because of my age. I was then forty-two, and the great flood of "nontraditional"—that is, overage students—had not yet started. I continued to teach art in order to pay tuition bills, my children's as well as my own. After four years as a part-time student, I received a BA in art history and anthropology at the age of forty-six, and six years later, a PhD in anthropology at the age of fifty-two. I cannot say that these ten years were very much fun or particularly easy, but they were certainly interesting.

When I went back to school I had not yet decided whether to become an "archaeologist" (that is, an art historian) or an "archeologist" (an anthropologist). I embarked on a double major in art history and in anthropology, both in order to help me reach a decision, and because neither the art department nor the anthropology department offered all of the requirements of their majors at night. Somehow I managed to finish the requirements of both, discovering in the process that anthropology was the way to go. Somehow, too, I managed to convince the graduate admissions committee that I was serious and that, despite my age and other commitments, I would finish the program. The committee accepted me but stated that as a part-time student I would be ineligible for financial aid; I saw no problem with this. The university was selling knowledge, and I desired to purchase it.

I was fortunate in my choice of an advisor, Charles W. McNett Jr. McNett was my undergraduate and graduate advisor and chairman of my dissertation committee. He was as skilled an advisor as he was a teacher, and I took care always to advise him of my plans—which courses I was going to register for, what papers I wanted to write, which sites I wanted to investigate, where I wanted to do my dissertation research. He usually assented to my choices, giving direction without seeming to. In addition, he served as a buffer between me and the rest of the department. Unfortunately, McNett's research interests lay in the preceramic Paleoindian Shawnee-Minisink site on the Upper Delaware River, and I had to go elsewhere to seek advice about ceramics.

The ceramic mentors I found were two of the best, George M. Foster and Frederick R. Matson. Foster, who had visited Acatlán in Mexico, encouraged me to use the village as a site for my dissertation research, made time at American Anthropological Association meetings to discuss my work with me, and wrote to me in the field. He agreed with me that the best way to find out how people made pots was to make pots with them, the same way they did. Matson, who had worked with village potters in the Near East, agreed as well. Matson patiently answered my stupidest questions by phone or mail, suggested sources, read my papers, and advised me about courses. As the outside member of my committee, he came down to American University from Penn State in eight inches of snow to attend my dissertation defense. Thus, I became an ethnoarcheologist. It was the best of both worlds: as an archeologist, I was not required to take more linguistics courses; as an ethnographer, I was not expected to go out into the hot sun and dig holes.

I have always found my age and various facets of my experience an asset in the field. My years as a waitress/bartender taught me to listen to people. Almost everything I learned in the building trades was helpful while working as a contract archeologist in downtown Washington and Baltimore. My background as a potter made it relatively easy to fit into life in a Mexican village pottery. Even motherhood taught skills useful to an ethnoarcheologist—I can be trusted to keep the dinner from burning, I know how to change a baby or watch a toddler, and when to clear my throat at older children's misbehavior. Further, someone of my advanced years does not present a threat to the young women of the community.

Age has both advantages and disadvantages. Despite affirmative action, one unfortunate consequence of finishing a PhD so late in life is that I never found a "real" job—a tenure-track position in a college or university anthropology department. Nevertheless, I do not think of anything that I could, or would, have done differently. Many women today defer marriage and children until they have finished school and have become established in their fields. Some wait too long and find that it is too late for one or both. I would suggest that these important steps not be deferred, if for no other reason than that a graduate student needs all the help he or she can get. My husband, a geographer, instilled in me a respect for the tools and materials of learning, such as original research, and careful documentation of this research. He taught me how to construct a scientific argument and typed all of my papers, including my dissertation. My children washed their own clothes, did most of the cleaning, and did quite a lot of the cooking. We may have become very tired of Tuna Helper, but we all learned a great deal in the process.

Since I got off to such a late start, I feel that I have barely reached midcareer level. I am not retired and doubt that I will ever have time to do so. I do not think I would like retirement anyway. I have been working in the state of Puebla, Mexico, for eighteen years, documenting traditional pottery-making methods before they become extinct and am currently researching the tin-glaze tradition in Spain and Mexico. When this project is completed, two more await, one in West Virginia, the other in Staffordshire, England. Meanwhile, while not in the field, I live in Baltimore, teach part time at the Maryland Institute College of Art, and, on occasion, rehab an Edwardian row house.

~ Epilogue: Into the Twenty-first Century[2] ~

After I finished my dissertation, I continued working in the state of Puebla, Mexico, for almost twenty years, documenting both traditional pre-Columbian pottery-making methods and Talavera Poblana, a Spanish-introduced tin-glaze tradition. When the owner of the Talavera fabrica I had been working in died, I was forced to change the direction of my research. I am now working with contemporary potters and ceramic artists in the United States. Using the same research methods

I developed in Mexico and Spain, I am trying to answer Michael Cardew's famous question: "Why make pots in the twenty-first century?"

My appointment as research scholar in the Department of Ceramics at the Maryland Institute College of Art in Baltimore facilitates these investigations. Since this midlife career change, I have written a number of articles for *Ceramics Monthly* and the *Journal of the National Council on Education for the Ceramic Arts*, as well as a book, *Rudy Autio*, published by the American Ceramic Society in 2002. I have not completely abandoned my roots, however. These publications are all really ethnoarcheology thinly disguised as art. In any event, contemporary American ceramic artists are better able, as well as more likely, to buy a girl a beer.

~ Endnotes ~

1. Louana Lackey's narrative first appeared in the *National Association of Student Anthropologists Bulletin* in the Summer 1992 issue under the heading "Elder Views." It is reprinted here with permission.
2. Written especially for this volume.

Family Involvements

Earning a PhD while Raising Children

Molly G. Schuchat

HAVING BEEN married and a parent for two-thirds of my life, I find that my "self" includes my husband, children, other kin, and friends in a very phenomenologically interpreted world. I see the real, the ideal, and the remembered chaotically intermixed. Instead of maintaining contact with a variety of important ideas and people only through letters from a distance, sometimes written by a third person and read to the recipient by yet a fourth, our support systems include immediate telephone, television, and, now, Internet connections, radically shrinking time and expanding space. All of this has affected the meanings traditionally embedded in the term *culture* and influenced my interest in studying anthropology in the middle years of my life.

Finding Anthropology

Ever since I learned to read, travel and history books have thrilled me. We had many such books in my parents' house, and I particularly remember Geoffrey Parsons's *The Stream of History*; the charming histories in Hendrik Willem Van Loon's *Van Loon's Lives*; and C. W. Ceram's books, foremost among them the *Gods, Graves, and Scholars*.

Molly G. Schuchat: PhD 1971, American University. Dissertation: "Hungarian Refugees in America and Their Counterparts in Hungary: The Interrelations between Cosmopolitanism and Ethnicity." Molly taught at a historically black college as part of the American Anthropological Association's outreach program and was editor-in-chief of the *Anthropology News*, 1985–1988. She has many published articles and has maintained an active stance on social issues.

In the summer of 1946, I visited Mexico, Guatemala, and the Yucatán with my parents. I came home fired up to return to the Maya with an archaeological group. However, people at the Carnegie Institution in my hometown of Washington, D.C., which funded much of the Yucatán work, discouraged me, saying, "Finish college before you do anything about anything." Back at Vassar, I wrote a long story based on a Mayan tale I had heard. A few years later, I did additional research in Spanish from original documents at the Library of Congress for a children's book of Incan and Mayan myths. But the publisher who had encouraged me discontinued the children's series before the book was finished, and I never pursued it further.

I received my undergraduate degree in economics from Vassar College in 1948, as I celebrated my twentieth birthday. My plans were to become a writer, preferably a foreign correspondent. Further formal education was not a part of this scheme, so I left my notes behind as I departed for the real world. On the other hand, from childhood on, I have kept one or another form of journal, and from that I have never parted. They provide a check of sorts on the memories on which I draw in this essay.

The overwhelming majority of my classmates married almost immediately after graduation and shortly thereafter moved, with their growing families, to the suburbs. But I remained single and spent the next five years working in advertising, public relations, and politics in American and European cities. In 1953 I married Michael A. Schuchat, an attorney in Washington, D.C. Mike and I had five children in the next seven years, during which period I also did a few public relations and related freelance jobs.

My father died suddenly soon after the birth of our fourth child. His death left me with the terrible understanding that there is no eternity. Realizing that greater familiarity with something would be necessary to establish myself in anything, it seemed imperative to work toward a master's degree. But in what? A political mentor, hoping to focus me more on my future than on my loss, sent me as her representative to a National Day Care Conference, where a cultural anthropologist, Ethel Alpenfels, gave the keynote address. Alpenfels observed that Mother's Day was the American National Day of Atonement because everyone, including mothers, who could escape childcare on a regular basis did so. This was not strictly an American phenomenon, she added, but held true throughout history; she cited as examples wet nurses, nannies, and governesses, as well as boarding schools. Alpenfels's anthropological approach to the subject excited my interest.

I was still interested in the Maya and decided that I wanted to learn more about pre-Columbian archaeology. I knew that it was separate from classical archaeology, but how was I to find out about the field? I went to the Castle, the Smithsonian Institution's headquarters, but didn't know what to do next. However, never underestimate the power of a guard. He asked me who I was looking for and immediately suggested I go upstairs and inquire at the Bureau of American Ethnology. So I did.

Several men were sitting around in ties and shirtsleeves. They welcomed the stranger and talked with me for an hour, at the conclusion of which the director,

Frank Roberts, suggested that I was possibly more interested in ethnology than archaeology. It was then that I recalled that I had actually taken one anthropology course at Vassar, about Bronislaw Malinowski's *Coral Gardens and Their Magic*, and did not like it at all, although I was impressed by the ideas brought up by the instructor, Mrs. Dorothy Lee. Dr. Roberts suggested several persons with whom I should speak about graduate study in anthropology in Washington and recommended that I audit an undergraduate course first to see how I liked the subject at this later date. We had our fifth child in the summer of 1961, and a month later I registered for the introductory anthropology course at American University. I loved it.

In 1962 I began graduate school, mostly part time, at the Catholic University of America, which had a small but well-established anthropology department. I wrote a master's thesis concerning the Bureau of Indian Affairs and the Northern Ute Indians and their experiences with development. In 1965 I began teaching a section of introductory anthropology at Howard University while continuing (still part time) toward the PhD at Catholic. During those years, I had several full-time job offers in the federal government and area community colleges, but I was not interested in working full time because of our children. I found that graduate school, with or without part-time teaching, did offer me "the freedom and flexibility and the chance to do the work of [my] choice" that Wendy Kaminer associates primarily with women volunteers.[1] Now, part-time work is sometimes comparatively well paid. It is also far more available, as are fellowships for part-time study, compared to the situation in the 1960s and even in the 1980s.

According to Virginia Kerns, my graduate time marked a central transition in my life from childbearing adulthood to nonchildbearing adulthood.[2] Was this corroborated by a young male grad student who sputtered, "Why, you're almost old enough to be my mother" when I celebrated my fortieth birthday? While it may be that with this transition many women experience heightened mobility, power, and authority,[3] the last two are sadly lacking to a graduate student, no matter how favorable other conditions.

~ The Great Years: Graduate School ~

I began graduate school in 1962 and received the PhD in 1971. From the beginning, I responded differently to graduate school than I had to college. I typed all my notes (and I still have them all!) and did all the reading. But I always felt fractured and rushed. However, I think that all my life I have chosen to be a juggler, trying to fit in many things at one time and accomplish them all by bedtime. I loved having kids, loved having people at our house, loved being involved in the outside world—and also loved getting away from all my responsibilities in the library, any library.

I wrote term papers based on my participant-observation experiences in my "other" life with my children in their nursery school and on their elementary school playground and on language styles I encountered teaching at Howard University. Independent of graduate school and anthropology, I always kept notes on the children, their activities, and behavior. Reviewing for this essay, I found one about the eldest, then eight, who firmly told a caller that his mommy couldn't come to the phone because she was studying for a test. Attending school myself seemed to provide a formidable excuse *not* to participate in most PTA-related activities. The other mothers (almost always mothers) thought of my schoolwork as something special and sacred and a perfectly reasonable excuse. So I didn't bake cookies, but I did act as room mother and drove car pools for field trips.

When it came time to pick a dissertation topic, I wanted to do something where I could stay in the Washington area, since we had five little children and my husband's well-established career to consider. I was interested in immigration and cultural change. I thought a study of the Hungarian refugees, the Freedom Fighters who had settled in the Washington area, might be useful. I gradually narrowed the topic to focus on their food patterns as a way of maintaining identity while also adapting to the way things were done in the United States. In doing this fieldwork with Hungarian immigrants, I was constantly juggling events and experiences while trying not to neglect family responsibilities. I attempted to involve my family in my research, but they had their own priorities. On the other hand, one or two of my major informants wanted to have me take on their family responsibilities along with mine and I could not let that happen, either. My dissertation director, Michael Kenny, took this more calmly than I did: "You win some and you lose some, but that's par for the course" is how he more or less consoled me.

Priscilla Reining and her husband, Conrad, a professor at Catholic University, said that I really would have to go to Hungary for part of my fieldwork, to participate in another language and culture. Bela Maday, at the National Institute of Mental Health, was extremely helpful in arranging for me to go for the summer of 1969 and associate with persons in the catering trade, as they called it, in Budapest and in Debrecen, a city famous for its bread. Bela introduced me to Tamas Hofer, Hungary's most prominent ethnographer, already well known in the United States.

Fieldwork in Hungary was, of course, an exciting anthropological experience, but it also offered a period of several months with no family responsibilities. For once, I could be completely self-centered. For me, there was no hurry in Hungary. I could take the time to walk everywhere. But after a while, as I watched other family groups and husbands and wives together or had dinner with a whole family, I began to wonder about this insanity that engaged me, and I cut two weeks out of my projected three months away.

~ My Children's Views ~

In writing this story, it seemed to me vital to interview my children, upon whom my student years probably had had the most profound effect. That, too, has been a learning experience, bringing home to me how strongly egocentric children are.

Our oldest sons were in second grade and kindergarten when I began graduate school and say they were not too aware of whether I was a worker or a student or what. As one put it, "I was pretty occupied with my own life." He does admit that in his early years, he was aware that, when I was not taking care of his needs, his mother was doing things that other mothers were not doing. The younger three, all under five when I began, were never aware that it could be any different. They all agreed that I was never gone all the time, but that in various ways I was not there, either: "Dad was gone all day, but you were always at work." "You were sitting at the typewriter, totally focused, didn't know I was in the room asking a question," one daughter said. On the other hand, she never remembers my having a test or deadline that prevented me from doing "what we needed done, except that from early years we were pretty independent. You weren't in the kitchen making snacks for us when we came home from school; we did that for ourselves."

When she was in junior high school, one of my girls was interviewed about having a working mother. She was quoted in the *Washington Post* to the effect that she didn't like it at first because I never went to school functions, but now it was wonderful not to have me in the way. She also expressed outrage that some of her friends' brothers didn't even know how to fry an egg and expected to be taken care of by their sisters, if not their mothers.

My other daughter said that she was proud of her mother, taking care of five kids and also studying and working professionally. She was appalled that some of her school friends thought of their future as getting married to take care of husbands. But this may not be due to her mother or anthropology, because "I have the most nonsexist brothers, and that is a value from both parents."

All of the children agreed that they knew that I was not studying business or accounting—"not that there is anything wrong with accounting." They knew that anthropology was not chemistry or physics, though they were not sure what it was except that it "involved Indians and foreign places, exotic places. There was no CNN back then." The youngest said he was always explaining to his elementary school teachers that I didn't study bones but how people live. He was eight when I went away for the summer, and remembered that he thought Hungary was a funny place to go to study how people enjoyed food.

They all mentioned the variety of students and other anthropologists who came to our house for parties and informal visits. An African priest spent a fair amount of time with us because it offered him a chance to play with children, something he sorely missed from life back home, where he was one of twelve children enmeshed in a large extended family. He used to tell our children about growing up with his family in Nigeria.

The older children recalled how my fellow students enlarged their intellectual life. One son is sure that his interest in Chinese and Japanese was first kindled by one of my dissertation advisors, Marjorie Whiting, who replied to his question about which languages were difficult to learn that those two East Asian ones were the hardest for westerners. This son also felt that there was a lot of tension in the house during his growing-up years, though he recognized that there is always a lot of tension involved in getting a graduate degree under any circumstances, and that five children—as well as a husband—must add a lot to that. But, reflecting on his own graduate school years, he thinks that my having a husband and his income must have also been a help.

Most of the children were very interested in travel, but not as tourists. Our daughter the doctor suggests that watching me getting trained and then working as an anthropologist probably helped propel her toward epidemiology with its anthropological component, which is both more exotic and diverse than hospital work. She was always interested in travel and other cultures, but unlike some of her friends in high school and college who went traveling as tourists, she only wanted to go where she could have working-in-the-country relationships. All of the children took some anthropology courses while in college, and one actually majored in the subject as an undergraduate. None became an anthropologist, but all have lived and worked outside of the United States.

Now it is my grandchildren's turn. Three of the five have studied anthropology in high school—an option not available to my children. One granddaughter, a junior in college, has just returned from a term in Ecuador where she lived with a variety of families as she studied anthropological issues. Another has developed a strong interest in anthropological film. All five grandchildren have had experiences outside the United States, opportunities that were not available when I was in high school and college.

~ My Family Support System ~

When we married, Mike said that after the children were born, he expected that I would work outside the house, as his mother always had. I suppose I outmaneuvered him by going to graduate school instead, but he was quite willing to help me go. My mother certainly encouraged me to go back to school. She paid for my first year of graduate training, Mike paid for the rest of my MA, and I paid for the PhD with part-time teaching.

My mother was always "working," but as a volunteer. She was usually president of whatever she was engaged in—something I have seldom been. Both she and my mother-in-law, who worked as a shoe saleswoman and had previously owned a dry goods store in West Virginia, had flexibility in their hours. For me, graduate school and college teaching permitted the kind of flexibility that makes it more possible to enjoy raising children as well as indulge in intellectual endeavors. Studying and preparation can be done at home. The Martin Luther King Central Library had many of the books I needed, and the Washington library system delivered them to the most convenient neighborhood library. If a child was ill, missing two hours of class was less disruptive for everyone than missing a day of work or trying to make alternative arrangements.

As far as support systems, until her quite-untimely death at sixty-five, my mother and her housekeeper helped out when other systems failed. The summer I went to Hungary, my mother-in-law, in her mid-seventies and not well, came to stay. Especially in the early days, with children in preschool and elementary school, I had the most regular assistance from an elderly neighbor up the street. Mrs. Ritchie would babysit for two or three hours at her home or mine for very little money while I went to class. Several of the courses were taught in the evening, and my husband, Mike, arranged his work life to cover those. It was a complex field organization, but it worked. It was probably responsible for some of the tension that one of the kids mentioned. I did seem to be always in a tearing hurry. But as I appraise this and other parts of my life, there has always been a surfeit of areas to investigate and goals to achieve.

Most of the time, even when agonizing over my divided life, I was gratefully aware that my personal and economic situation were such that I didn't have to struggle financially while raising children and pursuing the PhD. I had financial and every other kind of support and encouragement from my husband, a lawyer in private practice who was also, from 1969 to 1997, legal counsel for the American Anthropological Association.

Mike was in his mid-thirties when I started graduate school over forty years ago. Without his involvement and concern for the children and for me, my studies and research would not have been possible. Perhaps he was ahead of his time? But perhaps he was not. His profession, and his approach to it, permitted him maneuverability that many people do not have. He has always been certain that the primary part of life is home and family. He usually walked the children to elementary school on his way to work, which is, by the way, a privilege of urban living and neighborhood schools. He was self-employed and could set his own hours. We ate dinner together as a family unless I had an evening class starting at 6 p.m., in which event he was there to eat with the children and frequently to cook the meal as well.

But most of all, he listened, over and over, to my problems, my excitements, my hesitancies—and he never tuned me out. The times I had to accommodate to his priorities were so rare that they stand out, like the evening I was trying to finish the final revisions of my master's thesis but had to break off to join Mike at a client's fund-raising dinner for an association in which I had little interest. On the other hand, he joined me at events, like a debutante's ball sponsored by the Hungarian Freedom Fighters Association that I am sure was just as peripheral to his interests.

~ Life Experience and Academic Life ~

When I entered graduate school, I was welcomed and, I believe, taken seriously. A number of the other graduate students had also had postcollege experiences, and one was a single working mother of four. This being *the* Catholic University, several priests and nuns were fellow students. Unusual among universities at the time, Catholic offered advanced degrees in nursing and social work, so we also had a number of nurses and social workers in our classes. This being Washington, D.C., there were always foreign students who wanted not only to study but to be where the national power was. I had little time to socialize at school, but I did manage to attend the student anthropology club meetings. There was absolutely no time for me to attend outside lectures or have allied experiences. I suspect that my not knowing people beyond the department was not unusual for graduate students, although I certainly felt that those from other departments who took courses with us added immensely to my understanding of the various subjects under discussion. There was time to attend, with my husband, the parties for graduate students given by one or another faculty member. I think these gatherings were partly impelled by the number of graduate student priests who were in the city for their schooling but who had few other ties in the area. The anthropology department was small and sociable, encouraging close ties among students and faculty.

I think school and children make an excellent combination; in addition, my feeling is that graduate school directly after undergraduate school leaves a lot to be desired, at least in the social sciences and humanities, when there should be some grounding in the real world to underpin theoretical studies.

Interviews with family members and others as to what they learned and loathed have convinced me of the rich rewards for everyone in combining child-rearing with social study and with the comparative values of fieldwork at home as well as away from all of them. I think it is a useful approach to achieving the Good Society by bridging the "profound gap in our culture between technical reason, the knowledge with which we design computers or analyze DNA, and practical or moral reason, the ways we understand how we should live."[4] Children learn from their parents. When the latter go to school, too, it may help the children learn what education has to offer.

Of course, Bellah et al. call for the educational institution to recapture a well-defined sense of mission and a willingness to connect education to the common weal. I am uneasy that many anthropologists today study anthropology from undergraduate days straight on through graduate school. I think many of them have a very narrow understanding of their own culture beyond what they know from their formal education. No matter what their upbringing, such students are frequently not well acquainted with their own society and are poorly equipped to interpret or understand it. Perhaps this is merely justification for my having done a number of other things before going into anthropology, with its comparative approach as well as its particularistic focus. Nevertheless, I do believe that having some life experience before graduate school is particularly valuable in a social science that is also a humanistic endeavor.

In any event, the day after I turned in my dissertation to the graduate school office in the late winter of 1971, I joined the antiwar pickets at the White House. A short while later, I was turned down for a teaching job because I was "too old" (at forty-four!). Six months after I received my PhD, our oldest son went off to college. By that time, I was teaching adults, full-time workers at the National Institutes of Health, who were enrolled in an Upward Mobility College run by the then Federal City College. This was an on-site program, partially during work hours, to assist lower-level employees who could not proceed up the career ladder without college. These eager students confirmed my beliefs about the value of life experience to formal study.

~ Being an Anthropologist ~

Since becoming a fully qualified anthropologist, I have concentrated on applied anthropology, doing evaluation and program planning with a group of psychologists and social workers, counseling and educational consulting, and occasional college teaching. I have also continued my interest in food habits research, studying areas like camping food and who uses it, Good Humor salesmen and their customers, and the status meaning of chili peppers and other specialty foods.

From 1985 to 1988, I served as editor-in-chief of *Anthropology News*.[5] This certainly broadened and integrated my understanding of the entire field and its practitioners. Through that editorship I was privileged to watch the development of a small program to encourage minority participation in anthropology through the use of volunteer professors at interested institutions. I became such a volunteer, teaching and living at a historically black college in rural Mississippi, for three terms between 1991 and 1996, with continued involvement since.

I have always believed in volunteering in the community, no matter what else I was doing. In 1984 I spent some time in India. Upon my return, I participated in a church-sponsored program to feed and house homeless and unemployed women. Poor, overpopulated India was one thing, but rich America allowing her citizens to go hungry and live on the streets was and is an outrage. This program challenged a number of us to do more, and I was a founding member and first president of a home for formerly homeless women. The home opened in early 1989 and is still in operation, although some of its goals have been modified and none of the original members is still in residence.

I formally retired from most consultancies in 1998 but became more active in volunteer work. For several years, I have been a "professor" in a "traveling university" that brings informal courses to elders in assisted-living and nursing-home situations, and have taught more mobile seniors through a "lifetime learning" university. I have continued as the cultural consultant for a group in northern Virginia that trains aides and nurses in developing better communication skills for their work in hospice and chronic-care residential living. This has deepened my admiration for adults, mostly immigrants, who have taken up these helping roles with enormous compassion and patience. Their work is vital but mostly underappreciated by outsiders—and almost always dreadfully underpaid. Working in this project has also given me additional skills with programs of distance learning.

In my retirement years, I have also returned to a high school love: playwriting. I find that the anthropological understanding of group interactions carries over into plots and relationships imagined for the stage. Writing is very gratifying, and so are the local staged readings of some of my work, including scenes from my plays taken to the seniors in some of the programs mentioned above. The participants seem to like having a playwright to interact with!

Anthropology has offered me a way to meet and try to understand, and sometimes to assist, a wide variety of people. It provides me with intellectual and social stimulation and a continuing opportunity to try to see the world, just as I wanted to as a child. But it has also shown me that America reflects the world and I can find it all here, at my fingertips. As airplanes and autos become more obstacle than magic carpet, or perhaps as I get crankier and less accepting of the discomforts of travel, that is all to the good. Most of all, though, I am grateful to have become an anthropologist, because it has provided me with a focus for seeing and being part of an ever-brave new world.

~ Endnotes ~

1. Kaminer (1984).
2. Kerns (1992).
3. Brown (1992).
4. Bellah et al. (1991:44).
5. Editors' Note: *Anthropology News,* published by the American Anthropological Association, is read by about twenty thousand anthropologists.

~ References ~

Bellah, Robert N., R. Madsden, W. M. Sullivan, A. Swidler, and S. M. Tipton. 1991. *The Good Society*. New York: Knopf.

Brown, Judith K. 1992. Lives of Middle-Aged Women. In *In Her Prime: New Views of Middle-Aged Women,* 2nd. ed., ed. Virginia Kerns and Judith K. Brown, 17–30. Urbana: Univ. of Illinois Press.

Ceram, C. W. 1951. *Gods, Graves, and Scholars.* Tr. E. B. Garride. New York: Knopf.

Kaminer, Wendy. 1984. *Women Volunteering: The Pleasure, Pain, and Politics of Unpaid Work from 1830 to the Present.* Garden City, NY: Anchor Books.

Kerns, Virginia. 1992. Female Control of Sexuality: Garífuna Women at Middle Age. In *In Her Prime: New Views of Middle-Aged Women,* 2nd ed., ed. Virginia Kerns and Judith K. Brown, 95–111. Urbana: Univ. of Illinois Press.

Malinowski, Bronislaw. 1935. *Coral Gardens and Their Magic.* London: Allen & Unwin.

Parsons, Geoffrey. 1929. *The Stream of History.* New York: Scribner.

Van Loon, Hendrik Willem. 1942. *Van Loon's Lives.* New York: Simon and Schuster.

Career Constraints and Enhancements

Marriage, Family, and Age

Ellen C. Rhoads Holmes

Two Steps Forward, One Back: Becoming an Anthropologist

A few years ago, during an anthropology meeting in Columbus, Ohio, a sudden spring snowstorm trapped us all in the meeting hotel. The distinguished lecture had to be canceled as the speaker could not get to the meeting. Since it was too late to cancel the postlecture reception, the program chair suggested we entertain ourselves by each telling how we became an anthropologist. It was astounding to me to learn that almost none of us had originally planned to be anthropologists but had "discovered" the field on our way to some other career.

In my case, I had entered college in 1953 with a major in accounting and visions of becoming a certified public accountant. Women in my family were expected to go to college, but there seemed to be less concern about actual graduation. I recall comments to the effect that going for a couple of years was a good idea "in case you have to take care of yourself." After my sophomore year, I discontinued my education to get married, a common trend in the 1950s. My husband was an air force pilot at the time and was hooked on aviation, in spite of a college degree in a completely unrelated field. Ultimately, he decided to pursue a degree in aeronautical engineering at the University of Colorado in Boulder. In the fall of 1959, we moved into half of a Quonset hut in married student housing with our daughters—a two-year-old

Ellen C. Rhoads Holmes: PhD 1981, University of Kansas. Dissertation: "Aging and Modernization in Three Samoan Communities." Ellen, now professor emerita, taught in the anthropology and gerontology departments at Wichita State University. She has written numerous publications, including *Other Cultures, Elder Years,* cowritten with her husband, Lowell Holmes.

and a four-month-old baby—and remained there for four years, during which my husband completed both BS and MS degrees in engineering.

It was during this time that I was first exposed to anthropology. I belonged to a students' wives organization that regularly scheduled lectures at their meetings by faculty from the university. At one of the first meetings I attended, anthropologist Omer Stewart talked about peyote and the Native American Church, its cultural significance, and the associated legal problems experienced by Native Americans. I found his comments fascinating. Over the next few years, I heard other anthropologists and met some anthropology students and always found the subject matter more appealing than other disciplines. I vowed that if I ever returned to school, I would take a course in anthropology.

It is probably relevant that as a child growing up in a small town in Mississippi, I was interested in people and places different from those in my own experiences. In fact, when I saw movies about cowboys and Indians, I was always rooting for the Indians. My husband was from upstate New York and had traveled widely in the United States. After our marriage, we lived in Montana, where our first daughter was born, and Oregon, birthplace of our second daughter, then Colorado, Washington, and Kansas. I had opportunities to learn about different regional lifeways, foods, celebrations, and activities. Perhaps I just had to find anthropology to give me a label for my interests.

It was not until I was widowed at age twenty-eight that I began to give serious thought to resuming my education. After a brief stint as an aeronautical engineer for Boeing in Seattle, Washington, my husband had found his dream job as an engineering test pilot for an aircraft company in Wichita, Kansas. Unfortunately, only six months later his career ended with his death in a plane crash in August 1964. My daughters were seven and five years old at that time, and we had a modest but sufficient income so that I did not have to work immediately. Over the next year, we began to adjust to the changes in our lives, and I considered returning to school as a logical possibility, especially since there was a state university in the community. The plan was to arrange my class schedule around my children's school hours, thereby using the public school system as my source of daycare. In the fall of 1965, I enrolled and began classes at Wichita State University. At age twenty-nine, I felt certain that I would be the oldest student on campus, but I soon learned that there were many other "mature" students at this urban university in the largest city in Kansas.

Almost all the credits from my first two college years a decade earlier transferred. I was a junior with a need to decide on a major soon. I had long ago abandoned the idea of continuing work toward an accounting degree in favor of interests in social science. And the desire to explore anthropology was still there. Spring semester found me among the five hundred students in Anthropology 124, and the course confirmed that I had indeed found my niche.

As my daughters progressed through grade school, I gradually increased my course load and completed my BA in 1968. My only sibling, a brother almost ten years younger, had finished his degree only a few months before I did. At that point, I had not given much thought to continuing my education and spent a few months being "Mom." About the time I began to realize that I was spending most of my time doing the same amount of housework that I had previously managed to do along with going to school, one of my mentors in anthropology spoke to a church group I was attending. Afterward, he asked what I was doing since graduation and suggested that I should consider graduate school. It was all I needed to motivate me, and in January 1969 I reentered Wichita State University to begin work on an MA in anthropology, which I completed in 1971.

At the outset, I had not even considered going beyond the BA, but at the age of thirty-five, I was beginning to consider seriously the possibility of pursuing a PhD. While working on the MA, I had had an opportunity to work as a lecturer in anthropology at the local air base and to serve as a teaching assistant on campus. This teaching experience brought an offer from the anthropology department at Wichita State to teach for a year. This allowed me time to think about my future options and decide on the best course of action.

The nearest institution offering a PhD in anthropology at affordable cost (i.e., in-state tuition) was the University of Kansas in Lawrence, a 300-mile round-trip from Wichita by turnpike. Fortunately, some of the faculty there had interests that matched mine. My children were now teenagers, with the older one in high school. They had long-established friends in Wichita. We had no family living nearer than 900 miles. My parents both worked and were caring for my grandmother, who lived with them. No one in the family had ever earned a PhD, so I was entering new territory in that sense. My parents raised no objections, but I suspect they thought I was on some interminable quest for education that they did not really understand.

As a consequence of not having family available as an on-the-spot support system, I had developed a small, local support network of friends. These were the people who cared for my daughters while I took part in a two-week anthropology field trip on one occasion, when I attended professional meetings, and during a couple of hospitalizations. The mother of one of my close friends was even called "Grandma" by my kids. These factors influenced my decision that it would be simpler and less disruptive, especially for my children, to continue living in Wichita while I commuted the distance to the university for my doctoral work.

I was admitted to the University of Kansas (KU) to begin work toward the PhD in anthropology in fall 1972. I was thirty-six years old at the time and somewhat less concerned about being an older student than when I first returned to college. This was probably because Wichita State had been a comfortable environment for a student like me, and by the time I had finished my degrees there, a student my age was hardly unusual—the average age of students on the campus being about twenty-seven years. Although I often had been the oldest student in my anthropology classes, it never presented any real problems, and the department faculty were supportive of all of us, regardless of age. Fortunately, all of the faculty were older than I by at least a few years, and at least one person had completed his PhD in his early fifties. They encouraged me in my efforts with no reservations about age.

The University of Kansas presented a different atmosphere altogether. I was always more aware of being older there, since almost all of the students in my classes were considerably younger. It was a more traditional kind of institution, with an overwhelming majority of young, straight-from-high-school students. Older students were less obvious on campus. I felt the quality of education was good, and I was able to pursue effectively my interests in Polynesian culture, cultural change, and worldview. But I always had the sense that I was viewed as somewhat too nontraditional. And there was a vague feeling that the faculty were not too sure I was serious about getting the degree. I chose not to take more than six hours of coursework at any time in graduate school in the hope of providing as much stability as possible for my family and, to be truthful, retaining sanity for myself. Being in the position of raising my children alone clearly affected some of the choices I made and the speed at which I progressed through the academic system. In general, commuting was also a workable, if not entirely pleasant, experience.

The second year of my PhD work proved very frustrating. In addition to my coursework at KU, I was offered an opportunity to teach two sections of an anthropology course at Wichita State. Teaching was relatively simple because of my previous experience and knowledge of the required content, and it also provided some additional income. Unfortunately, early in the fall semester, serious problems developed as my younger daughter took a less-than-ideal approach to coming of age. This straight-A student became disillusioned with school and embarked on forms of rebellion quite typical of the counterculture at the time. Because I soon found it impossible to devote the serious concentration required by the coursework I was enrolled for at KU, I had to withdraw in midsemester, the only such instance in my entire academic history. Although the family problems continued for quite some time, I managed to make reasonable progress in my education in subsequent semesters.

In 1975, having completed all of my in-class work for the PhD, I took a job with a newly developed program in gerontology at Wichita State University. My oldest daughter had just graduated from high school and was ready to enter the university, so the time had come for generating more income on a regular basis. At that time, the development of multidisciplinary programs in gerontology was being encouraged and funded through grants from the Administration on Aging. Wichita State was fortunate to have several faculty (including an anthropologist) who had already done research or had strong interests in various aspects of aging and were able to develop the necessary courses with ease. I became the academic coordinator, who was the primary advisor for students and liaison with faculty who taught the courses. This position was initially half time, mostly administrative, and would allow me to take leave while doing fieldwork for my dissertation.

Leaving the country to do fieldwork, however, presented a major challenge. Lowell Holmes, one of my former professors at Wichita State, was one of the pioneers in the anthropology of aging. He offered me an opportunity to participate in a grant-funded research project in American Samoa and Western Samoa and with Samoan migrants in the San Francisco Bay area. The research involved a test of what gerontologists call the "aging and modernization theory." It focused on aging Samoans in three different situations: an isolated village; a more urban setting; and a highly industrialized, modern city in the United States. I left for American Samoa in late summer of 1976.

The fieldwork project went well, although not without what seemed an inordinate degree of culture shock on my part.[1] The basic problems related to unrealistic expectations about how systems such as banking would function in an American territory in the South Pacific. My research colleague, who some years later would become my husband, suggested at one point that perhaps age forty was a bit late to do first-time fieldwork. I think the implication was that I was being a little inflexible, a fair assessment at the time. However, by the end of the field period, I had learned well how to go with the cultural flow. The data we collected on the effects of modernizing change on the aged in Samoa and among Samoan migrants in San Francisco (in summer 1977) not only allowed me to write my dissertation, but also led to several publications and has been of great value in my teaching.

After the South Pacific component of the fieldwork, I returned to my work in the gerontology program at Wichita State for a semester before taking two months' leave in the summer to do the Samoan migrant portion of the research project in San Francisco. That spring semester also included planning and preparations for my older daughter's wedding, including making dresses for the bridesmaids. Two days after the wedding, my research colleague and I left for California to complete our research. When I returned to work in late summer of 1977, my position was full time and included teaching. Within a few years, it became a state-funded tenure-track position.

I finished the dissertation and defended it in September 1980, after which my advisor and his wife had a small cocktail party for me at their home. I received the PhD in May 1981, at age forty-five. My children insisted that I go through all the ceremonies. Afterward, I was reluctant to go pick up my diploma, thinking that it might not really be there, but it was. The next day I flew to Hawaii to present a paper at a conference on Asian/Pacific elderly—a nice graduation gift to myself.

~ Being an Anthropologist: Family and Career Interactions ~

I continued working in the gerontology program after completing my PhD and found that my background in anthropology was an asset in this multidisciplinary field. In addition to more general courses on aging, in which I always emphasized the importance of cultural issues in aging, I was able to teach courses on cross-cultural aging and qualitative research methods. While some might assume that age forty-five would be a bit late to complete a PhD and still accomplish much professionally, I did not realize at the time what an advantage my age would be in both teaching and research.

With the exception of my first two years in college, my entire academic and professional life has been shaped to a great extent by family-based experiences and events. Up until the time I received my PhD, it was primarily childrearing responsibilities that had the greatest impact. In the post-PhD years, it has been parent-care and other mid-to-late-life issues that have been most significant. Some of these events have been negative in that they impeded progress toward a goal or limited my ability to do my job as I thought it should be done. Others have been more positive in effect. In the long run, however, these various life crises or life-course events have all contributed to my career in a constructive way.

Being middle-aged and aging have brought firsthand experience with many of the issues that I dealt with on the job on a daily basis. In fact, over the years, many of the events experienced within the context of my own family increasingly paralleled the topics on course outlines and texts used in courses. For me, even though widowhood had occurred at what sociologists call an "off time" (at an atypical age), I could easily relate to many of the experiences of older widowed people. I was remarried the year after completing my PhD, only a month after becoming a grandmother. My husband is also an anthropologist, who had taught that first anthropology course I took so many years earlier and who made my first fieldwork possible. With his three adult children and my two, we both had to adjust to relationships with stepchildren, their spouses, and more grandchildren.

We have been concerned with aging parents who lived at considerable distance from us, a situation not uncommon in our society, but one fraught with difficulty. When my husband's father died in 1983, his mother, who had Alzheimer's disease, became our responsibility until her death six years later. And after my father's death in 1993, we were responsible for the care of my mother, who had Parkinson's disease, a heart ailment, and increasing evidence of dementia. While these kinds of events are hardly unique to my family or me, such experiences have had significant impact on my professional life. The experience of taking on the role of caregiver for an aged parent will illustrate this point.

When my father-in-law died in Idaho, we "inherited" my mother-in-law. She became a member of our household at the beginning of a school year. Her mental status was such that she could not be left alone, and yet my husband and I were both employed full time at the university. It was also the year I was up for mandatory tenure review, with my dossier being due in a matter of weeks after her arrival in our home. Our lives changed dramatically as we juggled professional and personal roles, lost contact with friends, and found ourselves more confined to home than ever before. Ever the anthropologist, and partly as catharsis, I wrote notes on our experiences. Looking back, I suspect that having a job in an age-focused program in a university setting saved my career. My colleagues were undoubtedly more knowledgeable about Alzheimer's and therefore more tolerant of my frequent emotional distress and erratic schedule.

Eventually we moved my husband's mother into a building where she could live somewhat independently. We still had some responsibilities, but shifting the day-to-day care to someone else was a tremendous relief. About two years later, she had to be relocated to a nursing home due to her decreased ability to cope with the more independent environment, where she lived until her death.

This experience was most advantageous in my work. I learned about the process of diagnosis of Alzheimer's disease and watched the progressive deterioration it brought. I attended different types of support groups for caregivers, primarily as an observer to ascertain how the groups functioned and what concerns caregivers were expressing. While my husband took care of his mother's financial affairs, I learned to interpret Medicare benefit statements. Over a period of six years, we observed and participated in activities in a retirement community and nursing home, establishing relationships that continued for many years.

Our experiences with his mother led my husband and me to work during a sabbatical leave with a colleague at another university who was doing research with ethnic caregivers of family members with Alzheimer's. For me, this research was what Jeffrey Riemer has called "opportunistic research," or studying familiar settings or situations in which one is personally involved.[2] I have referred to this experience as the "If you find yourself in hot water, take a bath" rationale for research. It was during this time that I discovered that whether interviewing caregivers in their homes, participating in support group meetings, or observing at an adult daycare facility that focused on Alzheimer's victims, rapport was instantaneous. Because I was a caregiver myself, they seemed to perceive my interest in their experiences and problems as only natural. I was, in that sense, one of them. For individuals contending daily with a somewhat nightmarish situation, finding someone who is not only willing to listen but empathetic further enhances rapport. It also provides an element of reciprocity in the interview—my understanding of the effect of Alzheimer's on caregivers was expanded and they were able to unburden themselves of some of their concerns.

Lest this sound too rosy, being an insider in a research situation is not without difficulties. I was an insider in the sense that I had been, and was still in a limited way, a caregiver. However, I was simultaneously an outsider in that I was aware of the need to remain sufficiently detached so that I could deal with the data objectively. We are all taught as anthropologists that we should strive for the insider's, or emic, view of a culture without "going native." Sometimes it is difficult to maintain that balance between emic and etic (outsider's perspective) or even to be confident about where the line is drawn. Barbara Myerhoff, who studied elderly Jews in California, stated it very well: "In the beginning, I spent a great deal of time agonizing about how to label what I was doing—was it anthropology or a personal quest? I never fully resolved the question. I used many conventional anthropological methods and asked many typical questions, but when I had finished, I found my descriptions did not resemble most anthropological writings. Still the results of the study would certainly have been different had I not been an anthropologist."[3]

My husband decided to retire at the end of 1990. Although he returned to teach a course now and then in the first year or so after retiring, most of his interests were pursued at home. Writing has long been his passion, and retirement provided all the time he needed to do it. Since I was still governed to a large extent by the demands of work, it was a bit of an adjustment for me in the beginning. I sometimes felt that there were things he would have liked for us to do, and that I would also have enjoyed, but my work prevented it. We did collaborate on a book in the first couple of years, and I took a full year's sabbatical another. During that time we spent about six months in the San Francisco Bay area, both researching another book and revisiting our Samoan migrant research.

Near the end of the sabbatical, my father died unexpectedly and this brought about our second episode of caring directly for a parent, including some new complications. It took several months to work out moving my mother to Kansas due to our commitments and her need to recover from some recent surgery. She was a very congenial person and quite fond of my husband, but she was not at all used to being alone. Since retiring, my husband had various projects he liked to work on, but not all of them were at home. Now he found it more difficult to pursue his usual routines as he was staying at home with my mother when I was at work. It seemed his retirement had turned into a parent-sitting job. This time I found a gerontology graduate student who agreed to spend several afternoons a week with Mother and became almost like a member of the family.

Some months later, my mother's deteriorating physical and mental health and increasing need for professional care resulted in her placement in a nursing home. A series of little strokes over a year and a half finally left her unable to communicate and seriously weakened. She had a living will, and our last caregiving act was spending the final hours at her bedside as the provisions of that document were carried out, perhaps one of my more painful learning experiences about aging.

~ Assessing My Career Choices and Outcomes ~

Other than a couple of years of teaching during graduate school, I was never employed as an anthropologist in an anthropology department. I sometimes felt like a fish out of water in gerontology, not because I did not belong there, but because there seemed to be so little recognition of what anthropology could and did contribute to this multidisciplinary field. Over the years, I became relatively comfortable in gerontology. It is a very important field, and I think I have succeeded in making some useful contributions to the literature. I hope some of my students have a more comprehensive view of the aging process by my having been there. But I have always identified myself as an anthropologist. No other worldview makes as much sense to me, and all of my work is informed by this perspective. Even the many personal experiences that related to issues I taught about were analyzed in terms of the larger cultural context in which they occurred. I received some of my best marks on student course evaluations for relating course material to real-life situations.

There were problems associated with being employed in a relatively new program on the academic scene—one that was somewhat nontraditional in structure (at least in the 1970s) and more applied in focus than most courses on the Wichita State campus. I encountered some difficulties that I also think are at least partly attributable to my employment in a nontraditional academic program and, to some extent, to my being an anthropologist. When I came up for evaluation for tenure and promotion a few years after receiving my PhD, a special committee had to be convened for the departmental level of evaluation. None of these people worked with me. The recommendation of the committee was in favor of tenure but not promotion, and after college and university committee consideration, I was the first person to be tenured solely in gerontology at Wichita State.

Several years later, after gerontology became part of a department in health sciences, I tried for promotion again. This time a more typical department committee, including one gerontologist who knew my work well, evaluated my record and recommended promotion. At this time I had more publications than most faculty in my department and the majority in the college, and had also served as program director for gerontology. I was astounded to receive a query from the college committee about "which of my publications were based on research." The problem in this instance was that my research approach as an anthropologist and my publications were very different from what these clinically trained faculty were familiar with. They did not recommend promotion, and I appealed to the university committee, which did not overturn the decision.

I later heard that there was an assumption by some on the college committee that, because my husband was a senior professor in the anthropology department and that we had done research together and sometimes coauthored articles, that he had really done the work and not me. This was certainly not true, but it again reflected a lack of knowledge about how research is often done by anthropologists. It is far from unusual that married couples who are anthropologists may have similar interests, work on the same projects, and ultimately write articles and even books together. I never thought the difficulties I experienced had anything to do with my age but rather were related largely to my being evaluated throughout much of my career by people with little comprehension of what anthropology encompasses, other than archaeology.

I persisted and did finally get the promotion to associate professor on the next attempt, but it was a longer ordeal than I would have ever anticipated. University policy was to give a lump-sum award (varied by rank) to one's salary after receiving a promotion; this was in addition to any raise based on other factors. The year my promotion became effective, we had hired a new person in gerontology, a middle-aged woman with a brand-new PhD. It was a bit demoralizing for me that the only difference in my salary and hers was the lump-sum promotion award of $800.

The decision to retire at age sixty-two was an easy one. I had gladly chosen an academic career and enjoyed teaching throughout most of it, especially the diverse ages of students attracted to gerontology. I also liked writing, and in the last half-dozen years had coauthored two books with my husband. But I became more and more disillusioned with the all-too-frequent mandates for new strategic plans and restructuring of departments and colleges, pressure on faculty to teach more hours and in more locations regardless of student demand, and freezes on hiring that left our program and others short of staff when someone resigned or retired. In addition to a nine-hour teaching load, for the last couple of years before my retirement I served as advisor for master's thesis committees in gerontology. The rewards of my job, particularly the monetary ones, were being overshadowed by the hassles. I learned that two women on terminal-year appointments because they failed to receive tenure had salaries approximately equal to mine. So with no hesitation whatsoever, I wrote a letter informing the director of the school that I would be retiring in December 1997.

I have literally not looked back after retiring, nor do I have any regrets. My husband and I immediately took advantage of this new freedom by spending the remainder of that winter (and subsequent ones) in our favorite beach area, Destin, on the panhandle of northwest Florida. We have become part of the snowbird culture that I used to discuss with my gerontology students. We also fulfilled a dream of exploring a remote part of Polynesia when we traveled for several weeks from Tahiti to the Marquesas Islands on board an interisland freighter, a truly remarkable adventure. It is fortunate that we took that trip when we did. Just as we learned from our experiences with our parents' health problems, we now find that our own health issues tend to dictate if, when, where, or how long we can travel.

When I return to the campus, it tends to be for a visit to the anthropology department or to attend a concert, a lecture, or an occasional function for retirees. I remain active professionally, but at a more leisurely pace. At the time of my retirement, I was a member of the board of a not-for-profit nursing home, serving as vice president of the executive committee during one year. I was asked to continue for another three-year term after retiring. I still maintain membership in several anthropological organizations, attend professional meetings occasionally, and do some writing, often in collaboration with my husband.[4]

When I first decided to major in anthropology, I really did not give much thought to what I would do with my degree. It just seemed like the right field of study for me. And even when I started work on the MA, I had no long-range plan in mind. My husband, who also discovered anthropology on his way to another degree, says it was like a "calling" for him. I can't argue with that—perhaps that is the way it is for many of us. When a neighbor and friend completed a bachelor's degree in anthropology, someone asked what she planned to do with the degree. She responded, "Frame it!" That's a valid response as far as I'm concerned. Anthropology is a way of life. If I had to decide again about proceeding with a PhD in anthropology, I would definitely do it again. I would hope not to repeat some of the difficulties I had in my career, but I would not choose any other discipline.

~ Endnotes ~

1. Holmes (1992).
2. Riemer (1977).
3. Myerhoff (1979:81).
4. Holmes (1999), Holmes and Holmes (2001, 2002a, 2002b).

~ References ~

Holmes, Ellen Rhoads. 1992. Culture Shock in Paradise. In *The Naked Anthropologist: Tales from Around the World*, ed. P. R. DeVita, 26–34. Belmont, CA: Wadsworth.

———. 1999. Review of *The Cultural Context of Aging: Worldwide Perspectives*, 2nd ed., edited by J. Sokolovsky. *Journal of Cross-Cultural Gerontology* 14 (1): 93–95.

Holmes, Lowell D., and Ellen R. Holmes. 2001. American Samoa. In *Countries and Their Cultures*, vol. I, ed. I. M. Ember and C. Ember, 35–44. New York: Macmillan.

———. 2002a. Ta'u Then and Now. *Notes from the Field*, Spring:3–4.

———. 2002b. The American Cultural Configuration. In *Distant Mirrors: America as a Foreign Culture*, 3rd ed., ed. P. R. DeVita and J. D. Armstrong, 4–26. Belmont, CA: Wadsworth.

Myerhoff, Barbara. 1979. Number Our Days. *Natural History* 88 (3): 77–84.

Riemer, Jeffrey W. 1977. Varieties of Opportunistic Research. *Urban Life* 5 (4): 467–77.

The "A-G-E" Effects on My Midlife Career in Anthropology

Esther Skirboll

IN 1998 I was promoted to full professor at Slippery Rock University, a state university in Pennsylvania. My climb through the academic promotion ladder was rather timely as these things go. What was unusual was the fact that I was sixty-two years old when I reached this level. The new title appeared so late in my life because I was a nontraditional student from my freshman year on. People like me share very special pleasures in the savoring of our education; however, the fact is that we also look forward to an abbreviated career. People who follow traditional timelines have the leisure to spread their careers over a much longer period of time, while those of us who get a late start must pack all our strivings for achievement into far fewer years.

In thinking about the motivations that brought me to this point, I can identify three forces that were vital to me: *anticipation*, *goals*, and *energy*. I call them the "A," "G," and "E" factors, or the "A-G-E" effect. At the same time, the acronym has the second meaning of an "age" effect, because there is no getting around the fact that as an older student I had concerns and issues that younger students lacked. More recently, as an older faculty member, I have experienced yet another "age" effect: the decline of my energy.

Esther Skirboll: PhD 1981, University of Pittsburgh. Dissertation: "The Transitional Period in the Central Highlands of Costa Rica: An Analysis of Pottery from the Curridabat and Concepcion Sites." Esther is a full professor at Slippery Rock University and has directed several summer archaeological field schools. Her research topics and publications include ceramics and women's retirement. She is active in campus women's issues.

For me, as is true for many of the older students I meet in my own classes, anticipation was a part of everyday school life. I definitely had "A." I loved being around the university, the library, and the other students. When I arrived at school, I had a lift in my heart.

I was not able to afford a college education right out of high school. It was necessary then for me to support myself and help to support my widowed mother as well. Therefore, it wasn't until I married and had two young children that I began my own university education. My husband and I lived in a very traditional nuclear family in which he worked in business and I took charge of the children and house. We agreed that I needed some personal time each week, and I was able to turn this time away from responsibilities at home into the start of a long-anticipated education.

I started college as a freshman when our son was just two and our daughter an infant and continued my college education throughout their school years. It took me nine long years to earn my undergraduate degree, taking classes part time most of the time. At first I was able to fit in two courses a semester by taking classes one evening a week. I had a good babysitter to give the children dinner and stay with them until my husband came home from work. When both children were old enough to be in school during the day, I transferred to part-time day classes.

My dream was to major in anthropology. I had discovered archaeology and anthropology when, as a child, I attended Saturday art classes at the Carnegie Museum in Pittsburgh. After class, my friend and I would wander the museum and library. The Egyptian exhibits were the most exciting, and the Saturday afternoon was topped off by a stop at the adjacent library where I would borrow as many archaeology books as was allowed.

As an undergraduate student, I was so excited about the idea of majoring in anthropology that the day I had an interview with the chair of the anthropology department, I dressed up in a suit with high heels as though I was interviewing for a new job! Yes, he said, I could major in anthropology!

While I anticipated each class, it wasn't until I was a junior and began to savor the fragrance of a bachelor's degree in anthropology around the corner that I felt the first twinge of the "G" effect—"G" is for goal.

During my last summer as an undergraduate, I decided to enroll in an archaeology field school. My university offered a seven-week field school in western Pennsylvania that turned out to be a very important early site, which is now world famous. I worked there during the summers for several years. I loved the fieldwork that first summer and did well enough that my professor suggested that I apply immediately for graduate school in archaeology. The University of Pittsburgh didn't offer a master's degree at that time, so I would be in a PhD program. If I did well the first semester, I would be eligible for an assistantship. This was important to me because my husband's salary had funded my undergraduate fees, but I was hoping to be able to support my own graduate education.

The only quick thing about any part of my education was the decision to enter graduate school. I consulted with my husband about it and he agreed that I should give it a try. My husband was and still is encouraging, supportive, and cooperative about every phase of my career. Six months later I was a PhD student in archaeology—who would have believed it!

I experienced graduate school with the heightened anticipation of spending hours in the library, reading the literature, and talking with other graduate students about anthropology. It was an exhilarating time. Also, the "G" effect was with me all the time now. The goal was the PhD—someday, maybe.

During these years, our children were growing up. While I was in graduate school, they were in junior high. My husband's and my life marched forward. His work was demanding and included my involvement in entertaining clients in our home and at theaters and restaurants. In addition there was our private social life, including family and friends. There was cooking, shopping, laundry, and care of the children in addition to coursework and archaeology field school every summer. I could do it all because my goal was before me and I had a lot of "E"—the energy required to do all these things.

~ Becoming a Feminist ~

The graduate school experience was very exciting from the beginning, but there were some unpleasant surprises. I was in for a rude awakening when I learned that as a graduate teaching assistant in archaeology, I was not permitted to assist in archaeology classes. At that time, only the male graduate students were permitted to march into class behind the professor. I was relegated to assisting in cultural anthropology classes, which were second class in the eyes of the small in-group of archaeology graduate students. I was being discriminated against! However, this discrimination had a benefit. Assigned to teach cultural anthropology recitation sections, I began to learn a lot about it, enough later in my career to teach courses in cultural anthropology. I also discovered that I liked teaching.

When I entered graduate school in 1974, the second wave of the feminist movement was well underway, but I had been preoccupied in the 1960s and early 1970s with marriage, babies, and classes. I wasn't unaware of social changes but had not given them a great deal of thought. I soon learned that anthropology, including archaeology, was organized by men and that its subject matter was men. Almost all of the professors were men, and in the courses I took and those in which I assisted, the subjects were presented from a male point of view. I will always remember a comment made by a very senior professor in a class in which I assisted in cultural anthropology. He was very kind and encouraging to me, and I respected him. One day, as he was lecturing about societies in which the men lived in men's houses separately from the women and young children, he began joking about how the men needed to get away from the women sometimes and really enjoyed their exclusive men's houses. He laughed, and the class also laughed at his little joke. I did *not* laugh because I was beginning to recognize the bias in such a presentation. The women were also living in houses without the men. What did they think? Were they lonely? Did they look longingly over to where the men were laughing and joking, or were they also happy about the arrangement? Later I was to learn that women who live in women's houses frequently gain strength and solidarity living with other women to whom they are related or with whom they share work. They also tell jokes and laugh as they enjoy their lives. Sometimes the sexes do not live together, but this does not necessarily mean that the women are kept away from the men against their will. It was around this time that I realized that I was becoming a feminist.

Over the years of doing field archaeology, I saw women being made the butt of humiliating jokes and being given jobs that were clearly subservient. I was mature, always older than the other students as well as the professors. I didn't accept gender discrimination easily. This led to some unpleasant situations and even a few confrontations. Although I sometimes thought of dropping out because of this, my husband's encouragement and my own persistence were vital in my continuing.

In my department, there was little encouragement of older women students. Some faculty members thought that although I was a good student, I was far too old to hope to get a faculty position. The few other older married women and I were sometimes referred to as "retreads." Even the sole tenured faculty woman once told me that since I was doing so well, I would be able to go on and teach in a junior college. By this time, I knew enough to be seriously insulted and angry. Many anthropologists and other academics do teach in junior colleges, but I was being told that I would never be able to get into a four-year college or university. Not only was I tied to the local area because of my family, but I was "too old"—a different kind of "age" effect.

Graduate school had many compensations, however, and my anticipation now included completing coursework. As I moved through graduate school, my husband's solid and loving encouragement through difficulties as well as through the best of times was vital to my success. The one time I seriously considered quitting graduate school, his encouragement and perspective were the supports that I needed to continue.

Eventually, the goals of passing the comprehensive exams and the language exam and finally beginning dissertation work were driving forces. As I moved along through the system, I experienced the tingling of new goals. I began to envision a faculty job, publishing, becoming involved in women's studies and women's issues. Toward the end of my coursework, I began to teach a women's studies course called Anthropology of Women. This was vitally important to me as it allowed me to study gender issues that were revolutionizing anthropology in the late seventies. I have never stopped teaching women's studies courses.

When I completed my coursework, I was made a teaching fellow, which allowed me to teach my own classes at branch campuses and in summer school and the evening program. I taught courses in archaeology, physical and cultural anthropology, and anthropology of women. Not only did I have the energy to do all this and still care for my home and family, but the goals and anticipation helped to energize me. The "A-G-E" factors were in full force.

~ The Long Road to Tenure ~

I was awarded my PhD in 1981, one of the first women to receive this degree in archaeology from my university. Like so many other academics in many fields, I was to spend too many years on the part-time teaching route. I was hired as a permanent part-time instructor in a small private college in Pittsburgh, teaching three courses a semester. This college did not offer an archaeology program, and since I wanted to continue research activities, I began to work with a colleague on a sociocultural project on retired women. During this time, I also took any other part-time coursework I could find in the hopes that one would turn into a permanent job. One semester I was teaching courses in three different universities.

By 1987 I became discouraged about ever getting a tenure track position. I was working hard and making about $10,000 a year with no benefits. My anticipation, goals, and energy weren't paying off. I had hoped to help pay college tuition for my children, but I couldn't get a full-time job and was giving some thought to leaving academia. I was vacationing at the beach with my family that July when I received a phone call from my dog sitter. She told me that Slippery Rock University was looking for a temporary full-time position for the fall semester and they had been given my name by someone at the University of Pittsburgh. They wanted an archaeologist. I was an archaeologist! They needed someone to start in two weeks. I could do it! The job offered benefits and a decent salary, but it was more than an hour's commute from my home in Pittsburgh. This meant a lengthy drive five days a week. I talked it over with my husband, Stan. He said, "This is what you've been working for—go for it." Other family members worried about what would happen to my social life; who would make Stan's dinner? In the end I said, "Yes, I'll do it."

I am a fortunate woman because, in spite of being older than most PhD graduates in anthropology, I finally did get a faculty position. After two years in a temporary full-time position at Slippery Rock, a permanent tenure-track position was approved. I applied for it but almost didn't get it due to the efforts of a few faculty members who didn't want an older woman. Perhaps they couldn't envision me helping the department grow, or perhaps they didn't like having an assertive woman around. In any case, with the strong support of the chair of the department and other colleagues, I was offered the job.

By 1989 I had achieved my goal of a permanent faculty job. In this new position, I felt that at last I would be able to accomplish all the things I had been anticipating. Teaching is the first mission of Slippery Rock University, and I am a dedicated teacher. Over the years, I was called on to develop a variety of courses for anthropology majors, as well as two that "swing" between the anthropology and sociology faculty. I now teach archaeology, physical anthropology, cultural anthropology, and women's studies courses and run a field school.

In 1990 I was asked to chair the first Women's Commission on the campus. I became deeply involved in women's organizations both at my university and within the Pennsylvania State System of Higher Education. I have also continued to carry out the research on women's retirement, which I had begun years earlier.

Being involved in so many activities is not unusual for faculty members, especially in small universities and colleges where teaching loads and service to the university are heavily stressed. Although teaching excellence is the primary mission of my university system, it is not possible to be promoted without research and publications. We must teach four courses a semester and carry out research as well. Of course, these activities require a high level of energy. This never presented a problem in the early years of my nontraditional career. I suppose I had thought there was an endless supply of energy, if I'd ever thought about it at all.

I purchased a house in Slippery Rock to reduce the number of hours spent on the road, especially in bad weather; I run it and the house in Pittsburgh. Each week I pack clothes and supplies for work (and my dog, Sadie, who was my constant companion until her death in 1998) and drive north to the Slippery Rock house, which I open and set up before leaving for work. I teach four courses requiring three preparations each semester. I serve on a number of departmental and university committees. In 1997 I became the president of the Women's Consortium of the Pennsylvania State System of Higher Education. I held this position for two years. I attend conferences, presenting research and taking part in discussions. In the past few years, I have concentrated on social research and am presently working on a research project on commuter marriages. For the past few years, I have also been researching retirement with a colleague. We have examined and published a study on white retired women and African American retired women, and have an unpublished study of retired professional women and men. In 2005 I undertook a new role as chair of my department at Slippery Rock. While this position carries a six-credit release time from teaching, it involves a great deal of administrative work and more time at the office.

~ Shift in Energy: The Age Effect ~

I am very happy doing these things for which I have worked so hard and long; however, now I am frequently very tired. The energy factor has changed. The late career-starter may have plenty of "E" to get through an education, get the job, and get started on the academic career; however, the fact is that she or he is faced ultimately with fitting a thirty-year career into fifteen or twenty years. And one's energy is simply not as great when one is fifty or sixty as it was at thirty-five or forty.

The pressures for publication, service, and promotion have been greater for me than for a traditional-aged individual because the career years available in which to assemble materials for each promotion are fewer, while the pressure to do so in a timely way is greater. I recently attended a gender issues conference at the University of Vermont and heard Johnella Butler of Michigan talking about ethnicity, race, and gender. She was worried about the fact that many African American faculty members not only work very hard in their universities in order to excel within their disciplines, but they also give a great deal of time and energy to helping African American students within their university communities. She said some of these people are working so hard, they are becoming ill and dying much too young. They are wearing themselves out. As I listened to her, I thought, "This is the 'E' effect and I can identify with this. As a nontraditional faculty woman, I am also in the minority, and I am doing much the same thing trying to work for equity for women, helping women students, and furthering my own career." For so long, I had counted on the "A-G-E" effect. Now I realized there had been a change and that age—the other "age" effect—had come into play.

There are always multiple responsibilities that complicate the life of a working woman with a family. Unless she is very wealthy, she must bear the burdens of her career and her home. Although our children are now grown and are no longer our direct responsibility, they have remained deeply enmeshed in our lives. I am frequently reminded of a well-known article by Judy Syfers, "I Want a Wife," in which she humorously outlines the service role of wives and how they ease their husband's responsibilities in the home and in social life. She believes professional women also need someone to fill this role for them. The fact is that, for my husband and me, there was no one else, no "wife," to shop, cook, pay the bills, take the dog to the vet, make social arrangements, and do the dishes. We were both working full time and more prior to my husband's retirement in December 1998.

I believe that while nontraditional working women often experience "A" and "G" factors, and benefit from them, they are often completely unprepared for and surprised by the "E" factor. We are using high levels of energy in fulfilling the goals we anticipate. However, we sometimes find that when we reach our goals, or begin to do so, high levels of energy are still required to maintain our position. This may cause a great deal of stress. As Butler worried about the effects of this level of energy output by African American faculty members, it may also be a health issue for the nontraditional individual as well. Recently, for example, I had pneumonia over Christmas break and bronchitis the following spring. I was very surprised that my health was being compromised. Perhaps this would have happened even if I had worked less intensely. However, it did draw my attention to the fact that perhaps I should moderate my activities somewhat.

How can middle-aged professional women deal with the "E" factor? Is education the answer? Should we be required to take a course somewhere along the line on How to Survive Your Career? It's unlikely that such a course will ever be offered; instead, each of us will continue to have to work it out individually. We know, for example, that women and minorities in the academy should learn to say no to some of the many requests to serve on committees. This is not always easy to do, however, when you know that representation on committees by such people makes a difference. Recently it was very difficult for me to say no to a request that I run for the promotions committee (an elected position in my university). When I did say no, I was told that strong women are needed on this important committee because all-male promotion committees frequently devalue the research and other accomplishments of women faculty. I held my ground this time because a considerable time commitment over the semester break is required, and I knew that I needed this time for my family and myself. This was not easy for me to do, and I felt somewhat guilty about it, although other women did balance this committee. As a person whose energy levels have decreased, I must consider my choice of commitments carefully. I intend to continue on as a faculty member and researcher for at least several more years, so I give the "E" factor some respect when making decisions.

In the coming academic years, I will serve on several committees that are concerned with women's issues on campus, and I also hope to get my recent research into publishable form. However, now I approach the coming years with the knowledge that I can and will do useful and important work, but that it has limits in scope. While anticipation and goals are still important, I must observe the "E" factor in a way that I had not anticipated when I started on this road.

As nontraditional workers will certainly begin to notice, as they reach their sixties, many of their friends and colleagues are retiring while they themselves feel they still have some years of work to achieve their goals. We begin to suffer from decreasing amounts of energy with which to accomplish our goals. Is this a call to reduce the extent to which anticipation and goals can carry us forward? Not at all! It is a recognition of the realities that face the midlife career enthusiast with the goal of enabling us to include the energy factor in our long-range plans, but in a different way, as we experience the "A-G-E" effect compounded by the "age" effect.

~ Reference ~

Syfers, Judy. 1991. I Want a Wife. In *The Gender Reader*, ed. Evelyn Ashton-Jones and Gary A. Olson, 341–43. Boston: Allyn and Bacon.

Section 4

Being the Other

Encounters with Difference

WE ANTHROPOLOGISTS famously (or notoriously) study "Others"—people different from ourselves in various ways, people of different social groups, ethnicity, religion, class, lifestyles, cultures. Because of assumptions of intellectual superiority and entitlement, traditional enthnographers (mostly white males) did not concern themselves with how they as anthropologists might be viewed as Others by those they studied. Confident of their findings, they wrote as omniscient narrators about "the such-and-such people." That approach has changed in the wake of postmodern interrogations and postcolonial stirrings. These forces have produced many concerns about intellectual property rights and giving voice to the formerly invisible Others who now may be choosing to study their own people and even, sometimes, us. The othering has been turned back on us, and we have become more humble.

The four authors in this section embrace and explore the concept of themselves as Other, but all the tellers of the tales in this volume know about being the Other in multiple ways. Our being Other has roots in various qualities. We know from our own experiences about being girls not worth educating "because you'll just get married and have children." We know about being girls who grew into women whose work as homemakers, wives, mothers, and caregivers went unpaid and unrecognized. We know about being put into the disregarded categories of "older" or "old" woman and "just a housewife." We know about being Other because of class, ethnicity, race, and religion; because we didn't behave according to familial or cultural norms; because we defied the norms of the academy by returning to school in midlife. We know about being subalterns, marginalized and invisible, and like other native ethnographers, we are now giving voice to our own experiences.

A Late Bloomer's Struggles with Discrimination

Ruby Rohrlich

I WAS a late bloomer, earning my PhD at the age of fifty-six after having had four previous careers. My late blooming and the relevant preceding and subsequent events were fueled by the gender system. Because of my role as a female, I have had thrust upon me experiences that changed my life negatively. Because of my socialization and also my biology as a female, I have rejected golden opportunities offered to me by men, the sex with the power. As a member of a college faculty and within the discipline of anthropology, I have encountered discrimination as a woman and as an older woman. However, no situation was clear-cut; contradictions arose from interventions by both women and men.

"You'll Just Get Married"

It began with the untimely death of my father, protector and earner for the family, when I was little more than a year old, in 1914. My mother insisted that my brother Arthur, at age sixteen, go on to finish his last year of high school and my sister Molly, at age fourteen, go to work as a salesgirl. Molly took courses at night in typing and shorthand and eventually became a stenographer. Although I didn't feel the impact of the gender system until I started high school, I knew, long before then,

Ruby Rohrlich: PhD 1969, New York University. Dissertation: "A Comparative Study of Sociocultural Variables and Stuttering among Puerto Rican Elementary School Children in San Juan, Puerto Rico, and New York, N.Y." Ruby was professor emerita, City University of New York, and research professor, George Washington University. An early feminist, Ruby published her book *Women Cross-Culturally* in 1975. She died in 1999.

that all of us six fatherless children had to become nondependent in a hurry. Arthur and Molly, who contributed the most to family finances and morale, were equally dominant; in fact, Molly was the only sibling who had a room all to herself.

It wasn't that I had an unhappy childhood, far from it. Compared with most Americans I have met who remember their young years as full of pain and grief, who hated their parents—particularly their mothers and sometimes their siblings—my Canadian childhood occurred in a fun-loving, noisy family. Our family enjoyed sports and celebrations and was held together by a mother who, though forced to be frugal in all ways, nevertheless fed us nutritiously and enjoyably, made our clothes, and was moral, religious, and intelligent. As the youngest, I grew up half-pet, half-slave, loved by everyone except my sister Anne, and I, in turn, loved everyone, even Anne.

Arthur, fourteen years my senior and in loco parentis, used to call me Ruby Rubina Rebecca Rohrlich as he scooped me up when he came home from work. He rewarded me with money whenever I ranked first in school. But it was also Arthur who decided that I should go not to the school that prepared students for university, but to a commercial high school, so that I would be equipped to earn money as a stenographer. If I had been a male, I believe I would have been allowed to choose. I got a job the summer after my junior year. Arthur, with three children of his own and barely keeping afloat, decreed that I should stay with the job and not return to finish the last year of high school. He said I was going to get married anyway, so why did I need more education?

Nobody insisted, as my mother had when Arthur was in the same situation, "She only has a year to go." I loved learning and screamed that I wanted to go to college, that nobody would have to support me or pay my tuition. But the fact was that with all the siblings either married or off doing their own thing, and the Great Depression just starting, I was the only one left at home and I had to help support our mother. Not that I didn't love her or owe her this. But if I had been male, Arthur and the others would have insisted that I finish high school, and in the face of my burning desire to continue my education, another source of support for our mother would have been found.

~ Culture and Biology Defeat Me ~

For the next five years, I dated, fell in love once or twice, became manager of the office where I worked, and found life unsatisfactory. So, mainly on my own, I studied the college matriculation subjects I needed and enrolled at McGill University. However, since I couldn't go to school at night in Montreal, I planned to go to New York, where I could attend college and live with my mother and sister Molly, who, after working for fifteen years as a stenographer, had finally achieved her own dream and completed a nurse's training course.

The following year I married the man whom Molly had adopted as a kid brother when she was a counselor at a summer camp where he was a camper. He had recently graduated from the Massachusetts Institute of Technology (MIT) in the first year that institution had not been able to place its graduates, and was looking for a job. Within a year, I left the horrible job I had been able to find, where the boss and his son brushed against my breasts at every opportunity. My dislike of the job so affected my speech that it was all I could do to say the name of the company when I answered the phone. I began to attend New York University (NYU) and at the same time had three part-time jobs. I had come to New York with some savings and was able to pay the tuition for the first full year of school; thereafter, I received scholarships for half the tuition.

In my junior year, I met and fell in love with anthropology. My teacher, Adamson Hoebel, found me a most interested student who took lecture notes in shorthand. He offered me a job taking notes at a seminar that brought together, for the first time, psychoanalysis, in the person of Abram Kardiner, and anthropology, represented by Ralph Linton. So pleased was I at the opportunity to attend these lectures that I would have done the work without pay. For taking the notes on Friday night and spending all day Saturday typing them, I received a munificent five dollars for each session. I also worked twenty hours a week in NYU's radio department, writing scripts and acquiring other skills at fifty cents an hour, eating my sandwich as I ran across campus in order to get to this job that started at 1 p.m., the same time my class ended. During winter and summer intersessions and other vacation periods, I worked for an advertising agency at sixty cents an hour. When I graduated, the agency offered me a job as an account executive, which meant I would have spent most of my time finding synonyms for *glamorous* and *casual*. I turned the job down.

During my senior year, Professor Hoebel offered to get me a fellowship in anthropology at Columbia University that would take me right through the doctorate. Of course, this meant going into the field; my husband was incredulous that I was elated at this possibility. He said, "How can you think of leaving for a year or two when we've been married for such a short time?" I would have been happy for him if he had been made such an offer, but as a dutiful wife, I turned down this first golden opportunity.

By the time I graduated from NYU in 1940, my husband had obtained permanent employment in the New York City high school system, a comedown for an MIT graduate, but a haven for professionals of all kinds in this period of dire unemployment. Never was the city's school system so laden with overqualified teachers, and never before or since did its high schools provide such superlative education. Now that we had a measure of economic security, my husband generously suggested that I leave any job I didn't like, and that's what I did. I then worked for a time as an editor for a pop psychology magazine and later did public relations for the Jewish Theological Seminary.

Then, with the coming of World War II, I got a job at the Office of War Information (OWI) as a propaganda analyst and, for the first time, didn't regret not studying anthropology at Columbia. Within the year, I became editor of the

Propaganda Analysis Department and acquired good editorial skills in a most exciting and difficult capacity. When the Allies invaded North Africa, I was asked to set up a psychological warfare office in Casablanca and accepted with alacrity (my husband had applied for a commission with the navy). The thorough physical examination I underwent revealed that I was anemic, and I was supplied with vitamins to rectify the deficiency. I had been trying, unsuccessfully, to become pregnant, and therefore was not using contraception. Lo and behold, the vitamins did the trick and, unwittingly, I became pregnant. This was the second golden opportunity I lost, deprived, this time, by my female biology.

~ From Motherhood to a Doctorate ~

The OWI gave me a year's maternity leave, and during this period I carefully observed the attitudes of nannies toward their charges. In the end, I decided not to return to the OWI because, in addition to nannies that didn't seem to care, there were no adequate childcare facilities. Besides, I fell in love with my baby, Michael. Two and a half years later, I had Matthew, whom I also loved, to keep Michael company. We followed the mob moving out to the Long Island suburbs, and I stayed home with my sons for eight years.

When Matthew was in kindergarten, I took a job as a teacher in Levittown, since the hours coincided with my children's school schedule. During the eight years I taught elementary school, I took courses in speech and hearing rehabilitation, received an MS in the field, and became a speech pathologist. When Michael entered junior high, we moved to Great Neck, which was reputed to have a first-rate public school system, although this meant that I had to continue working to help support our higher standard of living, including the ever-increasing needs of growing children.

Michael was a senior at MIT the year Matthew was a freshman at Boston University. The double college tuition we had to pay was too heavy for me to stop earning money in order to begin my fifth career as an anthropology student. The following year, with Michael in graduate school and on his own, we sold the house in Great Neck in order to acquire the wherewithal for the three remaining years of Matthew's college education. Then we moved back to the city, much against my husband's wishes, but now that the children were taken care of, my own needs had become primary.

I enrolled at NYU for a PhD degree in anthropology. While I completed my coursework, I worked for the Speech Bureau of the New York City Board of Education, dealing with the speech problems of Puerto Rican children. I then devoted myself wholeheartedly to anthropology, and during the next two years I completed my fieldwork and finished my dissertation. My comparative study of stuttering focused on Puerto Rican children in San Juan, Puerto Rico, and New York City. Twenty-nine years after I received my bachelor's degree, I was awarded a doctorate.

~ After the PhD ~

I applied for a postdoc, which offered a generous stipend to do a study of stuttering for the entire island of Puerto Rico. As one of five finalists, I was about to go to the final interview when my husband said, "What, are you thinking of going away for another year? I thought we would finally have a honeymoon." My backbone was still not stiff enough. I canceled my appointment, again giving up the possibility of a golden opportunity, this time to do original and significant work. How could I have done this again!

At the beginning of the academic year 1969–1970 a teacher in the anthropology department of Brooklyn College died, and I was offered his job. After receiving satisfactory evaluations from students and peers, I was told by the chair that since this was a tenure-track position, he could not hire me because at my age (early fifties), I could never complete the publications necessary to obtain tenure. I came as close to fainting dead away as I ever had in my life. I then applied for a job to teach Puerto Rican studies, which was surely up my alley. They turned me down because I wasn't Puerto Rican. But I was fortunate enough to obtain a job at Manhattan Community College, which needed teachers because the City University of New York (CUNY), of which it was a unit, had instituted open enrollment. My dissertation was accepted for publication by Colin Turnbull, editor of the Viking Fund's publications in anthropology, as number 51 in this distinguished series. Years later, I retired as a full professor with a much shorter career and a much longer list of publications than the Brooklyn College professor who would not hire me in the tenure-track position!

Before I retired, I was a member of a class-action suit brought by the female professors against the administration of CUNY because of unequal promotions based on gender. We won the suit. Each of the hundreds of members of the class action was given a cash settlement but, despite the tremendous expense incurred by CUNY, the inequities between male and female faculty did not disappear. The final insult of my teaching career came during the last semester when my course Anthropology of Women—one that I had instituted and taught for many years—was discontinued because of resentment over a grant I had received.

~ Retirement Years: The Struggle Continues ~

The most unfortunate aspect of being the youngest in a family is that in the normal course of events, the older siblings die first. This happened during the decade after I retired from teaching, and my son Michael, who lives in Virginia, invited me to move to his area so we could share each other's lives. I have been living in Washington since February 1993.

And so I come to the end of my saga on my late blooming and the discrimination I experienced because I was not male, because I was not young, because I was not Puerto Rican, because I was a female professor. But the issues are complex because men have offered me golden opportunities, several of which

I rejected because of my female role or female socialization or female biology, and have sided with me on occasion. Thus, while the primary basis of my experiences of discrimination was patriarchal, the issues as they developed were not cut and dried, black and white, but fraught with contradictions.

My Life Hangs by This Question

What Is a Human Being?

Elizabeth Dressel Hoobler

THE DEAN had given my dissertation his official signature of approval. I had delivered the obligatory copies of my too-long manuscript to members of my dissertation committee. The graduation ceremony was the only activity left. But I really didn't want to attend. My emotions were telling me that the graduation ritual seemed pointless and hollow.

Unfortunately, I had a very legitimate excuse for skipping the ceremony. My mother-in-law was in the hospital, dying of lung cancer. Her sister had kept a constant vigil at her bedside for weeks and needed respite from the sickroom. Therefore, instead of going to my doctoral-degree graduation at the University of New Mexico, I drove seven hundred miles to Kansas in order to take a turn at my mother-in-law's hospital bed. My escape from graduation occurred just weeks before she died. Her death, the arrival in the mail of my PhD certificate, and my sixtieth birthday occurred at the same time.

For me, the trip through graduate school and the doctoral-degree rite of passage had been long, exciting, humiliating, invigorating, and disappointing. How did I get started on such a mixed endeavor?

Elizabeth (Teddy) Dressel Hoobler: PhD 1986, University of New Mexico. Dissertation: "To Be Old or Not To Be Old: Exploring Life Style Variations and Their Implications for Age Identity." Teddy retired from teaching at the University of New Mexico in 1997. She continues to pursue her interest in the study and understanding of consciousness and its connection with anthropology and other disciplines.

~ Being a Christian Scientist ~

The original impetus for this journey began long, long ago in 1932, when I was six years old. My parents had been struggling with the deprivation and poverty of the Great Depression. Equally dismaying was their desperation over the health of our family members. As a baby, I had life-threatening bouts of pneumonia and had had my tonsils removed; my sister had almost died of diphtheria; my brother had continuous "colds" (allergies); my mother had recurrent periods of "nerves"; my dad suffered from exhaustion from holding several jobs at once.

Understandably, my parents began an urgent search for a lifestyle that would bring about relief from serious illnesses. Their search began with a popular health fad prescribing the exclusive consumption of raw food and eventually progressed through other health modalities. None of these changes made the family healthier. However, the golden promise of better health was fulfilled when my parents underwent a religious conversion to Christian Science.

Because my parents were serious and intense about being good Scientists, our religion permeated all aspects of our lives. As a child, I learned the Sunday school teachings, and I internalized passages from our regular morning readings from the Bible and our Christian Science textbook.

The religion of Christian Science provided a unique view of the material and spiritual world. It certainly seemed to provide me with a view of the world far different from that of our Catholic, Protestant, and Jewish neighbors. I felt different from other children. When I entered the teenage years, I developed endless epistemological and ontological questions, questions that in one form or another have lasted a lifetime. Oddly, some of these persistent questions helped to prod me to return to the university several times, culminating in a doctorate in anthropology.

For me, being brought up in the Christian Science religion in the first part of the twentieth century was both a wonderful and a puzzling experience. I was taught that human beings are expressions of divine, spiritual, perfect Idea—God. My religion's "scientific statement of being" said, "There is no life, truth, intelligence, nor substance in matter. All is infinite Mind and its infinite manifestation, for God is All-in-all... and man is His image and likeness. Therefore man is not material; he is spiritual."[1] We continuously affirmed that "God's perfect children" (that is, all humans) are perfect manifestations of perfect Idea, God. Everything material (the whole world) was "error" and had no reality.

As God's perfect children, we could overcome evil, illness, and death because they did not really exist. We no longer went to medical doctors, and we led a very ethical life. God's perfect children were neither fallible, evolving organisms nor mortal bodies. They were manifestations of the divine, omniscient, omnipresent, omnipotent God. Each child of God was expected to manifest this perfection. By doing our daily "mental work" (prayer), we reinforced in ourselves the Godlike qualities endowed by our Creator. We believed that our prayers were answered and people were healed of both emotional and physical illnesses.

The positive psychology of this transcendent belief system provided us with a tool to meet the anxieties and challenges of the Depression and World War II years. The health of each family member improved dramatically. Throughout the Depression, my dad always had a job. Unlike the fate of some of the neighbors, the bank did not foreclose on our house. We learned to tolerate the open religious antagonism and the isolation imposed on us by our ethnically diverse neighbors, and we developed our own psychological defenses of self-righteous correctness while trying to follow the Biblical advice to love our neighbors as ourselves.

On the negative side, however, in high school I was psychologically unable to study chemistry, physics, or biology. To me, the physical and biological sciences taught error and had no validity. By the age of eighteen, I was confident that I could live within my ideational world and avoid the false material world in which most other people lived. I believed that the best thing for me to do was to deny error messages and to hold on to my conception of an omniscient, omnipresent, omnipotent God who created perfect human beings and ran the universe. Little did I realize that life was about to hand me a first-class paradox!

~ Encountering Science—and *The* Question ~

In 1945, just before VJ Day—the day that signaled the Allies' victory over Japan and the end of World War II—and in direct conflict with my own beliefs, I married a remarkable young physicist whose whole approach to life was shaped by his professional training in the mechanistic, material, classical Newtonian world of physics. At that time, his universe was a dualistic, physically objective, scientifically verifiable one that included very material people. As he matured in his professional life, he remained abreast of the developing ideas in physics, and through succeeding decades his views of the universe and the philosophy of science were deeply influenced by the theory of relativity and quantum physics. But that was later.

Before our marriage, we had long, intense discussions about the nature of reality, about the nature of people, and about the origins of the universe. His arguments had a great deal of consistency. Annoyingly, his arguments also were supported by my five senses. My humans were perfectible expressions of Divine God; his humans were material, tangible, and oh-so-fallible. My humans were earthly expressions of transcendent Spirit, Mind, Soul; his were physical bodies with brains that could figure out the world around them without resorting to my ideational abstractions and "religious mysticism." Our discussions often lasted into the night, and most of the time I was outargued. Thus began my confusion and creeping doubts about my transcendent beliefs and especially my ideas about human beings. But I loved this intelligent physicist with all my heart, and despite our differences, I married him.

I knew that almost all the world agreed with my husband's view, not with mine. I also knew from past experience that I could not talk freely with most people about my belief system because they lacked my background. I didn't make sense to them. I gradually learned to live in the sensory, dualistic world of matter and mind and to cope in culturally prescribed ways. Nevertheless, the question of the *true nature* of human beings became a persistent covert question. I could not fully believe that humans were only physical bodies in the objective world of the five senses. But I had lost my sustaining confidence in the transcendent, God-encompassing spiritual realm that nurtured and healed us humans and gave us the heritage of God's perfect children. *What is a human being?* For me, the question emerged in young adulthood and in different guises has recurred insistently through the years.

In 1946 I went with my new husband to the University of Illinois, where he enrolled in the graduate physics program. With his blessing, I enrolled in college. What an eye-opener college subjects turned out to be! For the first time, I encountered historical geology and social Darwinism. Confusion confounded! What was real? Spirit or matter? Biblical creation or eons of evolution? Were people like us the expressions of Divine Idea or the results of survival of the fittest? Was governance by God's Law or by man-made morality and society? Where did these and other contradictory ideas come from? Endlessly the questions troubled me. Where could I look for definitive answers? (Forty years later, I taught anthropology and sociology students who were still troubled by these questions!)

In my confusion, I became a mixed-up, simultaneously spiritual and material human being who felt emotionally alienated from the rest of humanity. What were human beings really? What was I "supposed" to be as a human being? How could I feel like the rest of the human race? Hoping to find out, I majored in sociology. I was fascinated. After a couple semesters of reveling in the many facets of humans-in-society, I put my personal quest on temporary hold. I decided that college might not have the answers to my questions, but it certainly made this material world interesting.

Going to college with the masses of returning World War II GIs was both fun and a challenge. Class sizes ballooned, and the mostly male professors obviously enjoyed teaching these motivated young men. Many of the returning vets had wives and children, and these men represented a new kind of industrious, no-nonsense student. While the GIs were getting their degrees, the wives were celebrating their PhTs: "Putting Hubby Through." The wives were having babies instead of getting an academic education. As a young college female in a predominantly male college environment, I was again a minority person. Several times I was challenged about taking up crowded classroom space. After all, I wasn't attending college to find my man (a husband), so why was I there? Despite working half time to pay tuition and rent, I hurried through my courses and graduated in three and a half years. Contrary to the prevailing sexist attitude, a couple of my professors encouraged me to continue in graduate school, and I enrolled for one semester. But when my husband finished his PhD program, he said that it was time to move on. And in 1949 I didn't believe it was important for me to go to graduate school.

Alas, the mores of the early 1950s (and my physicist husband) believed that it was time to start a family. So, after he took a professorship in southern New Mexico, I enthusiastically played the role of faculty wife and mother, and we proceeded to contribute to the baby boom by having four children in five years.

However, in between the diaper-changing years and the junior high school years, I learned quite a bit about the intriguing Indian and Hispanic cultures of the Southwest. After I found books by Alfred Kroeber and Franz Boas in the library, I gradually became aware that I was intrigued by anthropological orientations, and that culture had to be reckoned with if one is going to figure out what goes into the makeup of a material human being. From then on, all kinds of human cultures and beings became my preoccupation. I reveled in the incredible variations of behavior recounted in the works of early anthropologists. A growing personal library of anthropological studies and books became my identity. The human variety was breathtaking! But what made a human being *human* still puzzled me. There was learned culture, there was environment, and there were prescribed and proscribed behaviors that accounted for continuity. There was cultural borrowing and innovation that accounted for change. But humans living within their cultures also had fears, inner anxieties, feelings, spiritual beliefs, intentions, motivations, inspirations, intuitions, exhilarating and transcendent moments, unexplained visions, instantaneous healings, and deep psychological certainties that were barely mentioned, much less explored. How was this internal world colored by culture? Didn't it somehow contribute to the definition of humanness?

~ Encountering Anthropology: More Ambiguities ~

As soon as my obligations to a traditional husband and four active children permitted, I took some courses in anthropology in the fledgling Department of Anthropology at New Mexico State University in Las Cruces. My professor exuded enthusiasm for his subject and encouraged me to continue. With these introductory anthropology courses and my sociology background, I was able to enroll in the MA curriculum at the University of New Mexico (UNM) in Albuquerque. The campus was more than two hundred miles north of my home.

For two semesters in 1965, I took a train from Las Cruces to Albuquerque on Sunday evening in order to get to Monday morning classes at UNM. I completed the round-trip home the following Friday evening to cook, wash, iron, shop, plan the next week's activities for the children, and listen to the endless problems my family encountered. Despite my husband's intent that I should have as much education as I wanted, he resented the extra burden of caring for the children while I was away. As a result, I stayed home for the next three years, but in order to finish my master's degree, I returned to the commuter routine in 1970. Looking back, I believe that the strain on our marriage during these years contributed to our eventual divorce.

I felt so fortunate to be back in school! There was a feeling of exploration and enthusiasm conveyed by the professors and the anthropology majors. However, I could not take part in their camaraderie because of my commuter status and lack of time on campus. Besides, the campus was in upheaval a lot of the time because of civil rights and Vietnam War protests and crackdowns. I was in a peculiar status as a forty-year-old person because I did not desire to protest and march with the students, but I also feared for my own teenage sons who would soon be facing the military draft. From Monday through Friday, I concentrated on devouring anthropological studies and theory and wrote endless papers for every course. In those precomputer days, I learned to write the final paper on the first draft because I had no time for revisions. Then on Saturday and Sunday, after riding two hundred miles south by train, I concentrated on my family's survival. I was living an exhausting but exciting adventure.

During this graduate school period, I don't recall any particular affinity, animosity, or interaction between my professors and me. Overall, these were the best professors of my academic career. I learned a great deal about material human beings. I explored the literature on the diversity of human belief systems and behaviors, and learned techniques and theory for studying human variability with the emphasis on culture. I marveled at the malleability of the human condition and tried to stop asking unanswerable questions. For inspiration, I kept a picture of Margaret Mead in my billfold long after she had dropped from anthropological favor. Years later, when I decided to discard her picture, I felt as if I were saying good-bye to a real mentor rather than a distant model.

I came to love human diversity in the abstract, not for romantic and exotic reasons, but because the ideation of many other cultures exceeded the Western psychological boundaries of rationality and objectivity. Despite their magic-ridden ceremonies and "primitive" social systems, these traditional humans were also viable and ethical in a relativistic way. If only the ethnographers could have explained their worldviews more clearly!

But alas! Studying anthropology in the 1960s and 1970s meant using anthropological writings and attitudes from the prewar and immediate postwar decades. For me, this meant coping with a new kind of ambiguity. Ethnologists were documenting indigenous cultures that almost always held beliefs in strange benevolent or malevolent nonmaterial worlds that frequently didn't appear to conform to the physical laws of cosmology, health, gravity, life, and death as we experienced them in the Western civilized world. The ideations, passions, dreams, enlightenment experiences, gods, beliefs, altered states of consciousness, and behaviors of these indigenous Others were very different from our understandings. From their strange beliefs evolved strange behaviors that begged for explanation.

During this period, to gain credibility in the academic world, anthropologists emphasized the need to use the scientific method. In order to be scientific when documenting other cultures, anthropologists had to maintain the stance of objective observers, yet they also had to develop the skill of empathy and insight while living among their informants. This technique of participant observation worked extremely well when documenting social, economic, political, and environmental information. But when indigenous cosmological, epistemological, and ontological belief systems were recorded, ethnographers found their informants' views of the material world and nonmaterial spirit pretty fuzzy and confused; they described the views as "primitive" (a term now, thankfully, out of vogue in anthropology). Understandably, when anthropologists inculcated with Western ideas and traditions tried to make sense of these strange beliefs and behaviors, they resorted to viewing them as nonrational, superstitious, and/or deviant. Of course, the researchers used explanations from the toolbox of their own culture! But it often seemed to me that the ethnographers' explanations made no more sense than their informants' concepts. I kept wondering why so many traditional cultures around the world resorted to nonrational ways of explaining and utilizing their origins, their environment, and the often-bizarre events of their lives and deaths. Even more important, why did all cultures seem to have to invent an explanation for their origins, and devise gods and spirits to explain the events of their lives? This universal inner need appeared to be part of humanness.

I believe that, subconsciously, my dormant personal questions gave me a feeling of kinship and empathy with some of those other cultures' worldviews. In those days, however, I could explain neither why I was fascinated by the uneasy contact of indigenous and Western cultural worldviews, nor why ethnographic explanations seemed more like *Alice in Wonderland* than real interpretations. But always, in the back of my mind, after my children were grown, I was going to be a Margaret Mead and study the esoteric, non-Western belief system of a heretofore undocumented culture, and *really figure out their inner world and beliefs*!

Graduate school teaches a vested interest in being an anthropologist. After I got my MA, I used my credentials to get a job in my hometown. However, in those days, being an applied anthropologist who worked in a mental health center did not meet the criteria for being a "true" anthropologist. I couldn't meet the test of having done research in a primitive society, nor was I devoting my life to the study and propagation of the discipline of anthropology. To truly be an anthropologist, I needed to return to graduate school.

~ Jumping Over Hurdles to the PhD ~

Eventually our daughter and three sons graduated from high school, and my husband and I divorced after thirty-one years of marriage. In late 1977, when I was fifty-two years old, I was passing through Albuquerque and decided to stop at the university. I soon discovered that both the anthropology department faculty and the curriculum had changed since my commuter days. One of the professors who had just gotten her degree later in life encouraged me to enroll for the PhD. Since I was at a crossroads, single, and without a job, eventually I applied and was accepted.

I certainly didn't feel old, but I soon discovered that I was older than anyone on the faculty. And there were only a handful of students in their thirties and forties. But though I was older than the students, I was just as poor. Most of the time, I couldn't afford gas for my car, but I lived near enough to campus to ride my bike. As much as possible, I acted like (and felt like) a bona fide student. As I enrolled once again, I told myself that this time I was going to become a real anthropologist and answer some of my dormant questions.

The first hurdle I encountered was a departmental decision that I must do my master's degree work over again. Since the decade of the sixties, there had been major changes in the field of anthropology and also revisions in the departmental curriculum and requirements. I had no choice but to conform to the new standards. As a result, I put in an extra year of coursework as I broadened my awareness of the linguistic, psychological, and cultural parameters of the human condition. But life wasn't all academic work. Most graduate students had part-time jobs. I worked at least half time throughout graduate school. Occasionally, we older students even had some fun, gossiping about who was sleeping around and involving ourselves in personal dramas.

The second hurdle was more subtle. For reasons unknown to those of us who were recent graduate student enrollees, the faculty conveyed to us that we were not inspiring students. They let us know that we were pretty mediocre compared to the faculty themselves. Over time, some of us felt intellectually diminished, and some students were resentful enough to drop from the program. However, most of us persevered. I decided to place my emphasis on psychological anthropology because it was the nearest I could get to dealing with my unanswered questions about what it was to be a human being.

With hurdle number three, my increasingly tenuous dream of being the next Margaret Mead vanished. My mother developed Alzheimer's disease. I had to move her near me in order to care for her. As her disease progressed, I realized that I was firmly rooted near the campus for an indefinite period. Going to some exotic place to do research was out of the question.

Conscientiously, I plodded through the courses and passed the exams, but I became too depressed to want to be an anthropologist any more. I tried to formulate a dissertation research project that could be done locally, but twice my research ideas were rejected as impractical. For another year, I registered in the graduate program but made no progress. In fact, I rarely showed up on campus except for my part-time job. I took care of my mother and pulled myself out of my doldrums by going square dancing and folk dancing, where I met a very nice person, whom I married. My second husband mistakenly thought I would have a terrific future and income when I got my PhD.

None of the faculty ever questioned where I was or what I was doing. I wasn't missed. By getting married again, I'd insured that I would not do research in some remote land. Sadly I took Margaret Mead's picture from my billfold and threw it away. I toyed with scrapping my PhD program, but my practical self told me not to throw away so many expensive years on campus. I decided to plod on.

In 1983 my third dissertation proposal was to study urban male and female retirees' attitudes toward retirement and then to compare their attitudes to their contrasting living conditions. This proposal was finally accepted by my faculty dissertation committee. By setting the research in metropolitan Albuquerque, I didn't have to leave my failing mother. It was on the cutting edge of the new field of the anthropology of aging. Because my major professor had become involved in another aging research project, she considered my research topic timely. I had finally learned what kind of research was fundable as well as how to carry it out acceptably. It took two years to complete my complex research interview schedule with one hundred people. In spite of my major professor leaving for another university position and the disinterest of the remaining committee members, I finally made sense out of a too-rich wealth of data, and during the following year wrote the too-long dissertation.

Hurdle number four turned out to be easy! My dissertation was accepted by both the department and the university dean. But the long odyssey through the PhD program left me with no desire to attend the final graduation ceremony. The original enthusiasm and zest I had felt for anthropology seemed like a chimera by the time I had jumped over all the hurdles. I had had to abandon my dream of contributing to the understanding of another culture's ideational life. And even then, anthropology didn't have a satisfactory answer to my question: What is a human being? After so much work for so long, I was tired of the whole academic scene. Instead of halfheartedly participating in the graduation ceremony, I drove off to Kansas to care for my dying mother-in-law.

~ Would I Do It Again? ~

I received my PhD just weeks before I turned sixty years old. I was a full-fledged anthropologist. I was a specialist credentialed to think and talk about humans-in-culture. I should have been able to do something with my degree. But I had several major problems to resolve first. Along with my new husband, I had picked up a teenage stepdaughter who needed personal attention because of her trauma from the death of her own mother. My husband's tenure meant that he could not leave his job to go with me if I were hired to teach or do research elsewhere, and I was not sure I wanted to go off without him. My mother was now in a nearby nursing home, and I was her available relative. And last but not least, I had no confidence that if I applied for a position, anyone would hire me at age sixty. No faculty member had shown an interest in my future, so I had no outside academic contacts. I decided to stay with my new family. Fortunately, after a year I was offered a part-time teaching job in the same department from which I had just received the degree. Teaching several courses to anthropology undergraduates turned out to be much more satisfying and fun than I could ever have guessed! Teaching those courses along with some sociology and gerontology courses, as well as doing some research, kept me occupied for the next decade until I retired.

In retrospect, I am sad to recall how I felt in 1986 when I received my PhD. I was angry and depressed. Why? First, there seemed little purpose in having dreamed so long and having done so much work and reached graduation without a sense of satisfaction. And second, I had spent so much time and effort without fulfilling my need to understand the as-yet-unstudied aspects of our inner humanness. I had only half an answer to what it was to be human in a constantly changing picture of our universe.

Happily, my anger at my PhD experience dissipated as I was able to put the experience into perspective. I had gained a priceless background with which to follow my subsequent psychological and philosophical interests outside the field of anthropology and outside of academia.

Am I sorry or am I glad that I got a doctorate in anthropology? Overall, I'm glad! I have learned so much about other people beyond my own limited experience. I appreciate my broadened awareness of the cultural place of language, economics, aesthetics, law, childrearing practices, ideologies, values, and worldviews. I know how flexible and adaptable humans have been in the past and are in the present. These characteristics are an irreducibly important part of being human. The study of anthropology has given me confidence that human beings have the ability and the intellectual imagination to make the necessary adaptations to survive the future. As I look back today, I say, "Yes, it was worth the roller-coaster ride!"

Would I recommend that other older women pursue the doctorate? I'd only suggest it to those who have an immediate practical goal and a tough psychological skin. To borrow from a pop phrase: "Graduate school ain't for sissies!"

~ Endnote ~

1. Eddy (1906:468).

~ Reference ~

Eddy, Mary Baker. 1906. *Science and Health, with Key to the Scriptures.* Boston: Published by The Trustees under the will of Mary Baker Eddy. Boston: J. Armstrong.

Not My Color, Not My Kind

Lessons in Race, Class, Age, and Gender in the Academy

M. Jean Harris

Full Circle

The scene: Spring 1999, outside the gymnasium–turned–commencement center at a midsize community college in the Pacific Northwest. I am garbed in a black faille gown, a thin, paperback novel secreted within the wide, velvet-striped sleeves of the gown, six-pointed crushed velvet cap firmly on head. Buoyed by a capricious wind, the blue and white hood on my back billows upward as if to join the white-cloud-kissed blue sky. Prodded by patient staff members, the lines of graduates and faculty slowly take shape. Suddenly, oblivious to stentorian commands to "Line up! Get in line," a slim, dark-haired woman breaks formation and runs across the divide between faculty and students to stand looking at me. "Wow," she says. "You look so good, like you were made to wear that gown!"

My former student in Introduction to Cultural Anthropology does not know this is my first opportunity to robe up since receiving the diploma that attests to my having "completed the studies and fulfilled the requirements of the Faculty for the degree of Doctor of Philosophy." She cannot know and there is no time to tell her how pleased I am at her compliment. Instead, I smile and squeeze her

M. Jean Harris: PhD 1998, University of North Carolina. Dissertation: "Crown and Glory on the Journey: Hair, Culture, and Self Construction Among African American Women." She was the first African American to graduate from the anthropology program at UNC. Jean, who had an earlier career as a social worker and personnel administrator, recently retired from teaching anthropology at Highline Community College in Washington State.

hand and respond to her comment about the gown. “Thank you. It does look pretty good, doesn’t it?” Enveloped by familiar strains, marching forward, we create pomp and circumstance.

I did not participate in the 1998 commencement ceremonies of the University of North Carolina at Chapel Hill (UNC). By the time of that commencement, I had earned tenure at one college in the Washington State community-college system and moved to teach at another two-year college closer to my home. The nine of us who in 1987 entered the doctoral program in the Department of Anthropology at UNC did not graduate as a cohort. I counted the climax of my career as a Carolina anthropology graduate student as the moment in April 1998, when my chair ushered me into the presence of my elder daughter and waiting doctoral committee members to hear the sweet words, “Congratulations, Doctor.”

~ The Beginning ~

The scene: August 1987, Seattle, Washington. With my fifteen-year-old daughter and two friends, I leave Seattle in a two-car caravan consisting of my aging Chevette and a “drive-away” car to be delivered to a student in Chapel Hill, North Carolina. I have traded a supervisory position in the human resources department of a local public utility for that of graduate student in anthropology. Our destination is an apartment I have leased, sight unseen, in Durham, North Carolina.

We arrive in Durham on an August day so hot the blacktop road is sweating. Bone-weary from the long drive, I glimpse our new home from the freeway but cannot find the way to it. I enter and exit the freeway again and again. Finally, near tears, I take a deep breath and exit yet again, and drive down one sun-bruised, deserted street and then another, relaxing now into the twists and turns in the road. One more turn, then there before us is the sign at the entrance to the pseudo-columned Colonial Arms Apartments. Looking back, my route from the freeway to the apartment is emblematic of my time in graduate school: much time was spent trusting intuition to find my way to a goal I saw but had no map to reach.

~ My Earlier Academic Career ~

Prior to enrolling in the graduate program in anthropology at UNC, I had always been a successful student. Mama, my grandfather’s sister who was the mother who raised me, had only gone through fifth grade, but she was a willing listener to the events of my school day and she corrected my homework assignments until they exceeded her skill level. From that point, Mama monitored my activities to ensure that I completed the work. Skilled in common sense, Mama early on explained to me that I, as a black person, would not always receive the grade I had earned, so I should work to satisfy myself. Consequently, though I received good grades, I did not put much stock in them. Grades were subjective, awarded by mercurial teachers, but standardized tests had meaning. Teachers themselves responded to standardized test scores, responses scored in distant locations without regard for responder. I came to believe that standardized tests were a fair measure of what I had learned. In elementary school, I tested into the gifted program; in high school, I was placed in the college-prep track. During my senior year of high school, I worked twenty hours a week after school; earned As and Bs; and, based on standardized test scores, earned a national scholarship to assist with college tuition.

The autumn after graduation, in the fall of 1961, I enrolled in a small, academically respectable, sectarian college. Supremely confident in my abilities and preparation, I turned a deaf ear to doomsaying faculty who in orientation told us, "Look to your left, now look to your right. One of you won't be here next quarter." I knew *I* wouldn't be the one who was gone! I believed that I could compete with students from the "better" (read "more white") high schools. Although I encountered instructors who initially discounted my abilities because of my race, I was right. My confidence was confirmed. By the end of my freshman year, I was eagerly sought out as a participant in campus colloquia. I still worked twenty hours a week and full time during breaks and summers.

Along the way, I discovered that courses at the nearby state flagship research institution were easier than at my college because the classes were so large that instructors administered multiple-choice tests. Periodically, I attended this university for a quarter's worth of "easy" credits. Away from home, away from my fundamentalist evangelical church, I joyfully balanced academic and social life. At the end of my junior year, I was inducted into the women's scholastic and service honorary. I worked a full forty-hour week during my senior year, yet my performance in independent reading courses encouraged two professors to advise me to consider graduate work.

I did not enroll in a graduate program immediately after college. Instead, I gave birth to a baby girl and went to work full time. After working for two years, I was accepted into the social welfare program at the University of California, Berkeley, and moved to California. For the first time in my life, I was studying in the company of a number of black students. Our first-year class was nearly 25 percent black. I was stretched thin by my workload—twenty hours of work a week, a full load of classes, and parenthood—but I was prepared for coursework at what I had heard was the most intellectually demanding university on the West Coast.

The heady, golden season of challenging professors and challenging study groups ended when my fiancé returned from his tour of duty in Vietnam, not to San Francisco as we had hoped, but to Tacoma, Washington, near my home and my seriously ill Mama. I transferred to the University of Washington, where I completed my Master of Social Work degree without difficulty. Marriage, the birth of another child, the death of Mama, and then a divorce delayed my half-formed plans to use my social work degree to finance graduate study in sociology. Still, I believed that I would someday become a graduate student in a doctoral program. I did not return to university for more than fifteen years.

~ Shifting Gears ~

Like most of the black women I knew, I had combined marriage, motherhood, and full-time work in a variety of settings. At the time of my divorce, I had obtained tenure at a local community college and gone on to a position as program evaluator at the State Board for Community Colleges, a job that required extensive travel. Faced with the logistics of arranging childcare with a heavy travel schedule, I obtained a job in the private sector and taught part time. I continued to explore possibilities for graduate study.

My older daughter exited college as the younger entered high school. The time seemed right for me to return to university. Friends introduced me to an anthropologist couple who encouraged me to explore anthropology, "the least restrictive of the social sciences." Carefully, I plotted my future. I used my degree in social work as leverage to enroll in a graduate course in tests and measurements, and used myself as subject for the course. The tests indicated that my interests matched those of college professors.

The process I used to select a graduate program was unorthodox. I did not evaluate possible programs based upon whether there were professors in my fields of interest. Instead, because I would be moving with a fifteen-year-old, relatively naive daughter, I eliminated programs in major metropolitan centers. Because I was a Northwesterner, I eliminated programs in locations that had extremes of climate. I then checked the ratings on programs that met my criteria and applied to those on my short list. I took the GREs, earning a score high enough to receive an honorable mention for a National Science Foundation fellowship and access to the foundation's computing center. My final choice of program was based upon a combination of my impression of the school during a campus visit and the financial-aid package. I felt confident I would complete the program in anthropology in time to be able to finance my daughter's tuition. With high hopes, I embarked on what proved to be, up to that point, my life's most painful journey.

~ Culture Shock ~

Shortly after I arrived in Durham, the university commenced orientation for autumn term. Faculty in the Department of Anthropology told our class, comprised of four white men, two white women, two international students, and me, that instead of admitting a large class with the expectation that a substantial number would wash out, they had selected us nine with the expectation that each of us would finish the program. This orientation certainly sounded better than the one I'd had as an undergrad! I recall thinking that graduate school was part hoop jumping, part endurance exercise, and part intellectual endeavor.

Initially comforted, I soon found my confidence eroding. My fellow students were, for the most part, the offspring or relatives of academics or other high-status professionals. Suddenly self-conscious, I felt I did not fit. I had returned to school after a long absence. My North American classmates were young recent graduates of selective colleges and universities. My professional training in social work and my work experience reinforced the use of the plodding, ponderous language favored in business and government bureaucracies. My fellow students had honed the elegant turns of phrase rewarded in academia. Several years had passed since I had last taught. There had been a paradigm shift—no more functionalism; Marx reigned! There I was—thousands of miles from home, far from friends who believed in me, desperately trying to support myself and my daughter on a stipend meant for one person—paralyzed by self-doubt.

I felt intimidated, terrified that I was inadequate to the rigors of graduate school, and certain I had ruined my miserably alienated (later diagnosed as clinically depressed) daughter's life. Unable to borrow enough money to live on, unable to hire a lawyer to obtain more child support for my daughter, I took a job as a part-time census enumerator, then felt torn because I had no time for my daughter, no time for my studies, no time for myself. It did not once occur to me that the graduate school program was not structured for a person of my age, class, race, gender, and marital status.

Although my performance the first year was more than satisfactory, I was thoroughly miserable and alienated from most of my fellow students and our professors. I learned that some faculty had reservations about admitting me and another mature student (their age-mates!) because older students were "not flexible." My daughter changed from an outgoing, enthusiastic, self-reliant student to a silent, sluggish waif. Without the self-monitoring skills that had buoyed my confidence in past times, I had no idea why on one paper I received an excellent grade, and on another merely an "adequate, light on analysis." Suddenly, I, who had been named copy editor of the high school creative-writing magazine, editor of an edition of the college creative-writing magazine, and yearlong editor of the student newspaper; I, who counted on grades in English to elevate my GPA, no longer understood how to structure an essay. I, elected in college to a national speech honorary, became tongue-tied. In a yawning divide where common understandings fail, one of my favorite professors told me that she was perplexed by my lack of interest in my work, and I, mortified, found no words to tell her that I was thoroughly interested but confused and utterly overwhelmed.

Class, age, gender, and race intertwined to form a multistranded rope of misery. A professor for whom I was a teaching assistant insisted that I come to her house to grade papers. I resisted because doing so brought back memories of accompanying my Mama to do "day work." A senior professor in the department introduced me to another graduate student, a young white woman. He introduced her to me as "Ms. So-and-so" and identified me to her by my first name. I was very aware that he was among a minority of professors, "Southern gentlemen," who practiced similar asymmetry of address when conversing with or identifying the black secretary and the white senior secretary. This Southern gentleman looked put out when I asked the student whether she wanted each of us to address the other formally, by title and last name, or informally, by first name.

I was likewise incensed when the same professor condescendingly told a female graduate student that it was about time she made some more cookies for the office. The giggly response made by this highly competent woman and her prompt compliance with his request helped me understand why I was viewed as not having been "raised right" as either a black person or a woman. At that moment, I was too involved to realize that I was encountering situations exacerbated by differences of regional culture, differently gendered upbringing, and different understandings of education as a merit system.

Well-intentioned but culturally insensitive advice further fueled my sense of alienation. Faculty members, sincerely trying to be helpful, touted the desirability of the public high school in Chapel Hill as the best school for my daughter. Only one professor understood that considerations other than SAT scores and extracurricular offerings could affect my choice of high school for my daughter. He provided me with the telephone numbers of black parents, who informed me of longstanding and intense strains between black families and the local high school. Likewise, an opportunity to live in the rural part of the county was a selling point to attract white students to the program, but black students told me that a single black woman not from the region probably wouldn't want to live in the county because of recent Klan activity.

Out of a desperate desire to improve my financial situation, much as one might buy a lottery ticket, I applied for a Ford Foundation graduate fellowship for individuals who were members of minority groups underrepresented in higher education. At about the same time, I enrolled in a community creative-writing class at a branch of the Durham Public Library. Faculty members were skeptical regarding my chances for the former and gravely doubtful regarding the usefulness and advisability of the latter. My advisor and the only other black American student in the department encouraged me, though they admitted that they sometimes did not understand my misery. During a long, solitary walk, I recalled an article written by Douglas Davidson, a sociology graduate student during my days at Berkeley, "The Furious Passage of the Black Graduate Student."[1] I located the article; Davidson voiced many of my frustrations. Slowly, I became less anxious and more able to think and write. Near the end of the first year of the program, I learned that I had won a three-year Ford Foundation fellowship! My advisor visibly relaxed as I informed her of the award. Her hug and forceful expression of joy at my good fortune made me know that she had felt both my pain and the frustration of the department at my maladjustment.

~ Reflections ~

Mine is not a story with clear villains or heroes. It does not have a fairy-tale ending. My reflections upon my time at Chapel Hill contain nearly equal parts joy and pain. In the midst of misery, I formed friendships among faculty and students that will be mine for the rest of my life. I reconnected with friends from my days at Berkeley who provided me with tangible support in the form of references, offers to read and comment on my research proposal, weekends away from North Carolina, and the equally necessary intangible emotional support. Recently, my elder daughter died from cancer. Members of the department called, wrote, sent flowers. Friends from Chapel Hill came to see us. One, stretching the limits of telecommuting, stayed with me for three weeks. Nonetheless, when I recall my graduate experience, my eyes still fill with tears. The assault on my sense of self, the intellectual insecurity are deep, slow-healing wounds that may color the rest of my career.

The value of reflecting upon my experience lies, in part, in analyzing my case to see how my experiences, though uniquely mine, are similar to and different from those of others like me. I am, to paraphrase an anthropological saying, like all other mature women who returned to school to earn a doctorate, like some other mature women who returned to school to earn a doctorate, like no other mature woman who returned to school to earn a doctorate.

The intertwining factors of age, gender, and race shape my view of the nearly eleven-year journey from graduate student to Doctor of Philosophy, but my perceptions are especially influenced by issues of class. I know well from black feminist theorists the folly of attempting to separate or privilege multiple oppressions like age, race, gender, class. If I keep in mind that, in my experience, these factors function always together, I can discuss them sequentially.

Observers from older cultures—from Frenchman Alexis de Tocqueville, whose *Democracy in America* was first published in the 1830s, to Chinese American anthropologist Francis Hsu's research in mid-to-late-twentieth-century America—have commented on the youthful brashness, exuberance, and informality of Americans. Our nation and culture are relatively young, and we value youth. In our fast-moving, innovative society, the knowledge of older people is not always immediately applicable. It is perhaps an easy step to equate being older with being obsolete. Certainly, that is true with technology; perhaps it is true with people, too. Although we are living longer as a society, our general expectation for developmental tasks for members of my generation was that young adulthood was the period when one "completed" one's formal education and settled upon a career. Returning students, those reentering formal educational programs in their late twenties or after, were somehow out of step with their fellow students. Perceptions of less time to contribute to a career could jeopardize admission to professional programs such as medicine. Within the academy, perhaps there was greater recognition that mature, even "old" scholars could make significant contributions, though generally such mature scholars had still been relatively young when they made the initial contributions that earned them the doctorate and admission into the academy. Late-entering graduate students were suspect. They had no track record. How could one evaluate their "promise"? Today, in the universities in my state, and I suspect in many universities elsewhere, we give lip service to life experience, but not much college credit for it. During my graduate experience, examples from life were minor currency, elaborations on scholarly concepts. Thus, I am sure, being older was no asset.

Apart from learning that my age and that of my fellow classmates were mentioned when we were being considered for admission, I have no evidence that my age may have negatively affected my status in the program, though it was true that my having a daughter who was close to most of my classmates in age made for a bit of awkwardness in social interactions. Some students partied with both of us, some with one or the other. When we were out drinking, sometimes faculty seemed unclear whether I was in a peer or subordinate relationship. Moreover, I had more-varied work experience than most of my professors and both less fear of and less tolerance for the traditional, ritual debasement of graduate students. Perhaps, too, because I was older, I was somewhat less awed by my professors and more likely to think them merely eccentric, rather than taking their eccentricities as evidence of brilliance.

Gender intertwined with age. The most senior faculty men seemed to establish rapport and mentoring relationships with men students more easily than with the women. Traditional role expectations for women were present in everyday interactions, from the earlier-mentioned incident regarding cookie baking to opportunities to earn extra money by providing childcare for faculty offspring. The unfortunate experience when I was expected to grade papers at the home of a professor would not have happened had I not been a woman. No male student ever had that experience, although other female students did. I am likewise certain I would not have had the experience had I been an African American man of my age.

Race. Race—the always-present, seldom openly-talked-about factor in the experience of people of color—permeated my experience at Carolina. When I entered the graduate program, the UNC system was still under a consent decree because of race issues. The anthropology department in its long history had never graduated an African American man or woman with the PhD. My classmate from South Africa was the first person of African descent to finish the program; I am the first African American.

The all-campus black graduate student organization included students in all disciplines, yet we were few in number. As one of my part-time jobs, I was hired in a program to provide support to African American undergraduates. I heard them lament many times that they were told, directly or indirectly, by students and faculty that they were only admitted because of affirmative action. The implication was clear that they were not perceived as intellectually qualified to be at the flagship research institution, a perception that I did not share based upon my experience as a teaching assistant in two different departments. Because African American undergraduates were the same race as I, I imagined that they could be my children enduring painful experiences, and many times I was thankful that I was well matured before I encountered the condescending, patronizing attitudes that were rampant on campus.

Before I went to North Carolina, I had been a successful personnel professional. Trained as a recruiter at a Fortune 500 firm, I had managed the recruiting function in a large, multiple-branch financial institution and had coordinated the employee assistance program at the same corporation. Immediately before enrolling in graduate school, I had supervised the employment department for a regional public utility company. I had excellent references, so I attributed it to racial factors that I was never called for even an interview for the numerous personnel jobs at various levels that were available at the university and in the town (I did not remove from my résumé such racial identifiers as professional memberships and volunteer experience).

Although I did not know all of the African American students, faculty, and staff on campus, there was an imagined community that allowed us to approach each other more easily than we did students of other "races." When I first visited the campus, the department introduced me to the only other African American graduate student in anthropology. Our relationship of mutual support was cemented by our racial experiences in the South; in our case, race transcended class and regional culture differences.

Multiple factors influenced my graduate experience, yet I recall class factors most vividly. Bowles and Gintis[2] and MacLeod[3] provide analyses of the role education plays in reproducing a class structure. In his writings, French anthropologist Pierre Bourdieu deals extensively with cultural competence, cultural pedigree, and cultural capital. Bourdieu, along with Marx and Weber, provided tools for me to apply to my situation. Had I had the objectivity to consider my social class before I enrolled in graduate school, I might have been far less traumatized, for I would have understood the limitations of my education to that point. Had I not suffered from "false consciousness," I would have understood that the notion that education is a meritocracy obfuscates its support for the status quo. I would not have been surprised that I, more than the other grad students, tried to give professors what they expected of me. I would not have been surprised that the rules were different in the arena I had entered. I might have understood that the knowledge that is counted on in standardized tests is not sufficient to succeed at the level I had entered, and I might have more confidently engaged the assignments. Surely, I would have understood which productions were rewarded, and why.

Workers are not rewarded for original thought. Working-class people enter the academy in spite of their class position, not because of it, and in general, they shed working-class thinking, working-class behavior, working-class loyalties if they are to succeed. In Weberian terms, I was not working class. The class I was raised in and identified with was clearly a lower class. I was raised "on the dole" and had long outgrown feelings of shame about that fact. Moreover, I strongly identified with the substantial numbers of working-class students I taught in community college and wanted them to gain tools to earn better wages. I was irritated when my professors gently countered my plan to earn a doctorate so

I could return to community college teaching, with suggestions that my ideas would change as I realized I could "do more." No wonder, too, that the professor with whom I most strongly identified and who most strongly supported me was a white woman whose class of origin was more similar to mine.

My preferred communication style, relatively direct and confrontational, and my emphasis on pragmatic applications of theory all marked me as Other, but worst of all, my bullheaded resistance to changing my style made me suspect. Either I did not know the rules or I was deliberately refusing to play. In any case, perhaps I should not have been allowed to join the host in the ivory tower.

My research interest, African people in diaspora, especially African people in the United States, was not yet fashionable in anthropology when I entered graduate school. Neither were my synthesizing, interpretive approach and my interest in being accountable to my ethnic community. I recall my chair's dismay when I told a member of my committee that my greatest fear was that black people would say my work was "some esoteric, peripheral bullshit." I did not know where I was off, and most of my professors could not articulate what was wrong. Mutually frustrated, I became increasingly alienated—and they began to doubt my potential. Had we recognized how my class background was influencing my experience, I would have made choices with more awareness of the implications and consequences. Who knows, I might have taken a different path entirely.

Cultures clashed during my graduate experience, and I was changed. I am neither the person who entered graduate school nor the person who exited. I cannot weigh the factors that influenced my graduate experience separately, and I cannot at this time guess how they interacted with each other. I do know that I should be less surprised that I had challenges than that I surmounted them. Education is nothing if not change, a "leading out," in the sense of the Latin from which our word *education* comes. Anthropology provides us with tools to understand ourselves and the Other. Despite the pain, I have met both goals.

~ Endnotes ~

1. Davidson (1993).
2. Bowles and Gintis (1986).
3. MacLeod (1995).

~ References ~

Bowles, Samuel, and Herbert Gintis. 1986. *Democracy and Capitalism: Property, Community, and the Contradictions of Modern Social Thought.* New York: Basic Books.

Davidson, Douglas. 1993. The Furious Passage of the Black Graduate Student. In *The Death of White Sociology,* ed. Joyce A. Ladner, 25–51. New York: Random House.

MacLeod, Jay. 1995. *Ain't No Makin' It: Aspirations and Attainment in a Low-Income Neighborhood.* Boulder, CO: Westview Press.

Understanding My Life

The Dialectics of Marketing and Anthropology

Barbara Olsen

My Self as Other

This is a narrative of a life in which anthropology has been the lens through which it all made sense. In the 1950s, I grew up in a one-room cabin without running water and attended a one-room school. From an early age, I knew there were different yet equally valid realities, and I wanted to experience as many as I could in one lifetime. This meant making conscious decisions that involved not having children, becoming an artist, homesteading in the Caribbean, founding an advertising agency with offices in the United States and Europe, and becoming an anthropologist and a professor.

In the back of my mind, I always wanted to be an anthropologist, to lead the life of an adventurer, but life's antagonisms got in the way. When I finally received my doctorate at age forty-four, colleges had fewer anthropology departments and more graduates were becoming "practicing anthropologists." Although the graduate journey took twenty years, I now see that it was the disruptions that made all the difference and nurtured the anthropologist I am today.

The antagonistic disruptions were *defining moments* in my life that called for reinterpretations of events, which in turn initiated new eras. Each of the

Barbara Olsen: PhD 1989, New School for Social Research. Dissertation: "The Personal and Social Costs of Development in Negril, Jamaica, W.I., 1970–1988." Barbara, a tenured professor in the Department of Marketing in the State University of New York (SUNY) system, turned to anthropology after a successful career as an advertising executive. Her current research and publications deal with consumer behavior from an anthropological perspective.

four eras of my life is characterized by experiencing my self as Other. The first consciousness of self occurred in a quaint, almost premodern context, when I attended grades three through six in a one-room school and lived in a one-room cabin with outhouse and pump. The second era was spent homesteading in Jamaica during my twenties. The third period involved maintaining a career in advertising during my thirties and forties while going to graduate school for a PhD in anthropology. The fourth era is the years since receiving my PhD in 1989, when I became a professor of marketing.

During each epoch, I was defined as Other by my contemporaries. As a child, my peers saw me as poor and disadvantaged. As an expatriate, I was white trying to live in an Afro-Jamaican world. As an advertising executive, I was an aberration to my colleagues, ahead of my time using anthropology to solve marketing problems, while to the Marxist anthropology faculty at my graduate school I was a capitalist entrepreneur. And now, as a marketing professor, I am often recognized as some kind of hybrid or Other because I do not have a degree in a business discipline. In my own story, I turn the convention of otherness around, using these experiences of being othered, of being stigmatized as exotic, for reflection to reconstruct my life.

Because I now research an expanding, global consumer culture using my bifocal lenses to understand how the evolution of marketing and consumption is transforming the human experience, I have chosen to analyze my life by looking at the dialectics of marketing and anthropology. It is in the resolution of the antagonism between the two, as each discipline has historically felt uncomfortable with the other, that my life makes sense on both a personal and an intellectual level. This sense comes from a personal search for meaning in a quest for survival and from integrating the two domains for understanding how the trajectory of my life fits within contemporary American culture.

Life History as Political Document

Beginning in the early 1970s, I have sat in the bush of Jamaica, collecting the life histories of aging matriarchs. I recognized our collective humanity by comparing their lives with the lives of my grandmothers, mother, and self. Many of our struggles were the same; only the contexts were different. For these women, survival came through an economic struggle among scarce resources. In gathering their histories, I realized that each life is inspired by defining moments that shape later decisions. Our personal interpretation of events gives particular meaning to people, places, and things, which become part of our cultural biography over time. At the same time, life history is a political document because social contexts often become contests for survival of body and will.

Valentine Winsey maintains that most women who matured after World War II have lives that appear "chaotic-seeming."[1] Having grown up in what is now termed a dysfunctional family that was indeed chaotic-seeming, in 1992 I began exploring the life histories of elderly female recovering alcoholics to look for common themes in family experiences. As I listened to their stories, I found they also redefined their states of being at certain junctures of self-awakening. I related to their self-making—their idealism, disillusionment, resilience, and survival—and again saw the "we" in me and the wisdom in our accumulated knowledge.

~ Becoming the Other ~

We are born into gendered lives that are also contoured by the attributes of race, culture, and class and significantly altered by age as we make our life journeys. It all seems so normal, so regular, so predictable, until, in a defining moment, we see ourselves through the eyes of another and become self-conscious or stigmatized, fixed in the glare of another's conception of who we should be. For me, the stigmas of class, gender, and race have been particularly poignant.

My first experience as Other came from living in a one-room cabin as a child. It was a period when my parents miscalculated their finances, and the interim lodging became a permanent residence until we could afford to build a house. Living in our one-room cabin with outhouse and well coincided with going to junior high school and leaving the one-room schoolhouse I had known for four years. In that school, each row of desks was a grade, and each year we moved over one row to the next level: four rows, four grades, four years in the same room with the same teacher and classmates. I thought living in the cabin would be OK because no one in my new school far away would know how I lived.

We lived in the cabin for three years. We pumped water by hand from the well and heated it on the Kalamazoo kerosene stove that was also our heater. We used the outhouse in the woods in all kinds of weather and, me in my modesty, in all hours of the night. It was not normal, but it was okay. When my seventh-grade English teacher became the substitute summer mailman before school ended that June, he announced to our class that he knew where Barbara lived. My heart fell out, my cover was blown, and for the first time in my life I felt abnormal. I was different. I was Other. That teacher, whether malicious or simply stating observational fact, instigated my first self-reflection, the first time I compared my life to that of other people.

During the 1930s, my father had worked with the Civilian Conservation Corps building Glacier National Park, and he told my sister and me tales of the Blackfoot tribe. His stories and the monthly *National Geographic* were my earliest exposure to different lives. I wanted to become an archaeologist, but was raised to believe that only men could be adventurous. But I came to admire strong women and used them as role models. Mrs. Behr, who taught high school history, told us we must study "his story" because it is the best way to understand who we have come to be. My parents wanted me to be a secretary, but, inspired by Mrs. Behr, I went to college and majored in history while working on an IBM assembly line. From then on, education became the ticket out of my social class and a predetermined small-town life.

There was personal power in 1960s idealism. We wanted to create our own reality. We believed we could change society. Old icons were toppled, replaced by our own vision of a future we would create. We were revolutionaries. During my third year in college, I discovered an anthropology class taught by Joan Campbell. She was a powerful spirit, a single mother, and an anthropologist. She inspired me. However, an esoteric career like anthropology was for wealthy dilettantes, not children of factory workers, and I got a depressing job as a caseworker for the Department of Social Welfare in New York City in 1968. After six months, I decided it was time to become an anthropologist. I entered the graduate anthropology program at Hunter College. At Hunter, another female anthropologist, Annemarie de Waal Malefijt, a specialist on the Caribbean, suggested I follow her track. I stayed a year short of completing the master's degree because I married my sociology professor instead.

The years 1968 and 1969 were among the most momentous and disastrous in the political life of my generation. Assassinations and student killings bloodied the landscape we were trying to cultivate. Many of us preferred to drop out of American society.

~ Jamaica: Discovering the Other ~

In 1970 my husband was denied tenure. That winter break, we took a vacation to Jamaica and discovered an acre of land on the cliffs of Negril overlooking the sea. It cost $7,000. I figured that having already studied much about the Caribbean, I would live the life of an anthropologist in the field. Negril became my fieldwork site, and I watched the community evolve from catering to the explorer tourist to marketing to the package tourist.

In 1970 I designed an octagon cottage with thatch roof, which was built using the remainder of our savings on a dirt road with no electricity. In this alternative lifestyle, we had indoor plumbing, with water running from a roadside pipe connected to the reservoir in the mountains, and a kerosene refrigerator. Having lived as a child with an outhouse and a well with hand pump, this was luxury. Roughing it was nothing new. I knew I could live under any conditions and survive quite well.

Miss Ina, Miss May, Miss Lynette, and Vivianne (who never wanted to be called "Miss") were matriarchs who befriended us and taught me the intricacies of living off the land. I learned to wash dishes with sand, to wash my laundry in two tubs of water, to keep the weevils out of the thatch by hanging a lobster from a crossbeam, to kill rats by leaving a pan of very salty rice mixed with cement, and to keep "duppies" (Jamaican ancestral ghosts) out of my house by building an X over each doorway.

Living in Jamaica among people of another color was easy and natural at first. We were accepted as part of their community, and I became aunt to our neighbors' children. At first we were the only foreigners living on the lighthouse road and had the only car besides the lighthouse keeper. The locals wanted to befriend us for the favors we could bestow, for trips to the market eighteen miles away, and for the extra material goods we no longer needed or outgrew. I wanted to live like a Jamaican and became friends with families that went back five generations in the community. I did not see them as Other. Many are still my friends today and inform my ongoing research.

Then I realized that *I* was the Other. It did not take long to feel guilt for our having more things and more money, and for being members of a tribe that conquered with a territorial imperative, taking not just their property but also their quiet, dignified, traditional way of life. By our presence and the presence of all who followed, these gentle people would forever be transformed.

By 1972 our house was complete—and we ran out of money. Scarce resources put a strain on our marriage, and my husband began to court a wealthy heiress who was visiting Americans up the road. They eventually married and built two more houses, turning the property into a villa rental business. During my estrangement, I was adopted by a neighboring Rastafarian family. Jamaican women were very sympathetic, as many of them had "visiting husbands" and were victims of spousal abuse. Serial abandonment was just part of life. In my later studies of Jamaican social structure, I came to appreciate how these Jamaican women incorporated particular behaviors for survival into their social fabric.

I was related to my Jamaican sisters through a shared gender experience that erased the racial and class distinctions between us. My Jamaican friends showed me how they traditionally used both family and religion to give them balance in a world set adrift, creatively adapting cultural formations to the necessity of their realities in order to ease discomfort and ensure survival as a people. As Clifford Geertz reminds us: "It is what lies beyond a relatively fixed frontier of accredited knowledge that, looming as a constant background to the daily round of practical life, sets ordinary human experience in a permanent context of metaphysical concern and raises the dim, back-of-the-mind suspicion that one may be adrift in an absurd world."[2]

When I realized I was being replaced as a wife, I returned alone to New York to pick up the pieces and make money to fight for my land. For me, it was the end of one era and the beginning of another.

~ Advertising and the Promotion of American Values ~

In New York, I worked initially as a freelance illustrator and graphic artist in the art department of an advertising agency. I soon moved to supervising the television syndication accounts of United Artists, MGM, Columbia Pictures, Twentieth Century Fox, and Lorimar, among others. It was a fast-paced life. I tried to return to graduate school, but work got in the way. The fight for the land through Jamaican attorneys was too expensive and emotionally draining. My future was in New York.

TV syndication, the resale of network shows by the original production companies, reached its zenith in the late 1970s and 1980s. I helped sell *Starsky and Hutch*,

*Charlie's Angels, Eight Is Enough, The Fall Guy, M*A*S*H, Dynasty,* and *Dallas.* Now, reflecting on this, I see that I helped promote the replication of American cultural values and lifestyle around the world. Television syndication exported not just entertainment, but also hopes and desires. It transplanted the wants and needs of an affluent society to families with televisions around the world. Whenever I could, I returned to my Rasta friends in Jamaica to retreat to their simpler, saner life.

During one of my trips, I found an early effect of the infiltration of television on a Jamaican teenager who had been impregnated by her father. She gave her newborn the last name of Carrington (learned from *Dynasty*), rather than reveal paternity. Life in advertising had become schizophrenic.

~ The Dream of Anthropology ~

One morning in the summer of 1977, I awoke to a dream that I was sixty-five and had not completed my doctorate. It was frightening. Although I was totally immersed in the corporate world, I enrolled that same day at the New School for Social Research.

At the New School, I found a mentor in Professor Gene Weltfish. She sympathized with my corporate life because her sister, Florence Goldman, vice president at Gray Advertising, supported Weltfish during her struggle to be an anthropologist. I liked Weltfish's strength of character, her politics, her personal fortitude. Every month or so, she would invite me to her one-room studio and cook spaghetti squash on the hot plate in her bathtub. Her lifestyle was urban camp, and it reminded me of my childhood in the one-room cabin. I'd sit for hours listening to her stories and taking notes while surrounded by floor-to-ceiling books. The books were her friends, an intellectual reservoir to retrieve references or show pictures illustrating her stories. I was amazed to see handwritten notes taken during fieldwork with the Pawnee in 1927 under the guidance of Boas. Her extension of friendship touched my heart and stimulated a desire to join her tribe.

Dr. Weltfish understood when I confided my angst in deciding on sterilization as birth control. She told me of her struggles as a single parent after her marriage ended and said women who are conditioned to procreate in an economically antagonistic society are caught in a cultural contradiction. Recalling how my parents strained to raise us, I chose to study the dilemma rather than become a victim. For two years, under Weltfish's tutelage, I wrote and illustrated an unpublished book, "Toting Tots Around the World," a study of how women in eighty cultures accommodate caring for children within their daily chores—something I found insurmountable in my own culture. It was a way of rationalizing my decision, interpreting other societies' solutions against the disease of my own society regarding childcare.

My growing resentment against American culture was increasingly intellectualized. Night classes in anthropology at the New School and art classes at the School of Visual Arts provided a balance to corporate life. I painted and drew to exercise my creative spirit. At school, Michael Harner became another mentor as I focused on religion as a track of study. I gladly accepted the favor to illustrate his book, *The Way of the Shaman*.[3] It was an antidote to coming of age on Madison Avenue.

All along, I was fascinated by the "Madison Avenue Clan." Most of the time, I felt quite comfortable in the world of advertising, and I loved creating campaigns. However, whenever I interjected an anthropological insight during client meetings, my business partner would kick me under the table and roll his eyes, embarrassed because he did not understand the marketing application of anthropology. I was Other in spirit. I was an anthropologist in a world of suits.

As my clients focused their marketing to different geographical targets, the agency I founded in 1979, IMC Marketing Group, became bicoastal and multinational. We expanded the New York agency to Los Angeles to handle some accounts. In 1980 ABC Pictures International decided to market made-for-TV movies as feature films in England. This took me to London, where I affiliated the company with an advertising agency and music-video production company. As the agency grew, so too did the responsibilities and the overhead. It was a delicate balance of constantly bringing in new business and producing the best ads, brochures, and promotions to keep my clients and the agency competitive. The concepts of gender, ethnicity, race, and class were transformed into segmentation bases. People represented target markets measured by rating points to be sold consumer goods.

At night, I studied anthropology to find out how we came to be this way.

At home, my new mate resented my determination to study and work on subject matter that he thought bore little relationship to the real world and my career. His favorite comment was "Forget it and get on with your life, no one's going to want a fifty-year-old anthropologist." It was during moments like this that I remembered my dream and the horrible feeling, that early morning in July 1977, that I was too old to finish my degree. I also remembered the encouragement of my role models: Mrs. Behr, my high school history teacher; and anthropologists Campbell, Malefijt, and Weltfish. I knew I could be whatever I wanted. Joseph Campbell's wisdom echoed: "Follow your bliss, and doors will open where you thought there were no doors." I followed my heart and hoped for the best.

~ Marketing and Anthropology Come Together ~

My advertising career represented an education on how American culture is produced, packaged, and marketed. It also sustained my academic interests and frequent trips to Jamaica. I finally obtained the PhD in 1989, with a thesis emphasizing the social costs of development for tourism, particularly in Negril, Jamaica, from 1970 to 1988. Significantly, I have continued to chronicle how overdevelopment has compromised the carrying capacity of the environment and infrastructure.[4] This fits the pattern noted by William Rodman that "many long-term researchers move increasingly in the direction of advocacy research over the course of their careers."[5]

The academic landscape of 1989, answering to the demands of the times, included more business than social science curricula and was vastly different from the 1960s, when anthropologists could freely chart their paths. But, as John Sherry put it, "Anthropology, marketing and consumer research are poised as linchpin disciplines in parallel intellectual domains.... Convergence is occurring. Fueled by academics and practitioners in search of explanatory frameworks and managerial applications, contemporary business has been drawn into the orbit of anthropology."[6] For me, this was a plus. I joined the faculty of the Marketing Department at the State University of New York at Old Westbury. It was a natural fit. Teaching and researching marketing and consumer behavior was an extension of all I had learned in anthropology, but now the focus was on contemporary American culture.

My current research on our consumer culture has grown out of studies with my marketing students, conducting ethnographies of product use with three generations of their families. When I realized there was a connection between brand loyalty and lineage, as many of our favorite brands are "inherited," I began research in advertising agency archives to write about the marketing history that promoted these heritage brands to our grandparents' generation.[7] There is a great wealth of anthropologically relevant data in advertising archives.

The years since obtaining my PhD have been the most exciting and fruitful of my life journey. I have not only discovered new kin among the marketing anthropologists studying consumer behavior, but through an analysis of consumer culture, I have been able to piece together a bit of the puzzle involving the factors contributing to American social evolution and our roles within it.

~ Convergences ~

My research at the end of the 1990s turned toward how we use consumer goods to enhance and make sense of our life journeys in the way that Jean Baudrillard understood how advertised brands help us complete our selves as we re-create the lifestyles that advertisements define for us.[8] Research in the advertising archives reveals how the advertising copywriters from the 1920s and 1930s portrayed their own elitist social-class attitudes in advertisements that our grandparents' generation tried to emulate and simulate with status brands.[9] For my own grandmother, many of these brands also helped her learn how to become an American.

My research with middle-aged women, however, reveals a deeper and more symbolic dimension to contemporary brand relationships.[10] While I initially thought interviews capturing five life histories would report a major concern with the physical and emotional effects of the change of life at age fifty, each woman was, in fact, unconsciously preoccupied with continuing to solve her own life theme. Each theme, established in childhood, was related to a traumatic or inspiring life-defining event that occurred during or prior to adolescence. Their themes, in turn, concerned aspects of control, comfort, status, a longing for Europe, and empowerment. The enhancement of each life theme was accomplished by forming specific relationships with particular branded goods that represented symbolic associations. Thus, advertised brands of the late twentieth century have become part of the tool chest by which we craft personal histories.

My continuing fieldwork in Jamaica involves an analysis of popular song lyrics to understand how the political economy and social structure influence the angst and tension inherent in gender relationships that surface in song. Jamaican music both records and reveals the history of its culture as it portrays the personal lament of a songwriter. Jamaican lyrics now advertise the populist philosophy of a culture caught in the web of international economics. This becomes more fascinating as I weave cultural history into my courses on consumer behavior and international marketing.

In an ironic twist of historical convolution, in 1999 I coordinated and chaired a special session at the annual meeting of the American Anthropological Association (AAA) titled "Caribbean Connections: Linkages of Marketing and Consumption in Historical Perspective." One attendee, Timothy de Waal Malefyt, introduced himself as Annemarie de Waal Malefijt's nephew. He has built a career in advertising and currently is director of cultural discoveries at BBDO Advertising in New York City. He invited me to participate in a 2000 AAA session, "Advertising and Anthropology,"[11] and later asked me to write a book chapter about my career in advertising using narrative ethnography.[12]

This intellectual journey of retrospection led me to revisit my own fieldwork using reflexive introspection.[13] From this, I now understand why my older female Jamaican informants were so open and revealing of their life stories for my thesis. I met them when my then-husband left me for another woman. Over the following years, these women gave me guidance and protection and shared their own very personal histories of love lost. My latest research continues the theme of exploring Jamaican gender relationships. Even though all of the elderly female informants have now passed on, they live in fieldwork data where I am able to visit, hear their words, and work on papers to keep their memories alive.

Anthropology has helped me understand choices made along the life journey. For my own life, the device of Other has organized my experience in those *defining moments* where I was cast adrift on a sea of uncertainty and had to reconstruct my place in the world. Wherever possible, I have looked for the commonality that joins us together while trying to understand the process that separates and defines us as Other. I have increasingly taken an advocacy role in my Jamaican research, supporting grassroots efforts to protect the environment through sustainable development. Through my research on consumption, I have bridged the anthropological and business disciplines looking for new meaning in the construction of culture. This continuing self-reflection has inspired a greater understanding of the human collective and how we, and I, have come to be.

~ Endnotes ~

1. Winsey (1992:xiii).
2. Geertz (1973:102).
3. Harner (1980).
4. Olsen (1997).
5. Rodman (1995); see also Fowler and Hardesty (1994).
6. Sherry (1995:10).
7. Olsen (1995).
8. Baudrillard (1988).
9. Olsen (2000).
10. Olsen (1999).
11. Olsen (2000).
12. Olsen (2003a).
13. Olsen (2003b).

~ References ~

Baudrillard, Jean. 1988. *America*. New York: Verso.

Fowler, Don, and Donald Hardesty, eds. 1994. *Others Knowing Others: Perspectives on Ethnographic Careers*. Washington, D.C.: Smithsonian.

Geertz, Clifford. 1973. *The Interpretation of Cultures*. New York: Basic Books.

Harner, Michael J. 1980. *The Way of the Shaman: A Guide to Power and Healing*. San Francisco: Harper & Row.

Olsen, Barbara. 1995. Brand Loyalty and Consumption Patterns: The Lineage Factor. In *Contemporary Marketing and Consumer Behavior: An Anthropological Sourcebook*, ed. John F. Sherry, Jr., 245–81. Thousand Oaks, CA: Sage.

———. 1997. Environmentally Sustainable Development and Tourism: Lessons from Negril, Jamaica. *Human Organization* 56:285–93.

———. 1999. Exploring Women's Brand Relationships and Enduring Themes at Mid-Life. *Advances in Consumer Research* 26 (1): 615–20.

———. 2000. Early Advertising Strategies and Socially Embedded Texts. Paper presented at annual meeting of the American Anthropological Association, San Francisco.

———. 2003a. The Revolution in Marketing Intimate Apparel: A Narrative Ethnography. In *Advertising Cultures*, ed. T. Malefyt and B. Moeran, 113–38. New York: Berg.

———. 2003b. Reflexive Introspection: The Participant in the Observation. Paper presented at conference of the European Association for Consumer Research, Dublin, Ireland.

Rodman, William. 1995. Book review of *Others Knowing Others: Perspectives on Ethnographic Careers*, edited by Don Fowler and Donald Hardesty. In *American Anthropologist* 97:380–81.

Sherry, John F., Jr. 1995. Marketing and Consumer Behavior: Into the Field. In *Contemporary Marketing and Consumer Behavior: An Anthropological Sourcebook*, ed. John F. Sherry, Jr., 3–44. Thousand Oaks, CA: Sage.

Winsey, Valentine. 1992. *Your Self as History*. New York: Pace Univ. Press.

Section 5

Being an Anthropologist, Living Anthropological Lives

ALL OF us acquired new identities from our studies in anthropology and becoming "certified" anthropologists, with the awarding of our PhDs and the right to be called "Doctor So-and-so." This shift was based not just on getting the PhD (that's only a beginning!), but also on our research, teaching, publications, and other professional activities. Each of us has documented this aspect of our anthropological lives in a CV—curriculum vitae, the academic form of a résumé. This is our public anthropological persona.

But being steeped in a particular discipline shapes a person's worldview. For anthropologists, this is likely to include taking a comparative and holistic approach in mundane matters, in our everyday reading, observations, and relationships. We try to understand people from their own perspectives and to put people and events into wider contexts beyond the immediate experience.

And deeper still, there is a very private sense of the self as anthropologist. Some of us wonder if we were born anthropologists, as even from childhood we had tremendous curiosity about other people and places that we experienced through reading, travel, and participant observation (even when we did not know the term or think about what we were doing as research). Others discovered that their personal interests were the stuff of anthropology after some formal encounter with anthropology. However we came to anthropology, the process of becoming an anthropologist gave us a transformed sense of self, a new identity, and a changed way of life.

From Prehistory to Culture History
My Anthropological Journey

Marjorie M. Schweitzer

A New Beginning

It was spring break 1972 and we were relaxing in a cabin at Robbers' Cave State Park. John and I and our friend Martin Schwarz were discussing the possibility of my returning to graduate school. The goal: a PhD in anthropology.

Earlier that year I had asked myself: Is there more to life than being a chauffeur? My life as a mother of three young children was beginning to seem more like a taxi service. I was not a club joiner, did not play bridge, and was not involved in the social calendar that interested many faculty wives.

Don't misunderstand me. I loved being a mother and the wife of a university professor. I was proud of my role. Being home with the children full time gave me pleasures and treasured memories that I would not trade.

But I remember bouts of "cabin fever." With three little ones who were close to each other in age, I often wondered how I could do something intellectual and still be a good wife and mother. I had recently finished typing and partially editing a sociology textbook for two professors in the Department of Sociology at Oklahoma State University (OSU). I thought at the time, with a bit of presumption, that if they could write that book, I could certainly do as well or better.

Marjorie M. Schweitzer: PhD 1978, University of Oklahoma. Dissertation: "The Power and Prestige of the Elderly in Two Indian Communities." In 1986 Marjorie retired as assistant professor at Oklahoma State University. Her publications include two books: a bibliography and an edited volume on American Indian grandmothers. She continues to be an advocate for the survival of American Indian culture.

This was not to be my first adventure in anthropology, however. I had had a long involvement, beginning in the spring of 1948.

~ The Call ~

My love affair with anthropology began at the end of my sophomore year. I had finished two years of undergraduate studies at DePauw University in Greencastle, Indiana, as a zoology major. My plan was to become a med-tech, related undoubtedly to my early childhood wish to be a nurse. It was a sunny day in late spring. I was standing in the middle of campus with friends, when one of them showed me a book with the magical words that were to become like a beacon for me for the rest of my life.

When I read the description of this new word *anthropology* for the first time, I knew immediately that it encompassed everything that interested me. What I did not know was how much more—ideas, perspectives, substantive knowledge—I would encounter as I pursued BA, MA, and PhD studies in anthropology.

~ Go West, Young (Wo)man ~

I transferred to the University of Colorado (CU) for my junior year, combining my love of the mountain west with the more practical issue of enrolling in a school with a program in anthropology. The Flatirons of the Rocky Mountains defined the western limits of the town of Boulder, and many times while studying for classes on the CU campus, I looked to them for inspiration. Because I began my anthropology studies as a junior, I had two years to begin *and* complete my newly chosen major. I took as many anthropology courses as I could, but also studied other fascinating topics such as geomorphology, German, philosophy, and museum studies. I worked for Omer Stewart, coding data from his research with the Ute Indians of southwestern Colorado, designed and helped create museum displays of material culture from the South Pacific, and took field trips to local archaeological sites.

I loved every minute of it, even the times in Ned Danson's after-lunch class when, overcome with drowsiness, I tried to keep up with a seemingly endless list of Southwestern pottery types. Learning about anthropology was an eye-opening and mind-expanding experience and instilled in me a feeling of awe for the enormously different and intriguing lifestyles and worldviews that Other Peoples and Other Cultures had achieved. Even today, having survived postmodernism and deconstructionism, a sense of dis-ease and controversy that seems to pervade the anthropological academy every few years (even to the point of asking whether or not the four-field approach is still valid), and the variable status of the anthropologist in the contemporary world—sometimes revered and sometimes reviled—anthropology has never lost its importance and its appeal for me.

~ Point of Pines ~

In June 1950, after a vacation that included a trip through the ruins of Mesa Verde, my folks dropped me off at the old hotel in Globe, Arizona, where I joined the University of Arizona's staff and other students going to Point of Pines, the university's archaeology field school. For eight weeks, we excavated intrusive Anasazi sites in the Mogollon region of eastern Arizona, learning techniques of archaeological excavation under the tutelage of the dean of Southwestern archaeology, Emil "Doc" Haury, and his popular dig foreman, Joe Ben Wheat. We learned how to shovel dirt without scattering it (an important skill, really!) and how to describe and catalogue the items that we unearthed. We mused over why the "burnt room" had been buried under a mound of dirt ten feet deep.

~ The Four-Field Perspective ~

In the fall, I moved to Tucson and began graduate classes leading toward a master's degree in anthropology at the University of Arizona. Although we students knew that we would write a thesis based in one of the four fields—archaeology, cultural anthropology, physical anthropology, or linguistics—we studied each of the four subjects in depth. I believed then, as I believe now, that being well versed in all four of the subdisciplines of anthropology leads to a broader understanding of one's own specialty, as well as a more fully developed view of world cultures, past and present.

We learned how to describe teeth and measure heads under the watchful gaze of Bert Kraus. We had classes in ethnographic fieldwork methods (believe it or not), and were told how we should act when observing the Yaqui Deer Dance and attending the Day of the Dead ceremonies at the local cemetery. Dr. Edward "Ned" Spicer guided these interactions with the Yaqui and Hispanic communities, our introduction to participant observation. In class and in conversations, Ned challenged our minds with discussions of pluralism, culture change, and cultural persistence, and broadened our understandings of the grand ongoing saga of immigration and immigrants' interactions with native peoples.

In Dan Matson's linguistics class, we learned how to analyze the phonemes, morphemes, and syntax of an unwritten language. After passing written exams in the four fields of anthropology, I used the techniques of anthropological linguistics to analyze the Seri language for my master's thesis.[1]

To be sure, these experiences fall under the category of *rewards*. They occurred long before I decided to pursue a PhD. The courses, the experiences in the field, and the influence of my professors are of utmost importance to who I am and what I think about the world. All were preamble to, as well as the foundation for, the continuation of my education and my obtaining a PhD just shy of turning fifty. Anthropology has sustained me in everything I do and think. It clarifies and defines my understanding of the world and of people's relationships with each other. Is anthropology my religion? No, but it helps create my world-view. And it compels me to try to be better than I am.

⁓ Anadarko and the BIA ⁓

I married John Schweitzer at the end of my master's studies and defended the thesis soon afterwards, in 1954. We lived in Anadarko, Oklahoma, where he was director of the Southern Plains Indians Museum and tribal liaison officer for the Anadarko Area Office of the Bureau of Indian Affairs (BIA).

We attended Indian dances at Binger Y and the Wichita roundhouse and participated in other events at the invitation of our Cheyenne, Kiowa, Comanche, Wichita, and Caddo friends. These were special friendships, some maintained over these many years since. I gained intimate understandings about some facets of the lives and history of the Indians living in southwestern Oklahoma, but at no time did I think about "doing field research." If you ask why, I don't have an answer. I too worked for the BIA. I used the secretarial skills that I had acquired—just in case!—while still in graduate school. I was content with my life

After organizational changes occurred in the BIA, John resigned his position and we spent a year in France. From there, we went to Ann Arbor, where John enrolled in the graduate school at the University of Michigan. In 1959 we moved back to Oklahoma when John accepted a teaching position at Oklahoma State University. While my stepson Kit attended and graduated from Stillwater High School, I was kept busy during the turmoil of the early 1960s, raising our three younger children. I found enormous satisfaction in doing so.

⁓ Opportunity Knocks ⁓

During John's sabbatical year of 1966–1967, everybody in the sociology department (except one) resigned, including the only anthropologist. When we returned from France in the spring, I approached the one remaining department member who was now the chair and suggested that they needed me to teach anthropology. I think he and the dean were very reluctant to hire a woman with only a master's degree who had never taught. They agreed, however, to hire me part time for one year to teach a course being produced at the University of Missouri. My job was to handle class discussions, and the professor at Missouri would deliver the lectures by way of TV. It was a good way for me to get my feet wet in this untried world of college teaching.

⁓ Opportunity Knocks Again: The Museum of Natural and Cultural History ⁓

In the late 1960s, OSU advertised for a director of the Museum of Natural and Cultural History. With all the chutzpah of a neophyte, I applied for the job. It was clear to me that the interviewer did not think I had the qualifications to be the director. The interviewer was Bryan P. Glass, a preeminent mammalogist, who was subsequently named as director.

Dr. Glass recognized, however, that I had the skills and knowledge to work with the material collections, and I was soon appointed as associate director in charge of cultural materials. The museum now had an office with a director, an associate director, and a secretary, even if it did not have a building of its own.

During the time that I worked for the museum, I catalogued and described many exotic pieces of material culture and created displays in museum cases that were located across campus. Many of these cultural items had come from Ethiopia, where OSU had had a faculty exchange program. My association with the museum was immensely satisfying. My kids were still in grade school, and the job fit my desire for part-time employment as an anthropologist.

~ Back to the Beginning ~

When I talked about going back to school, many people suggested that I could easily get a doctoral degree in sociology from OSU. But I knew that I could put out the required effort and make the commitment needed to go to graduate school *only* if I could study anthropology. In the summer of 1972, I enrolled in a directed reading course at the University of Oklahoma (OU). Steve Thompson, the chair of the department, loaned me his copy of *The Rise of Anthropological Theory* by Marvin Harris, published in 1968. Thus began my eighty-eight-mile commute from our front door to the parking lot at OU. I vowed more than once that if I thought any harm would come to our three younger children because of my returning to school, I would quit in a flash.

John helped with many chores around the house. He cooked meals and shopped. He organized the grocery shopping by typing a list of foods as they appeared in the aisles of the local grocery store. I have always said that the timing was just right in many ways for me to go back to school. Our kids were old enough to be able to stay alone if they had to, but young enough they could not run around.

I believe that in the long run, our children, Jehanne, Bob, and Roland, accommodated well to my being in school. I did not hear any complaints, and I still have a handwritten note from Jehanne: "I am proud of what you are doing." John was and still is my biggest supporter. Without the support of my entire family, I could not have even begun this journey, to say nothing of being able to finish.

~ Noam Chomsky and the Graduate Seminar ~

Reading about theory through the summer of 1972 was fascinating, and I looked forward to fall classes. At the first meeting of the required graduate seminar, each student was asked to research a topic with which they were *not* familiar and make a presentation at one of the fall sessions.

Eighteen years had lapsed between the completion of my MA and the fall of 1972, and much had happened in anthropology. Since I was well versed in the principles of descriptive linguistics but did not know anything about the new linguistics—to say nothing about the developments in archaeology, cultural anthropology, and physical anthropology—I decided to research and report on generative transformational grammar introduced by Noam Chomsky. But raising kids, working as a secretary, and arranging museum displays had not prepared me for the complexity of changes that had occurred in those eighteen years. Understanding this new and radical approach to language was difficult and there were days when I thought I would surely fail before I really got started. I *did* learn enough about the new theoretical approach to linguistics, however, to make a successful seminar presentation. After that, what could be so difficult?

A Superannuated Graduate Student

Some professors in the anthropology department at OU made it quite clear that they did not think I was serious and that I was too old—at age forty-four—to be pursuing a PhD in anthropology! How anyone could think that I was not serious when I was commuting 176 miles round-trip from home to campus and home again, teaching part time (beginning in 1973), and making sure that everything at home was running smoothly was more than I could comprehend. My ignorance of the attitudes toward women and their expected roles was enormous.

There were no women professors to act as role models in the anthropology department and informal conversations between professors and students were often shared over TGIF beers. Students, especially older women, who had lives outside of campus sometimes missed important clues about succeeding in graduate school. I gradually realized that it really was a "man's world"!

My role as an older woman student was still fairly unconventional in 1972, but my classmates accepted me as an individual and I became good friends with many of those who, if not young enough to be my children, were at least ten to fifteen years younger than I was. It was a more difficult task for the professors to accept me for what I was and what I wanted to be. I was older than most of them. And although I eventually reached the feeling of friendship and even collegiality with them, I don't think that the late Steve Thompson ever reconciled his view of me as a "superannuated" woman with being a PhD candidate.

Denigration was not something that I was used to either in my family of birth or my family of marriage. As a child, I had grown up in an atmosphere that was completely supportive, that had given me the feeling without being stated in so many words that I could do anything I wanted to.[2] However, my own views of what I wanted to do early in my marriage and family life were conditioned by the expectations for women in the 1950s and 1960s. I grew up as a rather quiet, passive individual. When I decided to step out of the usual roles that had been designated for women, this legacy of family support made me even stronger. I was not easily put down by negative reactions because I firmly believed in myself and in what I was doing. I was committed to succeeding.

~ The 1970s: Gains and Losses ~

In 1973, one year after the start of my commute to OU, the chair of the Department of Sociology at OSU offered me a part-time instructorship. The challenges compounded. Besides commuting to Norman and doing my share of the homemaking and childcare, I prepared lectures for courses I had not taken, and in some cases, topics I had not studied. But I worked hard and prepared well and I believe that even from the beginning I was a good teacher.

The decade of the 1970s continued to be a time of gains and losses in my life. Just before summer field school began in 1974 I took my PhD written essay exams. My mother died in the middle of those exams and I think this disruption was part of the reason that I retook some of them in the winter of 1975. In September 1975, my father died. But teaching and commuting and interviewing as well as family times went on, even as these unhappy life events intruded themselves.

~ A Decade of Action ~

My return to school and the courses I was teaching all were part of a nationwide movement that centered on the roles and rights of women. It was a time of turmoil, hope, and some considerable advancement.

In July 1970, the U.S. Office for Civil Rights informed OSU that "women should be included in the affirmative action plan"; the university was urged to "seek out more women students, particularly graduate students, and *more women faculty.*"[3] The OSU Office of Affirmative Action opened in August 1973, and the university worked to provide the data the Equal Employment Opportunity Commission and the U.S. Department of Health, Education, and Welfare had requested about employment practices at OSU. I mention these details partly because they relate directly to my being asked to teach in the fall of 1973 and partly because they chronicle some of the many changes that were occurring across the country at the time.

Through the efforts of a concerned women's group, originally formed in 1972, a women's conference, cosponsored by the vice president for academic affairs and the dean of students, was convened in 1976. A formal Women's Council was established, also in 1976, which ultimately became one of five advisory groups to report to the president of the university. I worked as a member of the council even while still a student, and often in other, more indirect ways, to support equal opportunity for women at OSU, serving as chair of the Women's Council in 1982–1983.

My involvement in promoting the rights of women did not garner any points in my favor among my male colleagues or the administrative hierarchy, either before or after I finished my degree, and in fact was most likely regarded negatively. In addition to this lack of recognition for promoting the welfare of women at OSU, the chair of my department refused to take my teaching and research seriously, even though he was the one who had asked me to join the department as a way to meet the pressure being put on the university for a broader representation of women on the faculty.

~ The Right to Respect ~

During the mid-1970s, I realized as never before that I needed help in confronting the many subtle and not-so-subtle biases against women that I was experiencing as one of those individuals stepping out of customary women's roles. I wanted to break out of my passive shell and stand up for myself. A short course on assertiveness training was a revelation and helped me begin to understand the behaviors of other people as well as my own. I began to learn how to deal with the expressions of male bias that confronted me in my interactions with my male colleagues.

~ Come, Grow Old Along with Me ~

The director of our 1974 summer ethnographic field school at OU requested suggestions from the class for possible topics for our research. My suggestion was to study aging. I knew about the lives of my relatives as they aged. My great-grandmother lived in her own home until her death at age ninety-five. My great aunt lived to be 102, spending the last two years in a nursing home. My mother's mother lived with us while I was growing up. My parents had moved to Florida when my dad retired.

But I wanted to find out "What is it like to age as an American Indian today?"

The field school adopted my suggestion to research the topic of aging in Oklahoma American Indian communities. Thus began my professional involvement in aging.[4]

Since I lived in an area close to many Indian communities, the professor in charge agreed that I could do my field school research in north-central Oklahoma rather than in the communities around the Norman area. Armed with the name of an elderly Ioway Indian couple, Franklin and Martha Murray, who lived in the little town of Perkins, south of Stillwater, I knocked on their door. I described myself as someone who was interested in elderly Indians. To my continuing amazement and gratitude, the Murrays invited me in and we had a fascinating discussion about being old in Indian country. They were my introduction to others in the Ioway community. Their friendship was invaluable in many ways, not the least of which was simply being friends with them. I honor their memory.

Little did I realize at the time how pertinent this topic of aging was to become in the following years. The numbers of older people in the United States (and worldwide) were increasing, but my interest focused on the cultural construction of aging, not on demographics and statistics. Not until I became a charter member of the Association for Anthropology and Gerontology did I realize fully how timely a topic it was and how trend-setting was this cross-cultural, qualitative research on aging.

In the spring semester of 1976, my husband took a six-month sabbatical that he spent in Lambesc, France. I had applied for a grant to research the lives of elderly rural French, but when the grant did not come through, I decided to stay in Oklahoma to continue the research I had begun in field school on the cultural dimensions of aging in two American Indian communities.

I defended my dissertation in the fall of 1978, six and a half years after that life-changing decision at Robbers' Cave.[5] In the spring of 1979, just after my fiftieth birthday, I was hooded at spring graduation ceremonies, thus completing this part of the journey.

Born to Be an Anthropology Teacher

When I was hired to teach at OSU, I began a long and personally satisfying tenure as the teacher of a course titled Racial and Cultural Minorities. It was a challenging but intensely interesting course. Not only did my teaching of the course span the time of much Black unrest, but it also overlapped a period of militant Indian action. Members of those minorities who took the course brought their own immediate interpretations of events and issues.

Since I felt that it was essential to know the historical and cultural contexts in which group relations evolved and existed, I included as much background as I could for each group that we considered. The topics and issues covered in the course and the lessons learned were and still are some of the most interesting to me. While solutions to the problems that exist among and for the many ethnic and racial groups in America in an ever-changing scene are often elusive and difficult to achieve, I am steadfast in my belief that there are ways that we can live together successfully in a pluralistic society.

Teaching brought many rewards: strengthening my knowledge of anthropology, learning how people think, meeting new people, and advising or consulting with them as they met the challenges of being in undergraduate school. My classes were always more interesting when there were older students. They brought life experiences to the class that twenty-year-olds simply did not have. They were not afraid to contribute to the discussions, and I knew they were there because they wanted to be, not because someone else wanted them to be there.

Associating with students in class allowed me to tell them what I believed, and still believe, anthropology offers to those who are willing to listen: a much-needed perspective on the world that all peoples can use to their benefit. What other discipline presents a holistic, cross-cultural perspective on the interactions between language, culture, physical characteristics, and the archaeological past?

What other discipline exhorts us to know the Other without making judgments, to learn in depth the perspectives of the other person and their community? If just *one* person in my Minorities class learned how the historical and cultural context affected the contemporary positions of Blacks or American Indians and let go of some of his or her prejudices, I felt that I had succeeded. If the students learned about stereotypes and prejudice and could somehow make adjustments in their thinking to become more tolerant and to focus less on stereotypical characterizations of people different from them, I felt my class was a success.

In connection with my job as an instructor/assistant professor, I was the faculty advisor for the Native American Student Association for eight years. In that capacity, I made long-lasting friends with the students and enjoyed being involved in their activities. The club held a powwow each year, and I met families who came from Indian communities across Oklahoma. These acquaintances and friendships merged with what I was doing in the field as well as what I was teaching in my classes.

My association with the students in my classes as well as the graduate students in the Sociology Department immeasurably broadened my perspective about who I was and what I was striving to impart to the students. I was a college instructor, a role that I held in high esteem and that I cherished. I loved sharing knowledge with my students, encouraging them to pursue their dreams, as I, in turn, was pursuing mine. Although I had been an anthropologist in different capacities for many years, completing my degree and teaching at the university level was the special goal I had envisioned in 1972.

~ New Courses on Women and Aging ~

My explorations of feminist anthropology and my development of one of the early feminist anthropology courses, Women: A Cross-Cultural Perspective, about women in different cultures (including women in American society), taught me much about the variable statuses of women in the United States and in cultures around the world. These studies helped me to learn about the different effects that various aspects of culture had on women's statuses and roles, including women's struggles and their strategies for coping in varying situations.

Looking at the influences affecting women's roles at home and in different cultures around the world opened my eyes to the false ideas (many of which are still around) that permeated discussions about what women could or could not do and should or should not do.

In addition to the course about women, I introduced an Anthropology of Aging course. Interest in both of these topics reflected growing trends, one as part of the women's movement and the other as part of the growing interest of anthropologists in aging as a topic in and of itself. The anthropology of aging illustrated that the constraints on aging and the supports for aging people were vastly different for different cultural groups. There *are* different cultural attitudes, for example, toward illness, frailty, and old age, and there *are* varied roles for older people that are not universally subscribed to by all groups. This perspective broadened our understanding of aging. With the continuing increase in the numbers of older people in the United States as well as in other countries, ideas about aging will continue to change.

Culture History and Indian Aging

I am passionate about culture history and its companion, life history research. I began my research with the Otoe-Missouria and Ioway communities in north-central Oklahoma by looking at the lives of contemporary elderly. I have documented many events in the lives of the Otoes and the Ioways, from powwows to hand games to funeral feasts to tribal princesses to elders' views on growing old in Indian country. In doing so, I have also documented the adaptation of the tribes to many cultural and historical forces over which they have had no control: the removal to Indian Territory, the allotment of their reservation lands, the changes in their livelihoods, and their experiences in boarding schools and public day schools.

I have known many elders whose lives have spanned most of the twentieth century, who were born on the reservation, moved to an allotment, moved to a house in town, and made adjustments to culture that changed drastically during that period. Each of these ideas and events forms a piece in the long history of Indian people, people who have adapted but who have endured beyond all historical expectations held by non-Indians. These elders experienced drastic changes and it is they who say to the younger ones, "Look ahead. Get ready now. This is the way it is supposed to be."[6]

Oklahoma Pioneers

In the late 1970s, I met and interviewed descendants of the Land Rush pioneers who made the Oklahoma Land Run of 1891. These early pioneers had settled in the portion of the old Ioway Reservation that was opened up to white settlers. Their descendants grew up in a raw, developing territory that eventually became the state of Oklahoma.

Being an older person engaged in the study of aging was, I believe, in some ways an advantage, particularly in the Anglo community. Those I talked to viewed me as someone similar to them at least in age and sometimes gender, even if we did not hold the same political or religious views. One preconceived idea I had to overcome when interviewing the Anglo senior citizens was their extreme discomfort at the thought that I might be a social worker come to take away some of their freedoms. The descendants of the pioneers were fiercely independent and self-reliant in all of the positive ways that are usually associated with those characteristics. Like their ancestors, they had to work hard and survive difficult times. Many of these people were born in the late 1890s and grew up in difficult, hardscrabble times. They outlived the Dust Bowl days of the 1930s and proved that they, too, were of strong pioneer stock.

Many of the Land Rush pioneers and their descendants—Anglo-Saxon in background—were from Nebraska and Kansas and are in a sense a part of my own English midwestern heritage. The faces that stared out at me from photographs, for want of a better identification, could have been my own ancestors.

Retirement! Already?

Just as I was promoted from a part-time instructor to a full-time assistant professor with tenure, my husband was talking about retirement. Of course, he had been in the teaching business much longer than I, and justifiably looked forward to taking early retirement. I admit I found that a bit discouraging as I was, so to speak, just getting started on my career. After teaching part time beginning in 1973, I became a full-time assistant professor in 1981. In 1984 John retired from the Foreign Language Department at OSU.

I continued to teach, but in the spring of 1986 the university offered a special early retirement package for anyone who had been with the university for fifteen years and who had reached the age of fifty-eight. By cobbling together the various positions I had held at OSU, I could get credit for seventeen years; I had just turned fifty-eight in March of that year. I thought long and hard about whether or not I should take advantage of this early retirement package. I made a list of the reasons *for* and *against* accepting it. The pro side was long; the con side was short. I decided to accept OSU's offer.

Always an Anthropologist

After retiring in 1986, I taught one class a semester in 1986–1987. In July 1987, we moved to Taos, New Mexico. I still had several unfinished scholarly projects at the time and settled in right away to complete editing the *Anthropology of Aging*.[7] I made several return trips to Oklahoma to oversee the uploading of entries to the mainframe computer at OSU. In 1989 I bought a PC and finished the data entry myself.

In the meantime, we were slowly getting acquainted with people in Taos, who, while not replacing the friends we had left behind in Oklahoma, became new friends. One particularly important avenue for both of us for meeting people was the Taos Archaeological Society (TAS), which in its present incarnation was chartered in the fall of 1987. John and I became charter members of TAS and were active in many capacities, thus continuing my interest in the archaeology of the Southwest.

I have completed other projects[8] and continue to work on others. Recently, I created CDs from Ioway Otoe-Missouria audio language tapes that accompany detailed language booklets, helping to preserve the voices and language of the elders and, in a small way, giving something back to the communities that have meant so much to me both professionally and personally.[9]

I am not sure that I can claim, as my gentle coeditor does, that I was an anthropologist from early childhood. However, my fascination with Indians began early. I can still picture myself as a kid in our old two-story yellow frame house in Whiting, Indiana, looking at pictures of American Indians—I was smitten. Was it originally a romantic fascination? I don't really know the answer to that. Perhaps it was. But my understanding of American Indian history, their lifeways and images and all they represent today, has expanded to a deep appreciation of them both as individuals and as communities.

Although I met many challenges throughout graduate school and as a faculty member, the rewards of being and becoming an anthropologist and a teacher far outweigh the difficulties. My initial infatuation with the exotic and mysterious deepened into a broader understanding of how social structure, ideology, and economic adaptations of societies intertwine and of how history is never very far away. One of my weaknesses and also one of my strengths is that I am vitally interested in many subjects and perspectives. Anthropology fits me well!

~ Endnotes ~

1. The thesis title is "A Preliminary Phonemic Analysis of the Seri Language."
2. My father, Robert Henry Gardner, and my mother, Gladys Mary Ayers Gardner, gave me an undeniable sense of confidence and security that has carried me through my entire life. I thank and honor them. Many times when I was struggling to get just one more task finished, one more test passed, one more paper written, I remembered my father's words, "You dig a hole one shovel full at a time."
3. Kopecky (1990:164), emphasis added.
4. The field research was supported by a research grant from the National Science Foundation (Grant #GY-11477); a report was given to the NSF in Washington, D.C., by Marjorie Schweitzer and Gerry Williams. A published report of our research appears in Williams (1980).
5. Schweitzer (1978).
6. Otoe-Missouria Tribe (1981:56).
7. Schweitzer (1991).
8. Schweitzer (1999, 2001).
9. GoodTracks (2004) and Schweitzer (2004).

~ References ~

GoodTracks, Jimm G. 2004. Text for *Baxoje-Jiwere Ich^e Ioway-Otoe Language*, CD I and CD II. Funded in part by the Kansas Humanities Council.

Harris, Marvin. 1968. *The Rise of Anthropological Theory: A History of Theories of Culture.* New York: Thomas Y. Crowell Co.

Kopecky, Pauline W. 1990. *A History of Equal Opportunity at Oklahoma State University.* Centennial Histories Series. Stillwater, OK: Oklahoma State Univ.

Otoe-Missouria Tribe. 1981. *The Otoe-Missouria Elders: Centennial Memoirs (1881–1891).* Red Rock, OK: The Otoe-Missouria Tribe.

Schweitzer, Marjorie M. 1978. The Power and Prestige of the Elderly in Two Indian Communities. PhD diss., Univ. of Oklahoma.

———. General editor. 1991. *Anthropology of Aging: A Partially Annotated Bibliography.* Bibliographies and Indexes in Gerontology, no. 13. New York: Greenwood Press.

———, ed. 1999. *American Indian Grandmothers: Traditions and Transitions.* Albuquerque: Univ. of New Mexico Press.

———. 2001. Otoe and Missouria. In *Plains,* ed. Raymond J. DeMallie. *Handbook of North American Indians,* William C. Sturtevant, general editor, 447–61. Washington, D.C.: Smithsonian Institution.

———. 2004. Production editor for *Baxoje-Jiwere Ich^e Ioway-Otoe Language,* CD I and CD II.

Williams, Gerry, C. 1980. Warriors No More: A Study of the American Indian Elderly. In *Aging in Culture and Society,* Christine L. Fry and Contributors, 101–11. Brooklyn, NY: J. F. Bergin Publishers, Inc.

In Pursuit of The Word

My Anthropological Life

Maria Gleaton Cattell

It's a half century since I used my maiden name. I put it here because writing this narrative took me back to the days when I was Maria Gleaton. Remembering that honors my parents, Munsey Sinclair and Anna Scofield Gleaton, and their gifts to me, especially my father for the love of words, and both for the dream—a dream it took me a long time to catch.

Emerging from the Egg

Springtime, a sunny day in mid-May on the campus of Bryn Mawr College. Commencement day. The undergrads were at the head of the line, the graduate students behind them. We were in reverse alphabetical order by discipline and surname, so as Anthropology/Cattell, I was the very last in line. I burst out in a loud voice, "Boy! I thought this day would never come!" Other about-to-be PhDs ahead of me looked back, smiled, and echoed a chorus of "Me, too!" None had waited as long as I. At fifty-four, I was the oldest person graduating that day. But I did not feel old. I felt new.

Since my dissertation defense a few weeks earlier, I had been experiencing a sense of birth or rebirth, of coming into being, as in legends where a people

Maria Gleaton Cattell: PhD 1989, Bryn Mawr College. Dissertation: "Old Age in Rural Kenya: Gender, the Life Course, and Social Change." Maria has many publications, including two books. She has continued her research in Kenya for a quarter century and is a research associate at The Field Museum of Natural History. Currently, she is writing her spiritual autobiography.

emerge from a hole in the earth or from the world's egg. I remembered Victor Turner's notion of a "fruitful dark."[1] Rainbows colored my thoughts, irises bloomed in my mind, and I wrote a poem in celebration.

Iris and Emergences

Iris...
rainbow flowers
unfurling from leafy swords
Iris...
goddess of storm-born rainbows
and other iridescences,
olympian messenger
carrying knowledge on fleet feet
and golden wings
Iris...
the eye's diaphragm,
opener of seeing
Iris...
rainbow light and shining colors
emerging from darkness
and hidden secret places
Iris...
you have been in my eye
and in my mind's eye
my symbol of emergences
and knowing
symbol of my self
since long before
this unfurling day

My life journey has been a path with branches and loops, forwards and returns, a meandering pathway through light and dark, rainbows and dark nights. The constant is *me*, as my own "interpreter of experience," constructing, reconstructing, transforming my self while maintaining a coherent identity over my lifetime.[2] I am writing my spiritual autobiography, which weaves together my experiences of place as a traveler, gardener, and anthropologist.[3] It is one of my stories. This narrative is another, the story of my life as an anthropologist, from childhood curiosities about different others through becoming, in midlife, an "official" anthropologist, certified by fieldwork and the PhD conferred on me that sunny day in May.

~ Outsiderhood and First Fieldwork ~

Sharon Kaufman found that her interviewees (older Californians) organized their life stories around what she called "themes."[4] My themes surely include love of nature, The Word, and outsiderhood. The love of nature has been expressed in many ways, most especially in my lifelong passion for gardening. "The Word" is my metaphor for another lifelong passion. My mother liked to tell and retell a story from when I was a little kid. I had a high fever and was perhaps a bit delirious. I was tossing and turning and moaning, over and over, "I can't find The Word, I can't find The Word." Well, I'm stilling looking for The Word. I've written stories and poems and a flock of academic papers, a sporadic journal, a book or two. When I was seven, I wrote a short story on the back of an envelope. In my early fifties, I wrote a 726-page dissertation.[5] Now I'm writing this story, still looking for The Word.

As for outsiderhood, feeling different from those around me, I have experienced it since early childhood, among farmers and working-class people, among intellectuals and middle-class stay-at-home wives and mothers, in the workplace, in academe. I have always been a "marginal native"[6]—though I am giving Morris Freilich's concept a twist. I wasn't an outsider traveling elsewhere to study an unknown people, trying to become at least marginally adept in that society. I was a native to begin with—but one who didn't fit in, a marginal person in my own culture, trying to understand those different others who were my neighbors in everyday life.

We were a peripatetic family, moving eighteen times before we settled for two years on a farm near Altoona in western Pennsylvania. I was four. The local farmers seemed wonderful and strange to the city kid I was. I loved going down the dirt road to our neighbors' house, to sit in their kitchen (the heart of home for farm families) and watch and listen. I learned to dunk bread in sweet milky coffee. Some days I walked up and down, up and down, with Mr. Clapper and his big plow horse, until finally he'd let me ride the horse for just one round when my mother came to bring me home. Today I regard those experiences as my first fieldwork.

In 1940 we moved to Lansdowne in suburban Philadelphia, where I started school in first grade (kindergartens were not widely available in those days). My mother told me that I could already read when I got to first grade—"I didn't teach you; you taught yourself." At the end of the next year, the United States entered World War II. In spring 1942, my father was seconded from his Social Security job in Philadelphia to the Office of Price Administration, which controlled prices and rationed consumer goods during the war. We moved to Williamsport, a small Pennsylvania town on the upper reaches of the Susquehanna River. Two years later, Dad was returned to Social Security and we moved to Jacobus, a very small community near York in south-central Pennsylvania—still in the valley of the Susquehanna River. From these years, I remember air-raid drills, food and gas rationing, our family's Victory Garden, the death of FDR (a great hero to my parents), the concentration camp pictures released from the conquering troops in Germany, and VJ

Day (Victory in Japan Day) marking the end of World War II. It was a world without computers, cell phones, TV, and instant everything—a leaner, preconsumerist society. It was a big deal if a girl became pregnant before marriage (she had to leave school), girls (but not boys—go figure!) were to be virgins at the time of marriage, marriages were supposed to last forever, divorce and living together were scandalous. It was another world, a world that believed education was wasted on girls.

In Jacobus I had friends, and it seemed all of them went to school on Sunday mornings. I was curious. What was this Sunday school? Why did my friends go to it? What did they do there? My own family had no religious beliefs or practices. My mother, raised in a New England "hard-shell" Baptist family, was a lifelong skeptic, an agnostic; but my ex-seminarian father (he had a BD from Yale Divinity School) was aggressively atheist. When I said I wanted to go to Sunday school, Dad derided my interest but did not forbid it. So I went to Salem Lutheran Church, where I learned to memorize Bible verses, sang doleful hymns, and heard a lot about God and Jesus, heaven and hell. After six months, I ended that research with a perfect attendance certificate and no further interest in Sunday school or church, God or Jesus. (Later I became a Quaker, a non-Christian nontheistic Quaker.[7])

In 1946 we moved to a farm in eastern York County, about ten miles from Jacobus. There, we Gleatons were certainly outsiders, "furriners" in the local dialect. We were city folks with Connecticut Yankee and Deep South heritages living among Pennsylvania Dutch farmers. We ate rice and grits, okra and collard greens, and rare roast beef; they were bread and meat (well done) and potatoes folks. We were liberal Democrats among conservative Republicans. We were not religious, not even as much as the farmers who called God "the man upstairs" and didn't spend much time in church. Our speech patterns differed. We read books; they made fun of book learning. Of course, I was intensely curious about these strangers who were so different from my family, so I hung out in kitchens, followed farm women from springhouse to barnyard to kitchen, rode tractors, played in fields and barns with farm kids. For a while, I even wanted to "go native," to marry a farmer and be a farmwife. I became comfortable in that Pennsylvania Dutch farm culture but was not really part of it. I remained an outsider.

When I wasn't doing my research among farm folks, exploring the Susquehanna River hills, or doing home chores, I was often reading. I read the local newspaper and my mother's magazines: *Ladies' Home Journal*, *Farm Journal*, *Woman's Day*, *Family Circle*. I read fairy tales and myths till the books fell apart. I read other books with imagined worlds—the Oz books, Uncle Wiggily, Edgar Rice Burroughs's Tarzan and Mars books. I read Louisa May Alcott and Mark Twain, *Wuthering Heights*, the Twins series about children in other times and places, historical novels. I loved a book about Admiral Peary's daughter and Osa and Martin Johnson's story of their photographic travels in Africa. All were books about worlds other than my own, books I could not share with my schoolmates, who weren't given to reading much of anything. School was a one-room stone building with eight grades and one teacher. Our farmer neighbors didn't think much of books and saw no reason for anyone to go to school past eighth grade (then the legal age of school leaving for farm folks). But my parents expected me to go to college. So while my classmates left school after eighth grade, I went to a very small high school in the very small town of Wrightsville.

Again I was an outsider. Perhaps it was adolescent cliquishness plus my shyness that set me apart, but everyone else in my class had been in school together since first grade. Most of the kids were from working-class families, who, like the farm families I knew, did not place high value on education or a life of the mind. The cultural ethos and political and moral economy of the postwar 1940s and the 1950s pushed women back into the home after World War II, and it encouraged them to stay there.[8] Many times I heard people say things like "Girls! No use educating them; they just get married and have children." However, I never heard this from my parents. Indeed, all my life my father (whose daughter I surely am) told me I was going to go to Swarthmore College.

I did not appreciate then how unusual were my parents' expectations and their financial and moral support. They supported my sister's ambitions to become a doctor and my brothers in their pursuit of careers in art and ballet. In the 1950s, such career choices were all backward! Most doctors were men, and men who were artists or dancers were "strange." Neither our farmer neighbors nor the wider American society assigned much value to the education of women, nor were there common assumptions even among women who went to college that they would have careers. Heaven forbid! No, they would be good girls and become wives and mothers,[9] as expressed in the old ditty: "First comes love, then comes marriage, then comes Maria with a baby carriage." My parents had different ideas, and I went off to Swarthmore in 1952.

At Swarthmore I felt like the country mouse of Aesop's fable. Many "Swatties" were graduates of urban or private schools with elaborate academic and extracurricular programs. They were extremely articulate, able to engage in classroom discussions at an intellectual level for which I felt unprepared by my years at Wrightsville High, which had only a little over a hundred students in four grades and no frills unless you count the optional two years of Latin, two of French (which of course I took). When I got to Swarthmore, I knew no one else and often felt alone or socially awkward. But I enjoyed my classes—and I stayed, gradually becoming more socially adept and intellectually competent.

My great love at the time was English literature. At that time, there was no anthropology program at Swarthmore, and I probably would have ignored it anyway. Some classmates went to Bryn Mawr or Haverford to take anthropology classes, but I never considered it. (Ironically, years later I did go to Bryn Mawr to study anthropology—as a graduate student.) I studied English literature along with minors in history and art history. I read Chaucer in the original language and all of Shakespeare's plays. I learned to engage directly with literary works, paintings, and sculpture (we were discouraged from reading literary or art critics). I was doing textual analysis and "lit crit" long before postmodernism hit anthropology—and when it did, I did not go for it. I felt that I had not become an anthropologist in order to do what I had done as an undergraduate English lit major! I also learned something about history, the importance of dates and chronologies, and the flow of history as the story of change. As an anthropologist, I have often been frustrated or appalled by ethnographies without dates or any sense of change over time, especially as my own research in Kenya became long-term and I realized that good anthropology is also good history. So, in time, the intellectual threads of my undergraduate education have woven themselves into my anthropological life.

I cannot recall any hint from anyone at Swarthmore that women were less competent intellectually or less serious in their intentions than men. Founded as a coed school in 1864, Swarthmore has always taken women's intellectual endeavors seriously. So between my parents' expectations and Swarthmore's expectations, I had every reason to be a serious student. I didn't realize it then, but Swarthmore was preparing me for graduate school. Indeed, many classmates, women and men, went on for further studies following graduation in 1956. But the pervasive cultural expectations that women were destined to be housewives and mothers had their impact on many of us. Some women in my class were worried, in the senior year, because they were not yet engaged to be married—a notion that does not seem to trouble twenty-first-century women college students. Marriage was not a problem for me because I married Hudson Cattell in the middle of my senior year. So, after graduation, instead of following a vague dream of going to New York to become a book editor and writer, I stayed in Pennsylvania; taught high school for a year; held various secretarial jobs; did a lot of gardening, cooking, knitting, and volunteer work; and raised four children. But I did very little writing. I was not in pursuit of The Word.

This life was acceptable to the world at large but not always to me. Something was missing. When Betty Friedan wrote about the "trapped housewife,"[10] I recognized myself. During those years, I was also exploring issues arising from my relationship with my alcoholic father, a process that freed some creativity within me. I began writing again, mostly poetry. My children were still young and kept me pretty busy, but in 1969 I returned to paid work with a secretarial job at Franklin & Marshall College (F&M).

Today I regard my homemaking years as my First Career. Even then, I understood that coffee klatsches, popular back then and often denigrated as just women gossiping, were mothers and wives talking about their *work*—work still little recognized by society even in this new century. My own daughter stayed home for a few years after her twin daughters were born in 1990, but was working full time again by the time the girls were in elementary school. I do not know how supermoms do it, nor if it is good for our children to have other people raising them, nor whether women should view careers and family as incompatible and just not have children or wait until they are forty to think about having a family. I wonder if we Americans need to rethink the ways we value work—in the sense of remunerated work, that is, paid employment—and family life, and the ways we structure the life course, with education, work, retirement viewed as a linear progression when, in fact, many of us follow a zigzag trajectory. Sometimes I feel out of step in my views, old-fashioned. But that's okay. I'm entitled.

≈ Becoming an Anthropologist ≈

It was summer 1975, the year I turned forty-one. I was working in my Second Career as secretary in F&M's Department of Classics. In previous years, I had audited courses in geology and classics at F&M. That summer I was taking a for-credit religious studies course. I had thought about a return to literature, my undergraduate major, but I no longer wanted to write about what others had written. I wanted to write about my own things. One day I was chatting with Carl Boyer, a young man who was majoring in anthropology and religious studies. When I told him about the course I was taking, he suggested I try an anthropology course. "What is anthropology?" I asked him. "And how is it different from sociology?" Carl tried to explain, but all I got out of it was that both fields are concerned with the study of humans. "Just try it," he said. "I think you'll like it."

I took Carl's advice and signed up for the introductory course in the fall with a new faculty member, James (Jim) Taggart. And I liked it! Well before the end of the course, I realized that anthropology, as the study of everything human, was what I had been looking for. Sometimes I entertained idle dreams of graduate school, but mostly I was concerned with raising my kids. I wasn't thinking seriously about doing more than taking courses at F&M for intellectual stimulation. Perhaps I'd have thought differently had I realized then what I learned years later, that there'd been a Cattell before me who was interested in anthropology: my husband's grandfather, psychologist James McKeen Cattell, was the person who, in 1896, hired Franz Boas to teach in Columbia University's Department of Psychology and Anthropology.[11]

For the next few years, I took an anthropology course each semester, usually with Jim Taggart or Nancy McDowell. After a few courses, Nancy and Jim began suggesting that I consider graduate studies. "No way, I'm a single mom with four kids!" (Hudson and I had separated in 1974.) When I went to an Anthropology Club lecture by Jane Goodale from Bryn Mawr College, Nancy said to me, "Aren't you going to talk to Jane about graduate school?" Huh? But I did. In May I visited Bryn Mawr. Jane advised me to apply for the PhD program for admission in fall 1979. I did. I was accepted—with a scholarship that waived tuition and gave me a $2,000 stipend. It would not be enough money, even with child support from Hudson; but I already had two part-time jobs that could be expanded. Still, it would be a financial gamble. My daughter had just finished her first year at F&M, tuition free because of my employment there. Should I try to hang on to my job and do graduate school part time? After all, I had three more children coming up behind Kharran. I had just bought a house. There were problems with my father, and I was the responsible family member. But it would be another decade before my children finished college. I didn't want to wait that long. I took the plunge and resigned from my safe job with benefits and pension. I was forty-five years old and a full-time graduate student. I don't think of myself as a risk taker, but there must be one in me!

In making the decision, I told myself that I would "do" anthropology so long as I was enjoying it. Years later I was talking with a classmate, Prema Ghimire, who had come to Bryn Mawr after leaving her husband and two young children in Nepal. Since getting her PhD, Prema had taught in various schools as an adjunct—not a happy situation. But she wasn't giving up! She had told herself the same thing: "I'll do it as long as I enjoy it." We agreed that something had happened as we studied anthropology: we *became* anthropologists. Being an anthropologist was part of our selves. We had experienced personal transformations and were in it for the long run.

~ Professional Stranger: Anthropological Fieldwork and Beyond ~

For three years, I commuted the fifty-five miles between Lancaster and Bryn Mawr, somehow finding the strength and endurance to do that; stay up late studying; date the man who later became my second husband; and care for my family, including my father who did not live with us but was a persistent concern. My studies gradually focused on a geographic area and topic for my dissertation research: Africa and the anthropology of aging. I was interested in aging from personal perspectives because of my aging parents and my own aging. And I liked the fact that aging and the lives of older persons had not been much studied by anthropologists. I liked the idea of breaking new ground.

I opened my grant proposal to the National Science Foundation (NSF) with this sentence: "I believe that aging is mostly in the mind." When, after months of waiting, I called the NSF program director to inquire about the state of my proposal, she told me that the sentence had grabbed reviewers' attention—negatively. They wondered: Who is she to know anything about aging? They had assumed I was a twentysomething graduate student. But something in the proposal made them realize that I was nearly fifty and maybe did know something about aging! In the end, my attention-getting statement had a positive influence on their decision because I got the NSF grant and later, one from the Wenner-Gren Foundation for Anthropological Research.

In late 1983—the same year my youngest son went off to college—I flew to Kenya to begin two years of fieldwork. I had waited a year after completing my courses to get funding for this research, then postponed it for a few more months because my new husband, Bob Moss, had bypass surgery. Eventually I went off, leaving husband, family, home for an enterprise that seemed full of uncertainties, including uncertainty about my own ability to do what I had boldly proclaimed in my grant proposals I would do.

It was not my first trip to Africa. I'd gone with Bob in 1980 as a tourist to Kenya and Zambia, and again to Kenya in 1982 on a preliminary site visit funded by Bryn Mawr's Frederica de Laguna Fund. I flew the now-defunct PanAm Africa Service. We left New York around 10 p.m., arrived in Dakar, Senegal, with the dawn; and made two more stops in West Africa: Monrovia in Liberia, Lagos in Nigeria. With airport delays on the ground and our own continuing motion backward in time, it was dusk by the time we left Lagos to cross the wide body of Africa. We arrived at Nairobi in the night, with runway and city lights twinkling in the dark and dawn hovering in the sky.

My mind was playing with ideas of light and dark, black and white, and colors especially rainbows—and with ideas of my own strength, capability, power. Earlier in my life, I had conceived of myself as inhabiting dark places from which I emerged into a world of light and rainbows that was both astonishing and ephemeral. In the mid-1970s, I crocheted myself a Rainbow Cloak to replace the fairy-tale "cloak of invisibility" I had, till then, assumed I wore. (I thought—seems silly now, but I did think it—that I was in some way invisible, that when people met me they soon forgot me.) It was this cloak and the transformations of self it represented, which I came to see, on the long flight to Africa, as having become so much a part of me that it was now my own rainbow skin.

Rainbow Skin[12]

Dakar. Africa again. Land ho! my beauty:
waiting to ensnare—
a trap already sprung
on the one with white skin
who is hiding from the sun.
Monrovia, plush and green,
Lagos and lights, champagne takeoff.
Here's to! whatever—
wildness and elsewhere,
rainbow light:
white, all colors in one,
with all the power of the sun.
Once I wore it as a cloak,
now it is my skin.
And then Nairobi, dark and waiting.
Hello! good to be with you again.
Like home—but yours, not my own.
Soon the dawn, the rainbow sun:
white magic. Yours or mine?

Don't argue, Africa—we'll share.
Black too has all the light
and when it comes to magic
every color's right.
We'll wear each other's rainbow,
sun and skin,
knowing that the power comes
really from within.

A romantic perspective, yes. I know there are other, harsher realities—though as a gardener, mother, baker of bread, I choose to affirm life. If that's romantic, so be it. This poem was also, for me, a necessary statement of my intentions, determination, and capabilities, using the power of The Word to empower myself.

After three months of wrestling with bureaucrats in Nairobi to get my research permit, I finally went to dwell among Samia farmers in western Kenya. There, I was clearly an outsider, as anyone could tell by looking at my white skin. I was one of thirty-five or forty "Europeans" among the three hundred thousand very dark-skinned inhabitants of Busia District (county). But this time, I was not a marginal native trying to fit into my own culture. I was a "professional stranger,"[13] eager to learn about African people just as, many years earlier, I had learned about the Clapper family, Sunday school, and Pennsylvania Dutch farmers. By the time I left, I was still a stranger or visitor (*omukeni*, in the Samia language). But I was a different stranger from the one who arrived in Samia at the end of the dry season in February 1984. When I left in November 1985, I was no longer totally outside Samia culture, though neither was I totally inside it. I was, as several Samia friends told me, "almost a Samia person now."

I stayed in Kenya for two years, making friends and increasing my family. I first became a grandmother when two Kenyan "daughters" gave birth in 1985. Both named their daughters for me. The age that was a disadvantage to me post-PhD in terms of employment was, if anything, advantageous to me in the field. As the mother of grown children, I was clearly an adult woman and nearly age-mate to some of my old people. I did not need to put on the modest behavior a younger woman must use to show respect to her elders—though as a foreigner, a white woman, an educated woman, I was something of an anomaly anyway and not completely subject to local rules. Others have claimed that "mature woman" may often be the most advantageous age-sex category for a fieldworker.[14] Certainly, I found it no disadvantage, not in Samia nor in later research in Philadelphia and South Africa. As one young Kenyan man said, "You have raised four children; you can do anything you want."

~ My Anthropological Career ~

I had made it through the anthropological initiation rite of fieldwork! Dissertation time. For a while after my return home, I experienced unsettling culture shock in the land of supermarkets crammed with mountains of goods and new technologies such as scanners and VCRs. Even after I stopped drifting mentally between Kenya and America, I couldn't write about my Kenyan friends as if they were objects. But eventually I got down to writing and finished my dissertation in that season of rebirth in 1989, just a few months shy of being fifty-five years old.

Mine has been a career off the fast track, a nonlinear path of improvisations[15] in a world that heavily favors the traditional (or male) model of highly focused career advancement.[16] But my anthropological life has been rich and full, and there's no end in sight.

I taught in temporary positions at three colleges, but, though I submitted many job applications, I never got a tenure-track offer. Yes, the job market for cultural anthropologists was lousy then. But very likely the combination of my gender and age was involved in my lack of success in academe.[17] I spent a year and a half as a researcher at the Philadelphia Geriatric Center, doing a community study of older white ethnics in a rapidly changing Philadelphia neighborhood. But, as the years went on and grandchildren appeared, I wanted to enjoy family life. Nor did I want to participate in the academic slavery of adjuncting. I had come to realize, through my own experiences and conversations with colleagues, how hard it is to find time to write when you are a full-time professor—or a full-time anything. I had always wanted to write. My feverish childhood dream of not being able to find The Word was also my waking dream. Fortunately, by then I could afford to go my own way. So, around the time I became eligible for Medicare, I chose not to spend any more time and energy seeking formal employment. I "retired"—retired from making job applications.

I have continued my research in Kenya, with many return visits, most recently in 2004. In 1995 I was in South Africa at the University of Natal–Durban to carry out a research project on Zulu grandmothers and granddaughters. I have organized many symposia and made numerous presentations at professional meetings. I served two terms as president of the Association for Anthropology and Gerontology and a five-year term as co-chair of the Commission on Aging and the Aged of the International Union of Anthropological and Ethnological Sciences. In 1990 I joined the Interim Organizing Committee of what became the Association for Africanist Anthropology and have served on its board ever since. Currently, I am on the American Anthropological Association's Program Committee and am co-convenor of the Women's Caucus of the African Studies Association.

And the writing? I have a more-than-respectable list of publications, including refereed articles, book chapters, and encyclopedia articles. One of my more poignant experiences was in 1995, when I was working on a book chapter on African widows—and became a widow myself.[18] Art imitating life? I know the experience gave me a different understanding of widowhood. This present book is my third.[19] Perhaps this career direction should not surprise me. Philip Kilbride, my dissertation director, warned me that my age would be a negative factor in terms of employment. "You will make your mark through writing," he told me. "You write better than almost anyone I have ever known." In any case, I have the time and energy to write, and many things to write about. I think it is for me, as for Mary Catherine Bateson, that "[w]riting has been the constancy through which I have reinvented myself after every uprooting."[20] So I continue to pursue The Word, while also having time for gardening and my family. Though I still don't have time for everything I'd like to do!

I have made solid contributions to the anthropology of aging, especially in Africa. I have had opportunities to mentor emerging scholars in African gerontology. The reviewer of the manuscript of a book on aging in Africa, to which I contributed a chapter, described me as "really well known internationally" in the field of African gerontology. I take that as a measure of success. Invariably, when Africans read what I have written about them, they say, "You really know our culture." I take that as a measure of success. But those are external measures. For myself, I feel that I still have much learning and growing to do, more research, more thinking and writing—as anthropologist and poet, as mother and grandmother, as gardener, knitter, cook. Nor do I see those aspects of myself as separate from each other. My farm background and gardening experience in the United States contributed to my ability to do research among African farmers. Hanging out in the kitchens of American farm women was good preparation for hanging out in the kitchens of African farm women. Anthropology has made my life more interesting and exciting, brought me many friends, and encouraged my creative energies. Am I glad I became an anthropologist? Yes! Would I do it again? Yes! And yes!

Mentors, Models, and Family Support

Becoming an anthropologist and doing anthropology have been personally empowering and enriching for me. Of course, I worked hard, but I did not succeed entirely on my own. All along, my family has been wonderfully supportive. They were not perfect—my father's alcoholism was an ongoing problem, my children were not always expeditious in doing household duties, the occasional adolescent crisis took time from studies. One such crisis brought me a foster daughter (I missed a week of classes on that one!), bringing the teens in my house to five. But I always got support for my interests and activities from my mother, siblings, and significant others (including my third partner, Jack Mongar, who died in 2004). Once, I got so discouraged while in graduate school, I said to my youngest son, who was sixteen, "This is too much. I'm going to quit." "Oh, no you're not!" said Charley. "I want my mother to have her PhD." (Thanks,

Chazz!) In 1995 I wrote my sister Harriet that "I must be crazy to be starting this new research project in South Africa at the age of 61." My sister, three years younger than I, is a retired physician who never married nor had children. She replied, "You're not crazy. You're just doing what you want to do, like me. Why not do what you want to do?" Nowadays son Kevin bakes me lemon meringue pies, son David rescues me from computer difficulties, son Chazz babysits my cats when I travel. And my daughter, Kharran, has taken on the kin-keeper role, like her mother and her mother's mother before her.

My experiences in graduate school were equally positive. Never did faculty or other students suggest that, at my age, I was wasting resources because I was "too old" or that I might not be able to "pay back" the investment in my graduate training. I was in a college of radical feminists, after all! (At my MA graduation, the entire senior class stood and shouted, "Down with the patriarchy!" I loved it.) Philip Kilbride, who directed my dissertation, was just the right mentor for me. I have never liked people telling me what to do. Phil always gave me plenty of rope to try things on my own, but he also knew when to call me back—like the time I gave him a long chapter of my dissertation to critique and he had only a few comments on it, one of which was: "Fine, but where are the old people?" That made me rethink the whole thing! My teachers Frederica (Freddy) de Laguna, who founded Bryn Mawr's Anthropology Department; Jane Goodale; and Judith Shapiro were models to look up to—though neither Freddy nor Jane was ever wife and none was a mother. In her autobiography, Freddy describes the choice she made in 1929 to break her engagement because she believed marriage would have prevented full development of her career.[21] (My sister did the same thing in the 1950s.) Freddy remained a model right up to her death in 2004 at age ninety-eight: she was still writing and had just established the Northern Press. The "Bryn Mawr Mafia" (as the husband of one of us calls us), the relatively small number of women and men who got their PhDs in anthropology from Bryn Mawr, has been important over the years. They have been models to emulate and active colleagues in various projects.

~ Late Bloomers ~

I am fortunate to have lived this life. Though I have traveled, I have also remained close to home. I am blessed with good health, a penchant for reflection, a strong family life, and many interesting things done and to be done. Had American culture been different in the 1940s and 1950s, I might not have taken so long to find anthropology. But things were the way they were. I wish I had set out on the anthropological trail sooner, but I am glad, so very glad, that I did set out on it, however late. I am, as my crossword-puzzler mother, Anna Gleaton, used to say, an opsimath—a late bloomer, as are all of us contributors to this volume. As was my mother: my two older children went with me for her college graduation when Mom was in her mid-sixties. Now I wonder how my daughter, Kharran, now in her mid-forties, will bloom in her artwork when she again has time for it, when her own daughters leave the nest.

My friendly coeditor, Marge, in commenting on an earlier version of this chapter, objected to the term "late bloomer" as implying that "other roles/selves that all of us have had—e.g., mother, wife, secretary, teacher, etc.—are not important. It occurs to me that the phrase is buying into the common notion that some of us have encountered—that women who stay home are not important." I think my comments about my homemaking years as a First Career suggest quite the opposite. Yes, I bloomed late in anthropology. But as a passionate gardener, I welcome late bloomers, flowers we enjoy late in the season, with frost threatening and winter coming, without in any way denigrating the glory of spring and summer bloomers. I continue to practice other skills learned "on time" because they are still important to me and my loved ones: baking bread; growing and canning fruits and vegetables; knitting; and especially being mom and grandma, sister and aunt to my family. Yes, in anthropology I am a late bloomer! But surely a better-late-than-never bloomer.

Endnotes

1. Turner (1967).
2. Kaufman (1986:14).
3. Cattell (n.d.).
4. Kaufman (1986).
5. Cattell (1989).
6. Freilich (1977).
7. A story I've told in Cattell (n.d.).
8. Friedan (1963), Harvey (1993).
9. Cf. Harvey (1993).
10. Friedan (1963).
11. Wissler (1944).
12. Published in *Anthropology News* 38 (5): 60–61, 1997. Reprinted by permission of the American Anthropological Association.
13. Agar (1980).
14. Mead (1970), Wax (1986).
15. Bateson (1990).
16. Cf. Levine (1994), Weiner (1999).
17. Patterson (2001:137–38).
18. Cattell (1997).
19. See Albert and Cattell (1994), Climo and Cattell (2002).
20. Bateson (1990:223).
21. de Laguna (1977).

~ References ~

Agar, Michael H. 1980. *The Professional Stranger: An Informal Introduction to Ethnography.* New York: Academic.

Albert, Steven M., and Maria G. Cattell. 1994. *Old Age in Global Perspective: Cross-Cultural and Cross-National Views.* New York: G. K. Hall.

Bateson, Mary Catherine. 1990. *Composing a Life.* New York: Plume Books.

Cattell, Maria G. 1989. Old Age in Rural Kenya: Gender, the Life Course and Social Change. PhD diss., Bryn Mawr College. Ann Arbor: UMI.

———. 1997. African Widows, Culture and Social Change: Case Studies from Kenya. In *The Cultural Context of Aging: Worldwide Perspectives,* 2nd ed., ed. Jay Sokolovsky, 71–98. Westport, CT: Bergin & Garvey.

———. n.d. Earthworms Are My Friends: Gardening as Spiritual Journey and Other Dreams and Deeds of Self (unpublished manuscript).

Climo, Jacob J., and Maria G. Cattell, eds. 2002. *Social Memory and History: Anthropological Perspectives.* Walnut Creek, CA: AltaMira.

de Laguna, Frederica. 1977. *Voyage to Greenland: A Personal Initiation into Anthropology.* New York: W. W. Norton.

Freilich, Morris. 1977. *Marginal Natives at Work: Anthropologists in the Field.* New York: John Wiley & Sons.

Friedan, Betty. 1963. *The Feminine Mystique.* New York: Norton.

Harvey, Brett. 1993. *The Fifties: A Women's Oral History.* New York: HarperCollins.

Kaufman, Sharon R. 1986. *The Ageless Self: Sources of Meaning in Late Life.* Madison: Univ. of Wisconsin Press.

Levine, Mary Ann. 1994. Creating Their Own Niches: Career Styles among Women in Americanist Archaeology between the Wars. In *Women in Archaeology,* ed. Cheryl Claassen, 9–40. Philadelphia: Univ. of Pennsylvania Press.

Mead, Margaret. 1970. Field Work in the Pacific Islands. In *Women in the Field: Anthropological Experiences,* ed. Peggy Golde, 293–331. Chicago: Aldine.

Patterson, Thomas C. 2001. *A Social History of Anthropology in the United States.* New York: Berg.

Turner, Victor W. 1967. *The Forest of Symbols: Aspects of Ndembu Ritual.* Ithaca, NY: Cornell Univ. Press.

Wax, Rosalie. 1986. Gender and Age in Fieldwork and Fieldwork Education: "Not Any Good Thing Is Done by One Man Alone." In *Self, Sex, and Gender in Cross-Cultural Fieldwork,* ed. Tony Larry Whitehead and Mary Ellen Conaway, 129–50. Urbana: Univ. of Illinois Press.

Weiner, Lynn Y. 1999. Domestic Constraints: Motherhood as Life and Subject. In *Voices of Women Historians: The Personal, the Political, the Professional,* ed. Eileen Boris and Nupur Chaudhuri, 206–16. Bloomington: Indiana Univ. Press.

Wissler, Clark. 1944. The Contribution of James McKeen Cattell to American Anthropology. *Science* 99 (2569): 232–33.

A Lens, a Book, and a Compass

My Anthropological Life Tour

Jacqueline Walden

When I was eleven years old, I unwrapped two presents that Santa left me under the Christmas tree. One contained a laboratory microscope, the other, a ship's compass. Whether those gifts fueled new fires or fanned old flames, I'll never know, but they symbolize two of the three major interests in my life: the world up close and the world far away, the common and the exotic, the natural and the cultural. The third gift was not under the tree but on the shelf in the living room—a book. It symbolizes my lifelong pursuit of education. The lens, the book, and the compass are the threads that weave through my life tour. For I see my life as a travelogue, a series of minidestinations, temporary places of anchor that tease me with the promise of adventure and experience.

Journey's Start—Boston, 1935–1953: Being Sicilian

All four of my grandparents, seeking a better life, came from Sicily in the early 1900s and settled in Boston. I was the first child born to my parents. I was also premature. I guess I couldn't wait to get moving, even at that tender age. We were all very poor, living in the tenements of the West End near Little Italy, only a few blocks from Mass General Hospital. Its proximity was fortunate because I

Jacqueline Walden: PhD 1995, University of California, Riverside. Dissertation: "The New Menopause: Growing the Wise Woman." She has developed and led workshops on menopause and has been a long-term care senior ombudsman and a counselor for End-of-Life Choices. For eight years, Jackie owned a literary agency and a bookstore.

had severe asthma attacks as a toddler. In the middle of many nights, Dad would sprint those few blocks to the hospital with me, wheezing badly, in his arms.

My parents did not go to school beyond sixth grade. But not by choice. They had to work in order to help feed large families. One of my grandfathers was a shoemaker and cook, the other pushed carts of produce and delivered ice. Mom sewed at a factory, and Dad pushed a cart with fresh vegetables and fruits around Haymarket Square. "Buy for one cent, sell for two," his father had told him. Dad had street and business smarts. He washed celery in a basement across from Faneuil Hall, then sold it to grocery stores. His small business grew faster than beanstalks and eventually became a major wholesale produce company in the area. But work instead of school helped my parents realize that their kids must have an education to reap the rewards America offered. No pushcarts for us. My parents never told us to go to college. It was a given, an unwritten, unspoken commandment. The six of us never questioned the fact that we would go to college after high school. Consequently, we accumulated three PhDs, one MD, and two BAs.

When I was six, we moved to the suburb of Watertown. I remember hating to pick up after my younger siblings and begging Mom for a nickel for the movies. But I loved to swing from the nearby trees. At eleven, I remember bleeding, first from pricking my finger so I could examine blood under my new microscope, and second from menstruation. Menstruation was a taboo subject in those days, so all the girls in school huddled around me during recess, asking questions. I was very popular. I never imagined that forty-five years later, women would be crowding around me asking about menopause because I'd become an expert about it. The next year, 1947, in grade 6, I gave an oral report on cell division. It was elementary knowledge at the time. The Watson-Crick model of DNA molecules was proposed six years later.

I was only thirteen when I took my first trip to a distant place. I went to Quebec with my aunt, but took the train home to Boston by myself. My father must have been sleeping when that trip was planned! I wonder how many parents would allow a young girl to do that today! When I was fourteen, the family drove to Mexico City in the Cadillac. Seeing faraway places and different people was very exciting. Even the animals were different: I saw two horses doing something strange in a field. And then there were the funny balloon-type things I found in the hotel drawer in Monterrey. When I showed them to Dad, he quickly confiscated them. I had no knowledge of sex, so I didn't understand these erotic sights in exotic sites. Neither parents nor schools taught about sex back then.

My favorite reading material came from two books Mom had on the shelf. One was about the Hunzas, whose average life expectancy was over a hundred years. The author claimed that their pure, natural diet was the reason for their long lives. The other group from the South Pacific had no dental cares because they did not consume a refined diet. I read these books over and over, charmed by the photographs of natives and faraway places.

About the time World War II ended, I became aware that I hated my name, Eva Piazza. My closest girlfriend, a Swede named Dagmar (nickname Daggy), also hated hers. So we changed them. We announced the change to our parents; they must have accepted them for we have been Jackie and Vicki ever since.

The family moved to Belmont when I was twelve. In those days, Belmont was home to many families whose fathers were professors at Boston-area colleges. I applied to six of those colleges in 1952 and was accepted at all of them. My first choice was Simmons College for women. It was during a tour there that I first saw embryos preserved in large bottles of formaldehyde. I was totally fascinated. But for some unknown reason, at the tender age of seventeen, I attended Radcliffe instead. In later years, Mom said they wanted me to go to the most prestigious university ($300 per semester back then). Perhaps they wanted me to find a prestigious husband and a "Mrs" degree.

The career counselor at Radcliffe directed me to the Romance Languages Department. I don't recall having the presence of mind to say, "Wait. I want to go to the biology lab." So that interest was put on a shelf, like the embryo I saw preserved in a bottle. But I did enroll in a physical anthropology course taught by the formidable Professor Earnest Hooton. He lectured in front of a table heavy with craniums. There may have even been a cast of Piltdown Man because this was just before the fraud was exposed. Zinj and Lucy were still undiscovered. The class went on local field trips, including one to a museum that displayed Egyptian mummies. Later, I took my two sons through that same museum because I wanted them to experience the same excitement I had had when viewing antiquities.

I did not finish my undergraduate work at Radcliffe. I got all Ds my first semester because halfway through I stopped attending classes and studying. My parents couldn't help. They had no understanding of college except that that was where I should be, and they had just had their fifth child whom we all doted over. I was too immature and sensitive at seventeen to survive the peer pressure. Most girls lived in the dorms, were cliquish, and owned their own horses. I wanted to be in that in-group, but I lived at home and was labeled a commuter. Even though I drove to high school and Radcliffe in a Cadillac, it was not sufficient to be accepted.

Commuting was degrading, but freshman English was humiliating. I was the only female in a class of forty Harvard males. It should have been heaven. But the professor made a faux pas that made it hell. One of the rules of engagement was that the professor never revealed the name of the student he was critiquing. He broke that rule when he said "she." All forty heads turned their collective gaze on me. And I lost all my self-esteem. Today I would say, "Hey, you guys aren't perfect either." After a year, I had commuted myself right out of Radcliffe.

⁓ Key West, 1953–1954: Marriage and Loneliness ⁓

In July 1953, at age eighteen, I married Dave Hall, almost the boy next door. We spent our first year in Key West, Florida. Dave was an aerial photographer for the navy during the Korean War and was stationed at Boca Chica Field near Key West. Within three months of moving to Key West, Dave, age twenty-three, became very ill with diabetes, was close to a coma, and then was hospitalized for four months. Before leaving the hospital, we learned how to administer injections. After another four months, in April 1954, Dave was discharged from the navy, and we moved back to Belmont to live with his parents.

Key West was a very unhappy experience for me. From a fun-loving, athletic, social young bride, I became a lonely, sedentary woman with a very ill husband in the hospital. No family, no friends, no Cadillac, no piano, no skis, no bicycle, no microscope, none of the things that had identified me as Jackie, except a few books and my compass.

~ Belmont, 1954–1962: Motherhood ~

Dave and I worked in the daytime and went to college at night. This time around, though, I consciously wanted to go to school. This routine lasted for a year. Pheromones must have been in the air: almost everyone I knew—including me, my mom, my aunts, and my girlfriends—were pregnant in 1955. On April 24, my psychology class ended at 7 p.m.; our first son, Russell, was born at 5 the next morning. I stopped working, but I continued with school.

Belmont High graduates and their children were allowed to live in the Veterans Project. We were all dirt poor, but everyone knew each other and the days were full of fun. And work. I washed clothes with an old-fashioned wringer machine that Dave scrounged up. That was easier than scrubbing navy whites by hand in Key West. We pushed our baby carriages around town and played and swam at Walden Pond. And I hitched rides to Boston University at night with the guys.

After a few years at the project, our second son, Matthew, was born. I was a relaxed mother by now and enjoyed motherhood. We bought our own new house in Waltham for $12,000 and had wonderful years. In 1962 Dave decided to quit school and apply for work in the civil service. We carefully considered all the options and decided that the one with most promise was a position in Mobile, Alabama, at Brookley Air Force Base.

~ Mobile, 1962–1965: "It's Never Too Late" ~

I hated to go. The South just brought back bad memories. Dave and I compromised. If we stayed in Mobile for no more than five years, I would go. With a time limit, the thought of Mobile was bearable. So we moved. I resolved to extract the most I could from Mobile, and give it all I had. Surprisingly, it turned out to be a highly productive, rewarding experience.

I continued my education at the only college in Mobile at the time, the Jesuit Spring Hill College. It had just started to admit women, so I went during the day when Russ and Matt were in school. The course in the history of Western civilization opened my eyes like no morning coffee ever had. The faraway places became more than names on a two-dimensional map; they represented people who did significant things and events that shaped our lives today. And the English professor, instead of destroying my self-esteem, ratcheted it up a few notches. He was generous with his praise and suggestions. I worked hard to receive both.

The following year, 1963, the new University of South Alabama (USA) opened its Mobile campus. I attended USA for two years and studied biology. The bottle with the embryo was off the shelf and on the table, literally and figuratively. But could I study biology at the grand old age of twenty-eight? I asked my professor if he thought I was too old to become a biologist. He said, "Jackie, it's never too late until they pull the coffin lid down over you." Those words of wisdom, if nothing else, were worth the stopover in Mobile.

But somehow it didn't happen. I think I was too busy coping with two children, a house, and a sick husband, to handle all the physics, math, and labs required for biology. Dave developed high blood pressure and had occasionally severe insulin reactions that left the boys and me totally unnerved. As if that wasn't enough, there were rumors that Secretary of Defense Robert McNamara was going to close Brookley Air Force Base. The base did close in 1965, devastating the city, people, and property values. But we decided to stay with Dave's work unit, which was being transferred to Sacramento, California, so we sold our house and moved on.

~ Sacramento, 1965–1978: Rebirth ~

Something went wrong: I waited a whole year before I enrolled at California State University, Sacramento (CSUS). But once there, I launched a major assault to complete my undergraduate studies and went full time. I got so excited about every subject (except golf) I studied, that I changed majors every semester. At the start of my senior year, the administration forced me to declare a major, so I finished with a BA in psychology in 1968. I continued on at CSUS with a half year of graduate work, then a half year at McGeorge School of Law. But the tuition was getting high, and Dave was getting sicker, so I abandoned college and took a job with the welfare department as an eligibility worker.

I was also waging a public relations campaign to entice my family to move to California. Dad had just retired from the market at age fifty-seven and was ready to move. By 1970 my parents and siblings with their families had all moved to the West Coast. I no longer felt any loneliness. But later that same year, Dave died suddenly and unexpectedly from a heart attack. I think his angina pains were misdiagnosed as indigestion—the doctor had prescribed Tums. The boys were only fifteen and twelve; they seemed dazed but carried on. Fortunately, I had a job and we managed.

Two years later, I married a local writer, Duane, and started the first bookstore in the small city of Roseville. The bookstore was a challenge. I worked seven days a week and took only one vacation in five years. For six years, I was a bookstore owner, literary agent (I sold six book contracts), and wife of a popular writer. It was the zenith of my life. I actualized all my talents and interests to the max.

For our only vacation, Duane and I ferried up the Inland Passage in British Columbia. We camped out at the foot of Mendenhall Glacier and survived an earthquake on Sitka Island. That was exciting—dangerously exciting. But there is even more danger in a marriage in which personal and professional lives are totally entwined. If one thread breaks, the whole fabric can come apart, and that is what happened. The nasty divorce that followed was the lowest point of my life. My bookstore and agency were so bound up with my husband that, when we divorced, I shuttered the whole works.

I did learn about myself from the experience. My self-esteem could still be shattered with one blow, be it an English professor or an author-husband. My confidence in myself had not developed in spite of successes. Today I would say, "I can do it without you," but back then, my identity and worth were still connected to a relationship with a man. I promised myself that I would not subject myself to such pain again. I would learn to be independent. And I would, for the second time in my life, create my own name.

In the fall of 1977, I traveled to Belmont for my twenty-fifth high school reunion. I stayed with my girlfriend Vicki. We took walks around Walden Pond, where we used to build sand castles with our children. The trees were in full color. And the new name came to me in a flash, almost as though it had been waiting all those years to be born: I was Jackie Walden.

The passport agency would not accept my new name until I had used it for five years. So I had to use my former married name with "aka Walden" on my driver's license. That was fine—it got me to Europe for six weeks with my sister Joanne. While we were in Taormina, Sicily, Mount Etna erupted. The morning after, we took a trip up the volcano, which was about fifty miles away, and walked on crusty lava and wheezed from the sulfur fumes. My rebirth as Jackie Walden had been baptized by fire.

~ Houston, 1978–1980: Walden Reigns ~

It didn't take long to fall in love again, this time with a chemist from Sacramento who was moving to Houston, Texas. Russ, Matt, and I followed him and lived there for two years. Houston was booming, so the boys found jobs right away. For me, the best part of Houston was my new position with Walden Books as the assistant to the regional manager. I wore as many hats as I had in my own bookstore. I was in book heaven.

But the weather in Houston was from hell, nature's show of extremes. It changed from hour to hour, from cold to hot, from sun to fierce storms with lightning and tornadoes. The downpours terrified me. Once it rained eighteen inches within two days, and the bayou overflowed and flooded my car. After the sun shone and things dried out, I found weeds growing out of the carpet of my Mercury. It was time to move on!

~ Orange County, 1980–1987: Return to Anthropology ~

This move was easy. I packed up my nine boxes of worldly possessions, left Ken the chemist his keys, got in the car, and drove west, alone, until I reached the edge of the continent and a job managing a large Walden Books store in Westminster, California. This position lasted only a year because I sprained my back moving some heavy boxes of books during the Christmas rush. After I recovered, I went to work for a large developer in Orange County and used my compass a lot to travel with my sister Joanne. One trip was a tour of Peru, where we watched Haley's Comet from Machu Pichu in the moonlight.

The excitement I had felt for anthropology long ago at Harvard was renewed when I became a volunteer for the Natural History Museum of Orange County in 1981. While the focus of the museum was natural history, it included some culture history such as dioramas of Native American lifeways and their manos and metates. I was so caught up with the museum that I became a member of the board, public relations chairperson, assistant treasurer, and editor of the newsletter, again wearing many hats. I even designed a tour to New Zealand to raise money for the museum. A geologist with the museum arranged a tour to England and Scotland, where we collected 400-million-year-old trilobite fossils from Mortimer Forest, and ammonite fossils from Lyme Regis. I cherish every one to this day.

The challenge and excitement of developing a museum inspired me to resume my graduate studies, this time in museology and archaeology. The road back to college was fraught with dangers. Could I study and take notes at school after a twenty-year hiatus? Could I compete with twenty-year-olds? Could I compete with my three brothers who already had graduate degrees? Could I get by financially on a veteran's survivor's pension? The move to academia was as scary as the thought of a cross burning on my lawn. But I moved ahead.

To test the waters, I switched to part-time work and took advanced biology and chemistry courses at the local college. Coming in near the top of the grade list, I knew I should not fear being a reentry student.

Another concern was my rivalry and jealousy with my three brothers. There had always been differential treatment by my parents toward their three daughters and three sons. In Sicilian culture, like many others, girl babies are not as valuable as boys. Oh, my parents loved all their offspring, but they were in awe of the males. I was the firstborn, a princess for three years until my little brother arrived. Then I was dethroned. My parents sent my brothers to private schools in Belmont. All three got advanced degrees as a matter of course. Oh, poor

Jackie, she only went to Radcliffe—and she dropped out! It is true that I had the opportunity. I just didn't have the concept of a career. I had no role model. I lacked the expectations.

I felt so much angst and cried so many tears while trying to come to grips with my sibling jealousy. At first, I felt anger toward my parents for the differential treatment. In addition, I wondered if I wanted to go back to school for the wrong reasons, that is, to prove that I was as smart as my brothers and to receive that extra love and awe from my parents. After weeks of self-analysis came enlightenment. I realized that my parents had made the wisest decisions they could, based on their own experiences and what they thought would be their children's future roles: men were breadwinners and fathers, women were wives and mothers. In addition, I realized my parents were exceptional because, though not well educated themselves, they gave all six of their children a chance at college.

When I came to those realizations, it was easy to forgive my parents and my brothers. It freed me emotionally for returning to school. I knew I was doing it for myself, not to prove my worth to anyone else. I had reached a higher level of self-identity, self-worth, and self-actualization than ever before.

When I told my parents about my plans, they said I could live with them in Sacramento if I wanted to go to CSUS, which offered a museum program. I couldn't refuse. The final, financial obstacle had vanished, with the bonus of an opportunity to spend two years with my parents, getting to know them as people. And I didn't have to share them with five other siblings.

~ Sacramento, 1987–1989: An MA in Anthropology and Travel ~

The two years in Sacramento were devoted to an MA in anthropology and travel. My advisor, Professor George Rich, encouraged me to look into a specialization in gerontology, a growing field and industry. I took his advice. My research was on the Elderhostel program, and I interned as a long-term care ombudsman, resolving complaints at skilled-nursing homes and other facilities. It was rewarding to both the seniors and me. I was advised by Dr. Rich and my mentor and thesis committee member Professor Melford Weiss to continue on for a PhD. How could I go wrong with *rich* and *wise* on my side? It was a sign to plunge in and really test my mettle.

So I left Sacramento again, at age fifty-four, this time with a fellowship for the University of California, Riverside (UCR).

~ Riverside, 1989–1993: Getting the PhD—at Last! ~

My mom used to call me *pede longu*, a Sicilian phrase that means "long feet" or someone who is always on the go. Perhaps it has a double meaning: "a longing to travel." I have always responded to that longing by getting out my compass and going. My compass had not been neglected during my two years of graduate study in Sacramento. I spent time in England and Alaska and planned and took many trips with my mother and two sisters. We had such fun together, and I learned a wonderful lesson: carry out your dreams and enjoy life with your family and friends while you can.

At Riverside, classes in East Asian, African, and Indian cultures increased my longings to travel. So when the time came to write a research proposal, I switched from gerontology to tourism. The anthropology of tourism was in its infancy then. In 1989 I visited several prospective research sites, visiting two indigenous societies, the Ainu in Japan and the Ami in Taiwan. I was fortunate to have a Taiwanese American sister-in-law whose parents have homes in both Taipei and Tokyo. Those were my home bases as I ventured out with a niece who spoke some Taiwanese and Japanese. I saw a revitalization of culture among the Ainu on Hokkaido and an opportunity for research.

But when I started my second year at UCR in 1990, I was tackled by something bigger than sibling rivalry. It was polymyalgia rheumatica, a nasty type of arthritis whose symptoms are muscle weakness, joint inflammation, and lots of pain. The treatment for me was eight years of cortisone. With assistance and understanding from family, friends, and the anthropology department, I missed only a few beats during the fall and winter quarters in 1990, when I was the sickest and had to study by correspondence from home in Sacramento. When it came time to plan my research project, I asked my rheumatologist if I could spend a year in a remote area. The answer was a definite "No." I was extremely disappointed, but I knew the dangers of the disease and cortisone therapy. I changed my research plans back to gerontology and studied the cultural construction of menopause today. I spent a year in two major cities in the United States, where I had top-notch rheumatologists and hospitals to watch over my health and menopause clinics with subjects to interview.

~ Camarillo, 1993–1997: Growing from a Seed ~

As soon as I completed my research in 1993, I took up residence with a new partner, Joseph, and moved to his home in Camarillo, Ventura County, midway between Los Angeles and Santa Barbara.

It took a year and a half to write up the dissertation, defend it, and receive my PhD in 1995 at the age of sixty years and three months—just three months over my estimated date of arrival. My parents were too ill to attend the graduation ceremony, but they were as proud of my achievement as I was. There is a special type of process that I find most exciting and rewarding. It is a project that starts with an idea, grows into a seed, and develops to fulfillment. Babies, books, tours, and a dissertation are the largest long-term processes that mark my life. Russ and Matt are my seeds of life. I saw them grow in me, then outside of me. Studying about embryos and cell division, while exciting, doesn't compare to actually creating new life.

Owning a bookstore from its conception to its completion was a creation. But being a literary agent was even more exciting. I would interview an author about his or her idea for a book, assist during the writing process, negotiate a contract with a publisher, and eventually see the book on a shelf in bookstores, sometimes in my own store. A tour is the same sort of process. I start with an idea and a destination, then get approval from the travelers, arrange all the accommodations, and finally get those long feet moving.

Creating a dissertation was like being my own literary agent. I started with a research plan, got funding from an agency (thanks to Sonya Hamburger, director of the University of California, San Diego, Medical School and Menopause Clinic), collected the data, and wrote a book. And I got a bonus: a PhD.

Creations are the sunrises of life; they make living worthwhile.

Because I am a "Jackie-of-all-trades," a PhD in anthropology is most appropriate. An anthropologist sees and studies the larger picture, and I humbly believe that that is the way my mind sees the world. I always thought that psychology or biology or economics were too limited in their scope, reductionist in their worldviews. But the wide lens of anthropology makes me feel at home. I can study tourism, aging, Italian American internment during World War II, or the black circus, and be wonderfully excited about the projects and accepted by my peers. I wonder if other anthropologists are attracted to this profession because they have a holistic, systematic, relativistic worldview before they even start studying anthropology.

Life was good in Camarillo. I worked for a year as director of the Southern California student exchange program for World Learning. In addition, I gave workshops on menopause for various organizations and a university. In spite of my arthritic pains and reduced mobility, my partner Joseph and I toured China, Spain, Portugal, Morocco, the Great Basin, San Ignacio Lagoon, and New York. At Ellis Island, I cried as I thought of my four grandparents' arrival from Sicily. In 1996 I entered the political realm. I ran for senior assemblyperson in the California Senior Legislature. Campaigning, winning, and legislating at the Capitol in Sacramento are definitely high points in my life. As anthropologists know, in many societies when women are postmenopausal, they enter politics and the healing arts.

I thought my relationship with Joseph was forever. But it took only three years to fall into rifts we could not bridge. The straw that broke the camel's back was a dilemma for me, a cultural conflict: circumcision. I strongly believe in informed consent and had spent years of research and talking with menopausal women, encouraging them to be advocates for their own health and well-being. Circumcision of an infant, in this case Joseph's grandson, was neither informed nor consensual. But I tried to look at the occasion through an anthropological lens. After all, this was tradition, one that goes well beyond the physical body. I remained with Joseph after it was over, but the damage had been done. We severed our relationship.

There were many losses during those few years in Camarillo: my mom, my gallbladder, and part of a disc in my spine. And then Joseph.

~ Sacramento, 1997–2004: Death and Rebirth in the Liminal Zone ~

The old homestead looked beautiful when I returned to the Sacramento suburb of Fair Oaks. It was family time again. I came home to help my sisters take care of my father, who was eighty-seven. My son Russell joined us. My other son, Matthew, lived nearby in Woodland with his family, which meant I could play with my grandchildren more often.

The beauty didn't last long. Instead, I found myself in a black hole; a liminal zone of stress, fear, and love; a transitional challenge that eventually led to elderhood. I learned more than I cared to know about my family's and friends' diseases and conditions as well as my own. I acted more like an MD than a PhD. I constantly referred to *The Physician's Desk Reference* and *The Merck Manual of Medical Information* for help. I had two successful hip replacements and a dilation of esophageal strictures caused by so many first-generation anti-inflammatory drugs. But most challenging of all was keeping up with my dad's numerous, progressive conditions. His neurologist called him "a moving target." We all managed for four years until he could no longer swallow. We called hospice.

It was interesting, anthropologically, to observe the care of elderly parents in two different cultures. In my father's case, he chose not to prolong his life when he couldn't swallow any longer. We six siblings honored his wishes and gave him palliative care only. In contrast, my Taiwanese sister-in-law, Yuling, travels to Taiwan for months at a time to care for her ailing parents, who are in their nineties. Yuling maintains a shrine with candles, incense, and photos of deceased kin, to whom she often brings food. Yuling's family utilizes all the available high-tech life support and medications for very ill parents. Perhaps keeping parents alive and comfortable is necessary in a culture that believes strongly in ancestral spirits.

After it was over, I had to analyze, as is my wont and my forte, those four years. I was no longer in school studying gerontological anthropology, wrapping my hands around tomes, fretting over tests. Instead, this was hands-on people stuff, and failure could be life-threatening. This was real-time anthropology, participant observation at its most serious. The caregiver had to be both objective and subjective in order to stay alive, give the best care, and provide love for a father whose world was diminishing. It was a depressing situation, but the rare good moments with Dad filled me with an immense joy.

The last three years in the Sacramento area made up for the isolating nature of caregiving. I immersed myself in activities related to medical and gerontological anthropology. All were exciting, fun, or fulfilling. Disrespectful as it sounds, I felt free for the first time in years. I was living my own life. The first activity required a compass—travel with a group I called "The Fabulous Five," composed of my two sisters, my Taiwanese sister-in-law, my Irish girlfriend, and me. We traveled to see wildflowers, migrating butterflies, the Great Basin area in Nevada, Big Sur on the California coast, and numerous national parks. I also dubbed the group "The Club Sandwich Group." We were elite caregivers to our elderly parents, our children, and our grandchildren.

In addition to travel, I immersed myself in the theatrical group to which my mom had belonged, the Senior Players of the American River Community (SPARC). I joined as a tribute to her. Does this suggest a bit of ancestor worship on my part?

I worked with terminally ill members of End-of-Life Choices (formerly Hemlock Society) and interviewed World War II veterans for the national Veterans History Project. It felt like the old research days, when I interviewed hundreds of women about their menopausal experiences.

~ Grants Pass, 2005: Pede Longu Moves On ~

Oh, how I love "new." New state, new partner Drury, new way of life, new house. Now I live in a small town in Oregon and am guardian of five acres of trees, plants, and animals. Will I now reinvent myself as well as my surroundings? Will I stay active, travel, practice something I can call anthropology? Based on my history, the odds are high.

Fortunately, I have two wonderful role models to follow. The first is my mom. After she turned sixty, she spread her wings. She became a successful actress on stage and television, and studied art and music. For her, adulthood was a time for babies and a husband, but seniorhood was the time for self-development. She showed me the way to be productive after menopause.

My second role model comes to mind whenever I feel sorry for myself. I only have to think of Professor Daniel Crowley from the University of California, Davis, and I am injected with courage. He and I would chat at meetings of the Southwestern Anthropological Society and California Folklore Society. He contracted polio during World War II and was confined to a wheelchair. Later, with his degree in anthropology, he specialized in carnivals as practiced around the world. I shared in the despair that comes from pain and immobility, and the thoughts of giving up. But I also shared his thoughts of *growing* up, by adjusting and succeeding in the face of adversity. In spite of Dr. Crowley's wheelchair, he was not an armchair anthropologist. He was in the *Guinness Book of World Records* as the most-traveled disabled person, visiting over two hundred countries. It taught me that anthropology can be practiced in spite of obstacles. Dr. Crowley died a few years ago on the job in Bolivia. He is still my mentor, and I intend to travel on. I don't know the future, but I'm sure it will include a lens, a book, and a compass.

Section 6

Legacies for Future Generations

Surely, all of us hope to leave an intellectual legacy, some part of our anthropological work that lives on after us. But the legacies we think of here are the patterns of our lives, which offer models for our daughters and granddaughters and other girls and women—models to think about if not to follow. This alternative pattern—family first, anthropological career later—is demonstrated in our life stories. Of course, that way is not without its problems and struggles. But it did allow most of us to be home with our children in their early years, which in retrospect we see as a good thing for our children and families, though not always for ourselves. Doing it our way means having shorter careers—perhaps—though with today's life expectancies, many of us will have the opportunity for continued professional activity long past retirement.

We grew up with the gender ideology that reached its zenith in the postwar 1950s. If a woman went to college, often it was to find a husband. She might have a job until she had her first child; thereafter, she devoted her life to her children and husband. Though these ideas have not disappeared today, they must seem very strange to the baby boomers who are our children and to many of today's young women (sometimes called "millennials") who are their children!

All but three of us were formally employed in a variety of jobs before we enrolled in graduate school, and nearly all of us left employment to spend a few or many years as stay-at-home moms—again, for many mothers today, in this era of two-income families, a strange idea. And yet... women must still deal with the practicalities of managing both family and career, especially careers following the traditional (male) model of rapid and unwavering advancement. That this model may not be a one-size-fits-all is suggested by the fact that some women and men are now experimenting with alternative lifestyles, such as sequential careers and career niches that allow a better balance of family and work life.

A Time for Excellence, a Legacy for the Future

Jane Stevenson Day

In the Beginning

I was born in a suburb of St. Louis, Missouri, and grew up during the depths of the Depression. In the 1930s, even in my affluent community, life was simple in style and activity. St. Louis was more like a small town than a big city. In my memory, these years evoke a time of innocence and tranquility. Children walked to school, adults rode streetcars to work, and everyone walked to the bank, local stores, and church. Children were free to walk alone to visit friends and go to shops, the library, and, best of all, the movie theater. The 1930s black-and-white films of comedy and adventure provided an exciting window to another world. The movies cost a dime, and a nickel would purchase an ice cream cone or a candy bar, so for fifteen cents the outing was complete. I received a twenty-five-cent allowance weekly, its use carefully budgeted for me by my father: a nickel to church, a nickel to save, and fifteen cents to spend. It was a difficult exercise for a little girl, and the routine endured throughout my school years. As my needs increased, so did the allowance, but everything had to be accounted for. By the time I was in college, my father put a year's allowance into my account in a lump sum, which had to cover transportation, tuition, books, room and board, clothes, and extras—and I made it

Jane Stevenson Day: PhD 1984, University of Colorado. Dissertation: "New Approaches in Stylistic Analysis: The Late Polychrome Period Ceramics from Hacienda Tempisque, Guanacaste Province, Costa Rica." In 1995 Jane retired as chief curator of the Denver Museum of Natural History, where she developed and curated many exhibits including Aztec: The World of Moctezuma. After retirement, she led trips around the world to archaeological sites for the museum.

last the year. Having thus learned that responsibility can be instilled at a very early age, I repeated the pattern with my own daughters.

Many homes had servants, either girls from farms and small towns near the city, or men and women from the large black community in St. Louis, who cooked, laundered, and cared for the house and children. On Sundays most families, including my own, attended worship services, and the Presbyterian Church was one of the centers of my childhood. My father's Scottish family, arriving in the colonies in the 1700s, moved from the Scottish communities of Pennsylvania to settle in the Midwest after the Civil War. They were farmers, builders, preachers, doctors, and educators, and wherever they went they carried with them their steadfast faith. They were hardy, hardworking men and women of great integrity; they were responsible and loyal. While I have grown away from that early focus on faith, the moral and ethical personal behavior modeled in my childhood will abide with me always.

My beautiful mother was an adored child and grandchild of an old, respected family that, along with many other southerners, suffered the post–Civil War condition of little money but lots of gentility. She grew up in a world of loving acceptance and gentleness and, as a result, brought to her marriage and two daughters the gift of unconditional love, surely one of the greatest gifts that one person can give to another.

Like most other children in our community, I attended public schools. I loved books. I was read to throughout my earliest years, and I memorized poetry and rhymes to the delight of my proud mother and doting grandparents. Preschool attendance was uncommon at that time, so it was the lucky children who had been read to and challenged at home who got a head start. I spent only a couple of weeks in first grade and was skipped into second grade. From then on, I was never without something to read. My favorite early books were the series based on the lives of twin children in other cultures. They were written simply enough so that I could read to myself about the Eskimo Twins, the Dutch Twins, the English Twins, and the French Twins. I was fascinated by these stories of how children lived in places unknown to me. Looking back, I realize that these books were my first introduction to anthropology. I loved reading about how other people dressed, what they ate, and how and what they learned in parts of the world so different from my own. Soon I branched out into historical fiction in which children participated in the great events of history: adventure tales about boys who "went with Columbus" or "journeyed with Magellan," or girls who lived during the Civil War or the American Revolution and performed heroic deeds.

After reading, my favorite subject was geography. This was the closest any school came to teaching anthropology. The maps, the pictures of strange-looking people, and the stories about their lives in exotic climates and geographic settings fascinated me. Their homes, games, work, music, rituals, and clothes (or lack of them) were startling to a child of the Midwest. I wanted to know more. My aunt saved for me her old copies of the *National Geographic*. As many other enthusiastic readers will remember, it was one of the few sources of pictures and articles on faraway lands and people, and I eagerly awaited each one. Then, as I grew older, I discovered the excitement of real-life experiences in the books of exploration and adventure by men such as Richard Halliburton and Roy Chapman Andrews.

~ Growing Up: My Grandfather's Legacy ~

By the time I moved from grade school into junior high school, the world had begun to change. War had started in Europe and, on December 7, 1941, while my family was raking up the last of the fall leaves, the Japanese bombed Pearl Harbor. Cars, gasoline, tires, sugar, meat, butter, silk stockings, chocolate, eggs, shoes, and coffee were rationed. As the war progressed, many men, including my father, drew upon their boyhood farming education, raising chickens and planting Victory Gardens on lawns that had only recently been zoned against such activities.

At about this time, my father bought a rustic cabin on the banks of a river not far from St. Louis. Each weekend we loaded the car and spent two days "in the country." It was here that I picked up my first "arrowheads" and learned about the ancient people who once lived, roamed, and hunted in our beautiful river valley. A tenant farmer, his wife, and their three children worked the land. Their lifestyle resembled the farm life of a century earlier. They had no running water or electricity. Bathing was done in a large wooden tub, and the outhouse was at the foot of the vegetable garden. Cows were milked by hand, and mules were used to pull the plow and hay wagons. Children were expected to be part of the workforce. They fed the chickens, collected eggs, weeded the vegetable garden, and carried heavy pails of milk from the barn. At harvest time, hay was cut, sheep were sheared, and sorghum cane (the only reliable cash crop) was cut and processed with methods as old as farming itself, methods I have observed still in use today by farmers on the steppes of Russia and in isolated parts of Italy and Greece for pressing grapes and olives. As a child, I was envious of this rural way of life, but, as I grew older, I began to realize the terrible toll it took, particularly on women. Everyone had to work just to survive; there was little cash and no security for illness and old age except dependence upon other family members.

By the time I was ten, I was allowed to ride the train by myself to visit my maternal grandparents in a small Kentucky town on the Ohio River. As is rarely the case in today's more mobile society, both my maternal and paternal grandparents still lived in the houses in which my parents had grown up. My maternal grandfather was a railroad man who handled administration for the L&N Railroad, which his father had helped found. I loved best to visit in the summer, when I could make a nest for myself in the big roomy swing on the front porch and steadily read through stacks of books from the local library. Almost daily I played cards with my grandfather: first children's games, then gin rummy, and, finally, bridge. I took to the game immediately and, as I grew more proficient, loved to fill in as a fourth in my grandfather's evening bridge group. As I look back on the picture of a twelve-year-old girl sitting down at a bridge table with three elderly gentlemen, it makes me chuckle, but I considered it a great privilege then and still do.

I adored my grandfather and was so proud that everyone knew him and tipped their hats to him as he walked by. What I didn't know until much later was that he was basically an unhappy and unfulfilled man. At heart he was an eternal professor and, since he had no other outlet, I was his student and the eager recipient of all he knew and loved. He had graduated in the late 1880s from the University of Virginia, top of his class—a man everyone thought would go far and do great things. He was a classics scholar and a student of the Bible and the Greek philosophers, but above all he was a poet, and he read the works of the great poets to me throughout the years we shared. Each birthday he dedicated an original poem and mailed it to me wherever I was. One of the major sorrows of my life is that these carefully collected poems have somehow disappeared. My grandfather always seemed to me, even as a little girl, to be a man out of his time, not appearing to belong to his own era, but without the resources to allow him to live differently. His values and rather elitist worldview seem out of place today, but without his tutelage I would not have the appreciation I do of the beauty of words and poetry.

~ High School Years ~

During World War II, I attended high school and began to trade in some of my treasured "book time" for boys and a broader range of extracurricular activities. The theater became my passion. My school had a small but well-equipped theater and a drama teacher who taught the history of the theater and courses in reading plays, acting, and production. The culmination was a thespian club that put on three plays each year. We all felt very professional as we built sets; painted backdrops; learned the fundamentals of lighting, costume, and makeup; and naively performed onstage. This experience was the genesis of my lifetime love of the theater. Toward the end of my high school years, the war drew to a close, leaving our country elated over the return of our men but shocked by the death of Franklin Roosevelt and the explosion of an atomic bomb. Then, in my senior year, polio ravaged our class, leaving most of us devoid of a friend. It was a sobering experience because with the war over, we had felt fleetingly immortal.

May of 1947 was for me and my friends the ending of one world and the beginning of another. I had turned seventeen in April and, along with most of my classmates, was headed to college in the fall. Though my academic work had ranked me in the upper 10 percent of my graduating class, my record was not flawless. I had straight As in everything I liked—English, history, political science, theater, and even science—but I struggled through my four years of Latin and never fully understood why geometry was a necessary tool when spaces could be measured with a yardstick. However, I could attend almost any institution of higher learning that I desired and, after much deliberation, I applied to and was accepted at Colorado College, a small liberal-arts school in Colorado Springs. I was apprehensive but looked forward to the challenges of change.

~ Moving West: Colorado College ~

I loved the journey by train across the Great Plains between Missouri and Colorado. I had never been west before; everything I saw was new. My grandmother, whose life experience had been limited to her homes in Georgia and Kentucky, warned me about Indian raids, while my grandfather feared I would marry someone from that western world and never return. While Indians never raided, I did indeed marry a westerner and have lived the rest of my life a long way from my childhood home.

I arrived in Colorado Springs on a warm September morning, getting off the train in the shadow of Colorado's massive Front Range. During the first years after World War II, colleges were full of young men fresh from the military, many of whom would never have considered a college education without the aid of the GI Bill. This farsighted legislation was an instrument of incredible change for our country, and anyone who attended college in those years must recall the vitality brought to campuses by this unique generation of soldier-students. A philosophy professor once told me it was the best of all times to teach. The classrooms were filled with war veterans rather than high school boys. Many professors were themselves returning from war, bringing with them new issues and insights. Needless to say, this exciting atmosphere increased the quality of education for all students, including women. However, it wasn't until later years, when I began to teach, that I realized how challenging the discussions in philosophy, literature, and history classes had been in those postwar undergraduate days.

My college major was English, a logical choice for someone whose childhood had been spent with books. Even had there been a department of anthropology at Colorado College at that time, I suspect my choice would have been the same. For me a liberal-arts education was a guided adventure into the broad realm of human endeavor across time and space. This concept of multidisciplinary relationships began unconsciously to lay a foundation for my eventual introduction to the theories surrounding the discipline of anthropology.

Not surprisingly, academics were not my sole focus at college. Dorm life, good friends, and romance played a major role. My conservative, unsophisticated background needed expanding; I was delighted to throw myself into new experiences and did so with great gusto. I took fencing lessons, learned to drink beer, and, in typical 1940s style, attended the many sporting activities and social events that were the center of college life. Our daughters would find it hard to believe the clothes we wore, the dormitory curfews that were strictly enforced, and, above all, our required attendance at chapel services once a week. On Tuesday mornings, every student took his or her alphabetically assigned seat in the large beautiful chapel and a student monitor appointed for each row took attendance. Three absences and you were out of school.

~ Time for Marriage ~

By the end of my senior year, I was engaged to be married and a new war had started in a far-off place called Korea. Just six years after World War II had ended, young men were again being called or recalled to military service. Not intending to marry directly after college, I had applied for one of the government's newly established Fulbright Scholarships. I had planned for a year of graduate study at Oxford University, but, like many other women before me, when my fiancé thought he was being shipped to Korea, I changed my mind. We were married in a small chapel in the Webster Groves, Missouri, Presbyterian Church, in May of 1951.

Real life sets in for different people at different times in their lives. For me, it began at twenty-one. Reality was not grim and ugly but simply a realization that childhood and college were now behind me and I had to grow up. Being young and in love made it easy to accept adult status and even made it fun to live in a small California town just outside a Marine Corps base. It was an amazing learning experience. The rural community had only about five hundred permanent inhabitants; all the other people were imported Mexican laborers who came to work in the lemon-packing plants. I was turned down for jobs everywhere (including the packing plant), but finally found employment as office manager for the town's only physician. I didn't mention my mediocre math skills, but I could offer him my smattering of college Spanish as a desirable skill in the bilingual town. I bought a good Spanish/English dictionary, compiled a list of ailments and symptoms in both languages, and memorized the questions I would need to ask patients. Our finances were limited, but we were young and happy, though we waited in constant fear for orders that would move my husband's battalion to Korea—orders that arrived for many of our friends, some of whom never returned—but never came for us.

After two years, my husband was released from his duties in the Corps. From our small salaries, we had saved as much money as we could because we wanted to take a trip to Europe before we settled down in Denver. It was the time of the first economy-travel books, and *Europe on $5 a Day* became our bible and our budget. In the spring of 1952, we sailed from New York, then the least expensive way to travel overseas. Our resources lasted six months. We had no planned schedule and moved on or stayed as we pleased. When we were down to our last few dollars, we boarded a ship for New York, using the return tickets we had purchased before we left home. Instead of the neat and polished Dutch ship we had taken to Europe, our voyage home from Gibraltar was on an immigrant ship from Naples. Almost all the passengers were headed to Canada, looking for work in the wheat fields and a new start in life. As third-class travelers, we did not have private cabins but were in dormitories for six to eight people, with the women and children in some, the men in others. The ship rolled and lumbered its way across the North Atlantic from Cadiz to Nova Scotia. I was violently sick all the way. I assumed I was seasick, but it took only minutes for the five Italian women traveling with me to realize I was pregnant. They were delighted with my condition, and after two rocky weeks under their kindly care, I emerged from the ship at its first stop in Halifax ten pounds lighter and truly ready to be home.

~ Time for Motherhood ~

In the late fall of 1952, we arrived back in Denver with empty pockets but the security of an entry-level job for my husband in his family's automobile business. We moved into an apartment in a building filled with young couples. Eight first babies were born in the first six months we lived there, including our daughter Ellen. Our social life revolved around nursery concerns and husbands' job demands. None of us had money for babysitters or a second car, and as a result, we relied upon each other for support. We cared for and filled needs for each other in the way our families might have done, had we been living near them.

Not being an anthropologist at the time, I didn't realize that we evolved into a circle of fictive kin—sisters in all but blood. We met most mornings for "coffee talk" about our babies. As a friend of mine once said, it was a time when women talked about their children and men talked about their war. Almost once a week, we gathered casually with our husbands and children for a potluck supper. Deep and lasting bonds were forged during this almost-communal lifestyle, and those potluck dinners are still a part of our lives. Although circumstances changed and people went their different ways, the relationships remained intact and we still turn to each other for help in times of sorrow or for sharing in times of joy.

With a second child on the way, we needed a larger place to live. It was an exciting moment when we found a home we could actually afford. Here our next two daughters were born just fourteen months apart. It was an awesome and not always welcome task to care for three little girls under three. It was at this time that Gussie Mae came into my life. Gussie was and is a wonderfully strong and beautiful woman who loves children but was unable to have her own. She came to work for me almost fifty years ago, and my life and the lives of my daughters would have been very different without her.

Gussie is an upright and moral woman, a pillar of her church and community. She brought into our home a loving example of what it means to be a black woman in our city. Her love for our little girls was unquestioned and so was her stern authority. The girls and their friends loved her, but they stood in awe of her constant and strict supervision. She loved to have the girls visit for weekends when my husband and I went out of town. All four still remember her dressing them in their Sunday best and seating them in the front pew of her church so she could keep a strict eye on them from her place in the choir. As they grew older and learned to play the guitar and sing, Gussie signed them up to take their turn with the other children from her church to entertain the congregation with songs and hymns. Gussie was there for the girls and for me during the many crises of childhood and teenage years. She was there for the weddings and the breakups of marriages, the birth of grandchildren, and the endless needs and chores that underlie daily life.

Gussie Mae was one of the factors in my life that allowed me to move out of my world of family demands and back into the world of books and learning that still called to me and that I had never totally relinquished. Books remained a mainstay of life for me. I spent hours at the library, helping my children select books and, of course, at the same time keeping myself supplied with reading material. Once the children were in school, I took on the leadership of a Great Books discussion group. These discussion forums grew into a significant learning experience for adults during the 1950s and 1960s, and many people, particularly women, were experiencing renewal through reading and sharing their thoughts about some of the world's greatest ideas. The preparation for our weekly discussions allowed me to focus, albeit temporarily, on something other than my duties as a conscientious room mother, PTA president, nurse, chauffeur, and Girl Scout troop leader. I was not unhappy with my life: I had four healthy, bright children, a husband who loved me, and financial security. It was not a time when many women worked outside the home; in fact, almost all the women I knew were leading lives similar to my own. However, with my children in school, I resolved to add something new to my life of family and books. I experimented with a number of volunteer jobs, including political campaigns, hospital work, and the newly established Head Start program. Nothing seemed to quite suit my interests.

~ Time for a Change: A Volunteer at the Denver Art Museum ~

Over the years since college, I had been reading with growing fascination books and articles describing the new archaeological finds being made in Central America. While ancient New World sites had been known since the end of the nineteenth century, it was not until after World War II that in-depth investigations really began to take place. I was aware of the fine collection of pre-Columbian artifacts at the Denver Art Museum, and when I discovered that the New World Department, which was growing rapidly, was in need of volunteer help for their curatorial staff, I immediately applied. This step instigated my long and fruitful relationship with that fine institution. My experience would have been very different in a large, formal museum, but the Denver staff was still small, and serious volunteers were badly needed to work directly with the collections and curators. Twice a week, I faithfully showed up at an annex of the museum where the pre-Columbian collection was stored, ready to perform any duties requested by the curator. From the beginning, my main task was to help with cataloguing in preparation for an upcoming move to a new building.

Most of us were novices at the cataloguing process, so it was an overwhelming learning experience. Well before the cataloguing was finished, the collection had to be moved and installed in the new museum. I found myself part of a volunteer packing crew and, during the final weeks before the grand opening, was pressed into service to prepare the new exhibit cases for the objects. It was an in-depth education that few interns and museum students ever have. At the end of my first two years of volunteering, I had received incredible training and more hands-on experience and familiarity with objects than many art historians or archaeologists have in a lifetime. I was very fortunate.

From the beginning of my involvement in the department, I had read extensively in the literature of the pre-Columbian Americas, searching out the recent research reports and books that were rapidly appearing on the market. The move to the new museum brought with it a need for a corps of volunteer docents to tour the collections with groups of schoolchildren and be available to answer questions in the galleries. The curator prepared the docents for this task by presenting lectures and classes, and I took advantage of every opportunity offered. In addition, I began to seek courses outside the museum to enrich my understanding of pre-Columbian cultures. This led me to the anthropology department at the University of Colorado at Denver. There, in an evening class, I took my first anthropology class, The Archaeology of Mesoamerica, a course I, myself, was to teach many times in the future. I was hooked. The same combination that had so attracted me to the humanities in college—the blending of disciplines to recover and enhance knowledge of peoples past and present—also applied to my new study of archaeology.

By this time, I had spent five years as a volunteer at the Denver Art Museum. After completely inventorying the pre-Columbian collection and handling each piece for a second time, I decided that if I was really serious, I needed to consider getting a master's degree. So, with the concurrence of my family, I applied to the graduate school at the Denver campus of the University of Colorado. I was accepted and completed the degree in three years, taking most of my classes at night. Had I attended school full time, I could, of course, have finished in half the time, but I was still going to my children's school functions, helping with homework and research papers, and being an (almost) full-time wife, mother, daughter, friend, bridge player, and frustrated golfer. In addition, I was still volunteering at the museum and chairing the department's docent program.

~ Time for My PhD ~

For a while, I thought my master's degree in anthropology/museology would serve my needs, but it wasn't long before I realized that I wanted to pursue a PhD.

Unlike the situation encountered by many less-fortunate women, my husband and my family were supportive of my goal. They were unbelievably generous and encouraging, and their attitude enabled me to persist. Due to my family responsibilities, I applied at the University of Colorado's main campus at Boulder. It was not a time when older women were considered appropriate candidates for degrees in archaeology. While I was aware of this, I also knew that I was as well qualified or even better qualified in grades, background, and hands-on training than most applicants. Plus, I could provide my own financial resources; I was not going to apply for or be dependent upon scholarship monies.

Having completed the qualifying exams at the end of the master's degree and passed the GRE tests, I naively assumed that I would be readily accepted into the PhD program. Such was not the case. Instead of welcoming me as I had hoped, various members in the department made it clear that they thought I would be much better off if I forgot about a doctorate degree and returned to my volunteer work and social life in Denver. Today such a reaction would be grounds for legal action, but at that time it was fairly common practice to try to discourage older women from burdening the university with "unemployable" graduate students.

Fortunately, I had a few personal and professional contacts who were able to provide recommendations for me that were hard to ignore: Marie Wormington, one of the first women to achieve recognition in the field of archaeology, and Joe Ben Wheat, with whom I had worked at the University of Colorado Museum. Both were incensed that the department refused my application for reasons they felt were discriminatory. Eventually, with their support and my valid credentials, I was accepted as a PhD candidate.

I soon found that pursuing a doctorate involved a special kind of discipline for me. This included a daily seventy-mile round-trip to Boulder, regardless of weather conditions, a dedication to homework over social life, the sacrifice of leisure time reading, and an end to my golf and bridge games. There was also a growing dependency upon my husband and Gussie Mae for help with my youngest daughter, considerably younger than her sisters and the only one still at home. However, there was also the pleasure of finding I could still learn as well as, sometimes better than, students twenty years younger, plus a renewal of the excitement and challenge of new ideas.

During the next three years, I became a full-time student. I felt that if I didn't move quickly, circumstances in my life might change, or my enthusiasm might wane and I would never finish. For one of these years, my three older daughters and I were all attending the university at the same time. Our paths seldom crossed, though once in a while we waved at each other across the campus. Although my prematurely white hair stood out in any student group, I soon learned to become less conspicuous by wearing blue jeans and carrying a backpack.

During these three years of graduate study, I began to write and present a few papers at local professional meetings, and I came to know a number of people who were working in Mexico and Central America, areas of special interest to me. It became obvious that I should narrow my field of study and concentrate on combining my museum expertise with my archaeological interest in ceramics of the pre-Columbian world. As class work drew to a close, it was time to make a decision on a PhD dissertation topic.

~ Time for Fieldwork ~

Fieldwork, followed by the writing of a dissertation, is probably the most difficult period for anyone pursuing a doctoral degree. Due to the requirement of actual field research, it is particularly hard for women with families to find the right archaeological project. For many reasons, age being one of them, research interests another, I didn't really fit into any professor's ongoing project, so I set out to find my own. Over a number of years, I had the good fortune to serve as a private curator for a major collection of Costa Rican pre-Columbian art. I had become familiar with this region of lower Central America and I felt comfortable with the objects and the material culture generally. Due to the amazing depth of this collection, a number of archaeologists had visited Denver to examine the artifacts, and I had become acquainted with them. I decided to write to these professional contacts in Costa Rica to inquire about opportunities for fieldwork there. Their responses to me indicated that there were indeed several possibilities for a dissertation project based in ceramic research. So, relying on this information and on my confidence in my curatorial competence, I determined to go to Costa Rica to investigate the opportunities.

I set off for San José, not knowing where I was going to end up or even where I was going to stay, a very uncomfortable feeling for a conservative woman in her early forties. As instructed, I had tucked a copy of the current *American Antiquity* magazine under my arm so that I could be identified by the person meeting me. I was a bit frightened by the whole adventure. However, I was graciously met in San José and carefully instructed on how to take the local bus north to the town of Liberia in Guanacaste Province. From there, I found my way to the field camp where my colleague-friend was conducting an excavation. During the next week, we talked over a number of possibilities that might be appropriate to my expertise and interests, but nothing seemed just right.

Finally, however, the right project materialized. I was introduced to the owner of an extensive ranch that lay along the banks of the Tempisque River. His wife, Doña Carmen, was from an old Costa Rican family and had always been interested in the vanished indigenous cultures of her country. She wanted to preserve the past and had stored in an old barn thousands of pieces of pre-Columbian pottery recovered from ancient burial sites that had been uncovered accidentally by the hacienda's farming activities. Each time this occurred, Doña Carmen would take her umbrella and a folding stool to the field and oversee the removal of the archaeological materials to her *bodega* (an unused barn). Most of the objects were ceramic vessels, many of them looking as elegant as when they had first been made. Even when badly broken, the shards were carefully collected and stored together in individual sacks. There were several thousand whole or restored pots and hundreds more still in their paper bags plus many decorated and undecorated stone metates, some flint tools, a few gold and copper ornaments, and a handful of jade pendants and beads. The huge collection covered twenty-five hundred years of Costa Rican prehistory, with a repertoire of ceramic types from throughout the chronological sequences.

This fortunate meeting was one time when age and gender worked in my favor. Archaeologists and students had been requesting research access to this collection for many years, but the *duena* of the hacienda had been completely turned off by the bright, young students she considered "hippies." My white hair and accompanying twelve-year-old daughter appealed to her. My research request was granted, and I returned to Colorado to prepare and then successfully defend my research proposal.

The next spring, I returned to Costa Rica to begin the research project. In that diminutive country, the archaeological community is very small and everyone is interested in whatever projects are underway and whoever is new in the area. As a result, from the start I met many students and scholars with whom I would be interacting over the next few years. They would drop in for a chat and stay to look at the collection and compare notes on what they were finding and the latest work going on in the field. Needless to say, I learned an amazing amount from my new friends. In addition, I met the members of the National Museum staff and various government dignitaries whose duties included the preservation of Costa Rica's antiquities. They were eager to have this vast collection catalogued and photographed in compliance with the requirements of the recently enacted patrimony laws. While the family members were not completely satisfied with the final collaborative agreement with the government agents, I found myself responsible for numbering, cataloguing, and photographing each object in the collection and supplying final copies to both parties, enabling them to fulfill their obligations.

My very nontraditional field crew consisted of a pot washer (my twelve-year-old daughter), a volunteer photographer (my husband), a friend my own age working on her master's degree, and a graduate student in studio art. It was the first summer of the Nicaraguan civil war, and the Samosa and Sandinista forces were battling just twenty-five miles north of the hacienda where we worked. Volunteer soldiers with rifles walked north along the roads to join the rebels, and sightseers and journalists abounded. The locals were strongly supportive of the Sandinista cause. Neighbors, friends, and family members lived on either side of the rather-meaningless political border, sharing common interests and kinship ties that stretched back deep into the pre-Columbian past. The arrival of so many newcomers on their doorstep was unprecedented. The arrival of our own small group of four blond (or graying) North Americans and one blond girl seemed particularly remarkable. Our claim to be archaeologists was at first suspect because aliases had been used before. So, for the first month of our stay, we were assumed to be CIA agents. Finally, as we shopped in the markets and learned people's names, the novelty of our appearance wore off; and we slowly became a familiar, if rather strange, group on the local streets. From this inauspicious beginning the ceramic project moved forward.

Life on the ranch itself was almost as fascinating as the archaeology. The workers on the ranch were not unlike the tenant farmers I had known on the Missouri farm of my childhood. With their families, they occupied small houses on the periphery of the ranch, paying with their labor for the right to work some of the land and receiving a small salary from the ranch owners, along with supplies of coffee, sugar, lard, and milk. They were intrigued with our research project and, at the direction of the *duena*, happily provided us with constant refreshments and help as we worked in the upper level of a blistering hot barn. After two years and several long, very hot field seasons, the data from more than two thousand ceramic vessels were duly recorded for my research, documented for the ranch owners, and legally filed with the Costa Rican Department of National Patrimony. Ultimately, we had become a part of the community, and leaving was difficult. Our return visits still find a small, well-labeled museum in place in the barn of the hacienda and a warm welcome from old friends.

I returned to Colorado with notebooks full of copious ceramic data and thousands of photographs. I was glad to be home, but I knew my return meant facing the reality of actually writing the dissertation. It didn't take long for me to understand why so many PhD candidates in diverse fields finish with the designation of ABD (all but dissertation) rather than with a completed PhD. After the camaraderie and excitement of fieldwork, writing is a lonely pursuit. For women, the demands and interruptions of family life can make it a nightmare. However, in spite of some difficult periods, I did finish the writing and the successful defense of my dissertation.

~ Time for Excellence ~

After finishing graduate school, I was one of the few fortunate women who almost immediately found the right job in the right place. I went to work as a part-time curator of archaeology for the Denver Museum of Natural History (now the Denver Museum of Nature and Science). During my second year, the museum began to expand its staff and its role in the community, and my position became full time. A few years later, I was asked to take on the job of chief curator. At first I hesitated to accept the offer, knowing how time consuming it would be, but I couldn't turn down the opportunity to become a vital part of this expanding and dynamic institution. My responsibilities seemed to increase almost daily as I was given permission to hire seven new curators, restart the publications program, hire a conservator, and strengthen the library and archives. At first the five-year plans, the yearly budgets, and financial oversight of this major division of the museum seemed an overwhelming challenge, but once settled into the role, I found I had a talent for administration that I had never been aware of. The job and I were a good fit. I loved it.

No sooner had I become accustomed to this new position than another challenge came along. The museum decided to put together a blockbuster exhibition scheduled to open in 1992 as a commemoration of the voyage of Columbus and the first encounter of New and Old World cultures. We began the process of planning this massive exhibit three years in advance, and it took all those years to prepare not only the show but also the many facets associated with it. The subject was the culture and times of the final years of the Aztec civilization. Scholars from the United States and Mexico, including two major Mexican museums, helped with the exhibition storyline and the objects that illustrated it. Since none of us knew exactly what we were getting into, it never occurred to me, nor to the museum, that I might not be capable of acting as both chief curator of the museum and the curator of this enormous undertaking. Somehow, I managed to wear both hats. It was the most exhausting experience I have ever had, but also one of the most rewarding.

I was incredibly naive when I started the project, but perhaps it was just as well that I didn't fully appreciate the enormity of the complications involved, for if I had, I might never have begun. Needless to say, I was only one of many players. Particularly during the final year of preparation, the project required the enthusiastic cooperation of many departments in the museum. By the time the exhibition opened, I had presented a three-month lecture class to train our fifteen hundred volunteers and docents, organized a symposium, written a catalogue for the general public, and given lectures all over Denver to promote the exhibit. Opening day brought out the mayor of Denver and the governor of Colorado as well as a vast colorful parade prepared by Denver's Hispanic community. The exhibit was a resounding success: nine hundred thousand people walked through The World of Moctezuma, twenty-five thousand catalogues were sold in the shop, and literally thousands of Denver schoolchildren learned that America did not begin with the arrival of the pilgrims at Plymouth Rock.

I remained chief curator of the museum until I was sixty-five, at which point I decided for numerous reasons that it suited me best to revert to being the museum's part-time curator of Latin American archaeology. My husband's health had begun to demand more of my attention, I wanted some leisure time with my grandchildren before they grew up, and I needed some uninterrupted hours for writing. As a result, my job with the museum changed. Rather than the usual curatorial duties of cataloguing and working with objects in the collections, I was asked to continue my role as part of the public face of the museum. My duties entailed leading archaeological trips around the world, presenting lectures and short classes at the museum and in the community, and being available for consultation for the Departments of Anthropology, Exhibits, and Adult

Programs. It sounds like a dream job, and for eight years indeed it was. Then life changed and challenged me again in a different way—my husband of fifty-three years died in October of 2004.

I am now seeking my way out of the resulting grief and am aware anew of the strength of family ties. My sorrow is lessened as it is shared with my daughters, and we cry and smile together as we face the cycling anniversaries of a lifetime after the death of a loved father, husband, and friend. Christmas, birthdays, Thanksgiving—we deal with each one as it comes along and know that it will be easier as the years go by.

As I pick up my life again, I feel I have now come full circle. My newest position is not as an archaeologist but as a board member at the Denver Public Library and, in my "spare time," a reviewer of books. I have returned to my first love—reading, writing, and literature. Perhaps it is time for another new career. I've always wanted to write mystery novels, and I have always been taught to write about what you know best. So watch for a new series based on curatorial adventures in a large urban museum.

~ Looking Back ~

Despite the picture of my life laid out above, I find it somewhat difficult to identify the influences that drew me to the discipline of anthropology. Perhaps it brought together under one umbrella my interest in books, travel, history, and drama as well as feeding my fascination with peoples and cultures of the past. Certainly, it provided me with new tools and theoretical concepts to explore my natural interests. In addition, I never thought of myself as adventurous, but archaeology must also have filled an unacknowledged need as it led me to face new challenges, both physical and mental, that I had never dreamed of.

The aspects and events of my life that helped me succeed in this midlife undertaking are somewhat clearer to me. I am fully aware of the immeasurable value of the nurturing years of my childhood and the encouragement I received from parents and grandparents to be intellectually curious and observant. From my father and his strong, strict family I came to understand the values of self-discipline, integrity, and personal responsibility that underlie success and achievements. Later in my life, I received an excellent undergraduate degree, selected a volunteer opportunity that provided an amazing interim education, and eventually found a research opportunity that actually came my way *because* of my age and background. On a more personal level, I have also been blessed with health, financial security, a supportive family, fine daughters, warm friendships, and a good marriage.

However, I have not forgotten the trials that were part of the journey, such as the problems of a young marriage during the Korean War and the stress of the birth of four children in almost as many years—and the many stresses after their birth. However, these were offset by the thousands of books I managed to consume while my children were young, the many years of extremely valuable volunteer museum work, plus the often-unappreciated organizational and interpersonal skills developed in handling family finances, mediating quarrels, serving as a scout leader, disciplining and mentoring children, leading Great Books programs, and being a daughter, wife, mother, sister, and friend. In the end, the advantages far outweighed the problems, and, for me, the change in direction at the midpoint of my life worked.

Each woman's story is different, but as I look at examples of older women in midlife careers, there is one thing that stands out: there is no doubt in my mind that the most significant quality they bring to the field of anthropology is maturity. To know who you are, what you want to accomplish, and what is really important in your life is more valuable than being young. Accumulated life experiences by far outweigh the youthful search for identity. The rewards can be tremendous: the advanced degree itself, new friendships, professional contacts around the world, a fulfilled passion for the discipline of anthropology, and time to enjoy it. The downside is that discrimination does exist against older women in PhD programs; injustices occur; the right job is not always there; some marriages are badly strained, even destroyed; and old friendships are lost. Ultimately, for good or for bad, the years of a PhD experience change your life forever.

However, in spite of the problems most of us have faced, the time has come to take a constructive look at a cultural pattern that encourages a midlife change in career. Recently, men have begun to make such changes in their own lives. Unlike their fathers, who often spent their working lives with one company or business, many are striking out in midlife into new or more satisfying careers. While this pattern is clearly not a suitable choice for all women, it is a choice that those of us who have achieved PhDs in midlife can well speak to. My concern is that we do speak to it, that we acknowledge that change is possible and that it can be rewarding, not only for ourselves, but also for our children, our families, and the profession. Society needs to take a critical look at the future of our children and families and to reevaluate the ability and experience mature women can bring to the workplace.

We all have stories to share and advice to offer our daughters and granddaughters. Changes are needed, and our experiences, both negative and positive, concretely address some immediate anxieties many younger women have about their lives today. These anxieties often focus on their role in the workforce, the daily challenges of juggling career and family, and the inherent concerns about late childbearing. Most of us have "been there," though our childbearing years were in our early twenties, not early forties, and most often our children were of school age before we returned to the pursuit of new careers and doctoral degrees.

I have serious questions and concerns about the future of our grandchildren and the millions of other small children being raised by daycare centers and external caretakers. What will their future be? How well will they adjust and learn without the nurturing of full-time mothers? And, perhaps above all, how will they relate to their own children and families? The answers and the price we may pay are still unknown, but problems besetting society today suggest that all is not well. Men, of course, share these concerns. Many do their best to offer the support necessary for a two-job family to function. However, is this the best cultural pattern, the best lifestyle for our children? I suggest that the new social patterns in which women pursue a career until close to forty and then have a family, or have children in their twenties and upon returning to work, must endure the stress and competition between job and family, may not always be the best choices. The advantages of pursuing a career in later life begin to look very attractive when balanced against such serious problems as finding nurturing care for babies and small children, coping with childhood illnesses, finding time for school activities and teacher conferences, and, of course, dealing with our vulnerable teenagers. There are times when we just have to be there.

The advantages of being young with your children and avoiding some of the physical concerns surrounding late childbirth are clear to most of us. The question is, do late careers work? I think they do. The quality of life for both young and middle-aged women in the years ahead and the security and well-being of families may at least partly depend upon it. It seems to me that women in our profession have an obligation to communicate and demonstrate that midlife can bring a new "time for excellence."

Lessons for Today

Marjorie M. Schweitzer

MANY OF the young women who graduated during the past ten to fifteen years chose not to follow the paths of their mothers and grandmothers, but opted for work or graduate school right out of college. Because of advancements in the last half of the twentieth century in many dimensions of their lives, including the legal, social, educational, and reproductive areas, women believed they could be anything and do anything—that they could have it all—a career *and* a family at any age. While today's young women have many options for deciding their futures, the decisions facing them are complex in ways not imagined in earlier decades of the twentieth century. We look at a few of the questions that young women of the 1990s and early years of the twenty-first century ask. Some of the issues are new; others are much the same.

Medical advances have made it possible for women to delay having children until later in their reproductive lives; in fact, the decision to delay starting a family until a woman is in her late thirties or early forties has quadrupled since 1970.[1] A corollary to that statistic is the fact that the number of women in their early forties who become mothers for the first time is the highest since the 1960s, before the Pill attained widespread use.[2] When women who have established careers in academia, business, law, or industry now hear the "ticking of the biological clock," they may ask themselves, What are the options that medical advances offer? How long *can* I wait to make a decision? Once they decide to start a family, they are then faced with decisions about how to manage their lives.

Many women who have followed the career-first pattern leave the workforce soon after starting a family, either because they prefer to stay at home with their babies and young children or the demands of employers and the requirements of their jobs prevent them from continuing. They are giving up careers to raise their children without being able to foresee the future of a career after the children are older or have left home.[3]

Some women try "sequencing," where they put their careers on hold for a few years. But sequencing brings its own risks and dilemmas, as a woman wonders whether her skills will still be valued when she decides she wants to go back to work. Will she be able to fit in if she suddenly has to find a job if her spouse loses his?[4] Others are cutting back on the number of hours they work, as they go to part-time status in order to be with their children more.

The problems of careers and children in the world of academia are no different. As the number of women in academia continues to grow,[5] more women are joining the ranks of college and university teaching. However, motherhood and tenure-track jobs don't mix well—the childbearing years overlap with the tenure-track years. One option is to work fewer hours and take longer to reach tenure. That will depend on whether the university will agree to a part-time tenure track. In 1975, 46 percent of full-time female professors were tenured. This percentage had not changed in 1992.[6] Some women settle for non-tenure-track positions as part-time instructors or adjuncts to accommodate their needs.

Another option for career women is not to have children,[7] a choice made by one of the authors in this volume. Her decision echoes that of other anthropologists who have given up marriage or having children for the freedom of creating and maintaining a career.

Once a career woman makes the decision to become a mother, she faces social pressures today that focus on how good a mother she is. In their book about the current idealization of motherhood, authors Susan Douglas and Meredith Michaels argue that contemporary "standards of good motherhood" have been raised to increasing heights.[8] This process is especially "oppressive to women."[9] Society today expects that in order "to be a remotely decent mother, a woman has to devote her entire physical, psychological, emotional, and intellectual being, 24/7 to her children."[10] If she fails to conform to this ideal, she is looked upon with strong disapproval by society.

Ironically, this attitude echoes the 1950s when the message was the same—a mother was encouraged to spend all of her time and energy raising her children and was expected to focus on the "most minor details of the daily existence."[11] Anything less would be unacceptable.[12]

Judith Warner describes these extreme expectations as "perfect madness."[13] Women have often been viewed at one extreme or the other—as a saint or a sinner. They are once again cast in extreme terms as either too ambitious or not ambitious enough. These renewed arguments for extreme domesticity only add to the difficulties women and their families face.

While American society idealizes "mom and apple pie," attitudes toward the mother who stays at home to rear the children are ambivalent at best; she and her work are undervalued by society as a whole and by government and business in particular.[14] We often hear the statement that the mother who stays at home "doesn't work." The pervasiveness of this attitude toward the stay-at-home parent is ironically captured in an article about men who choose for one reason or another to be the at-home parent: "She Works, He Doesn't."[15]

One of the contradictions of our society today is that we speak in glowing terms about raising children, but we fail to create conditions that will help parents with the task of raising the next generation and ensuring continuity of the society with the best possible outcome. How are we to reconcile these views? Despite all of the advancements that have been gained for women in recent decades, mothers (and fathers) have been left behind.[16]

How is the stay-at-home parent—mother or father—undervalued? There is no pay, no Social Security, no time off, and no economic credit given or social acknowledgement made for the important work that they do. While the paid services of a daycare provider are part of the gross domestic product (GDP), staying home to raise children is not. Homeschooling your child is not listed as part of the GDP, but paying the teachers and the school system are. Hiring someone to clean for you is recognized as part of the economy, but doing your own housework is not. Stay-at-home mothers cannot qualify for Social Security even though they provide essential work.[17] Stay-at-home moms who decide to go to college or to enter the job market are urged not to mention their years at home in their applications. Those at-home years will be discredited.

When calculated in terms of what one would have to pay for a mother's services, a conservative estimate at the rate of a middle manager (plus other possible services such as a financial planner or a chauffeur) would result in an assessment of $100,000 a year.[18] By not being awarded any financial credit for all that she does, a mother—especially a divorced or widowed mother with young children—faces a reduced income, probably for the rest of her life.[19] The same challenges that women of the mid-twentieth century faced are amplified because society today believes that women can do it all, yet still does not consider in any meaningful way that what the parents at home do is worthwhile.[20]

If valuing and nurturing families and communities are realistic goals, how best might these goals be accomplished? How best to use the personal and professional contributions of both women and men to achieve "a good home" and "a good society"? Rather than promoting just one or two options—career first or family first—how can society support a variety of options without detriment to those involved?

Along with pointing out the challenges that abound, many of the publications we have cited offer a variety of solutions. At the top of the list are professional childcare, flexible work conditions, and a recognition by the employer—colleges and universities, corporations, law firms, and industry—that individuals can and do make contributions that are valuable even when working part time and with flexible schedules. While the life course of a woman is different from that of a man, the life course of men could benefit by reevaluation so that everyone gains—the wife, the husband, and the children. Some scholars suggest that until the men are included in the mix, families will continue to have a difficult time having and raising a family.[21]

Judith Warner argues that there are politically possible and economically feasible solutions that can give mothers, fathers, and families a break. These include tax subsidies for family-friendly corporations; flexible, affordable, and high-quality daycare; and affordable health insurance—all of these to be available to both full-time and part-time workers.[22]

Flexibility in job situations is a high priority for many workers. In 2004, 75 percent of employees were looking for new jobs, and over 66 percent of those job seekers wanted *flexibility*.[23] Social trends that reinforce equality and flexibility are advancements that would benefit both women and men,[24] and would promote the common good.[25]

Women seek flexible work situations more than men do, but only a few find flexible job schedules.[26] At least two-thirds of the women in two-career marriages "wish they could work at home."[27] World events have also changed men's assumptions about work in the twenty-first century,[28] and more men are jumping off the fast track as they consider how important the pacing of their own lives is to the lives of their partners and their children, as well as to society. Flexibility is happening not only at the workplace, but in the new career pattern that is occurring for men as well as women—most do not expect that they will stay with one job or with one firm their entire lives as their grandfathers and their fathers might have done.

Flexible jobs with professional childcare were on the rise in the late 1990s, but these perks are becoming less available in the twenty-first century as women (and men) are facing problems related to the current economic conditions—a slowdown in the market, layoffs, increased healthcare costs, and the drain on the economy by current wars.[29]

Some progress has been made, as many reports show.[30] But more than forty years after Friedan's seminal book predicting that social changes (such as professional daycare) would be common, it appears that less progress has been made than seemed likely in the 1960s.[31]

~ A Legacy for the Future ~

Is career first and family later the only alternative today? What lessons can we learn from the authors of the narratives in this volume?

Do late careers work? We think they do. Our experiences suggest that there are certain advantages in being an older woman entering college and/or the marketplace. An older woman brings maturity to a career and to schooling that a young person does not have. Having children during the younger years eliminates some of the concerns about childbirth that an older mother might have.

Are the issues faced by our authors any more difficult to solve than the ones women are facing today: being able to find a job after dropping out of the workforce, sacrificing pay and benefits when stopping work, having up-to-date expertise to return to a former job, working part time instead of full time?

Our daughters and granddaughters face challenges that in many ways are the same as those faced by the writers in this volume in earlier decades. Battling gender role stereotypes is still an issue for young women today, and basic questions remain: whether or not to have children, when to have children, and how to accommodate raising children along with the pursuit of a career.

There are no easy answers. Clearly, we need the resolve to support options for multiple choices, rather than limiting our young people to one or the other of two difficult choices. As Warner states, we need solutions that can give families a break.[32]

~ Endnotes ~

1. Kalb (2001:42; 2004); see U.S. Census Bureau (2002, 2003) for more details.
2. Tyre (2004:70).
3. Women with children *do* work, however. In 2004 “more than sixty per cent of women with children under the age of six are employed. Among mothers of children between the ages of six and seventeen, that figure rises to nearly eighty per cent” (Kolbert 2004:85).
4. Quinn (2004:6C).
5. Today women receive 42 percent of the doctorates granted (Kleiman 2002:11–12).
6. Kleiman (2002:I1–2).
7. Fisher (2003:2).
8. Douglas and Michaels (2004).
9. Kolbert (2004:86).
10. Douglas and Michaels (2004:4).
11. Chafetz (1978:194).
12. Nuss (2004).
13. Warner (2005b).
14. Crittenden (2001:2), Bauchner (2004).
15. Tyre and McGinn (2003).
16. Bauchner (2004).
17. Chafetz (1978:118), Crittenden (2001:71–78).
18. Crittenden (2001:8). It’s interesting to note that almost 50 percent of the women who make $100,000 or more in the United States are childless (Kiefer 2002:4).
19. Although a mother who is married and neither divorced nor widowed might be supported by her husband’s earnings, she would still be disadvantaged financially especially as she aged (see especially McCaffery 1999 for a detailed explanation of what happens to married women who work compared with those who do not).
20. Crittenden (2001:6–8, 77–78).
21. Wilson and Galinsky (2003:1–2).
22. Warner (2005a:48).
23. Nance-Nash (2005).
24. Wilson and Galinsky (2003).
25. Bauchner (2004), Fisher (2004).
26. Nance-Nash (2005:1), Kleiman (2005:4).
27. Brenner (2001:48).

28. Shields (2003).
29. Nance-Nash (2005:2).
30. For example, see Kleiman (2005).
31. Kolbert (2004:87). While California was the first state to offer a paid family-leave benefit (up to 55 percent of one's salary for six weeks) workers, especially women, still must negotiate their return and whether they will be able to retain their jobs with their employers. Often they meet with discouragement from the very beginning, as employers are not eager to hire someone who might at some point take advantage of this offer (Vesely 2004).
32. Warner (2005a:48).

~ References ~

Bauchner, Elizabeth. 2004. A Mother's Place Is in the Women's Movement. *Women's eNews,* March 10, 2004. http://www.womensenews.org/article.cfm/dun/aid/1744 (accessed March 16, 2004).

Brenner, Marie. 2001. Not Their Mothers' Choices. *Newsweek,* August 13, 2001.

Chafetz, Janet Saltzman. 1978. *Masculine/Feminine or Human: An Overview of the Sociology of the Gender Roles,* 2nd ed. Itasca, IL: F. E. Peacock Publishers. Inc.

Crittenden, Ann. 2001. *The Price of Motherhood: Why the Most Important Job in the World Is Still the Least Valued.* New York: Henry Holt & Co.

Douglas, Susan, and Meredith Michaels. 2004. *The Mommy Myth: The Idealization of Motherhood and How It Has Undermined Women.* New York: Free Press.

Fisher, Luchina. 2003. Working Women Delay, Forego, Rethink Motherhood. *Women's eNews,* November 7, 2003. http://www.womensenews.org/article.cfm/dyn/aid/1592 (accessed November 9, 2003).

———. 2004. Mothers Press for Care-Giving Work Credit, Respect. *Women's eNews,* April 7, 2004. http://www.womensenews.org/article.cfm/dyn/aid/1779/context/archive (accessed May 30, 2004).

Kalb, Claudia. 2001. Should You Have Your Baby Now? *Newsweek,* August 13, 2001, 40–43.

———. 2004. Fertility and the Freezer. *Newsweek,* August 2, 2001, 52.

Kiefer, Francine. 2002. Balancing Family and Work at the White House. *Christian Science Monitor,* April 25, 2002, 1, 4.

Kleiman, Carol. 2002. Tenure Overlaps Mama Track. *Albuquerque Journal,* December 18, 2002, I1–2.

———. 2005. Men Like Paternity Leave. *Daily Camera,* August 1, 2005, 4.

Kolbert, Elizabeth. 2004. Mother Courage: Kids, Careers, and Culture. *The New Yorker,* March 8, 2004, 85–87.

McCaffery, Edward J. 1999. *Taxing Women: How the Marriage Penalty Affects Your Taxes.* Chicago: Univ. of Chicago Press.

Nance-Nash, Sheryl. 2005. Fewer Employers Offering Flexible Schedule. *Women's eNews,* February 7, 2005. http://womensenews.org/article.cfm/dyn/aid/2109/context/archive (accessed February 7, 2005).

Nuss, Lisa. 2004. New Stepford Wives' Fuels Old Anti-Career Views. *Women's eNews,* July 7, 2004. http://www.womensenews.org/article.cfm?aid=1901 (accessed July 29, 2004).

Quinn, Michelle. 2004. A New Generation of Women Is Sequencing. *Denver Post,* May 10, 2004, 6C.

Shields, Julie. 2003. More U.S. Dads Balance Laptops, Kids on Laps. *Women's eNews*, June 15, 2003. http://www.womensenews.org/article.cfm/dyn/aid/1366/context/archive (accessed August 3, 2003).

Tyre, Peg. 2004. A New Generation Gap. *Newsweek*, January 19, 2004, 68–71.

Tyre, Peg, and Daniel McGinn. 2003. She Works, He Doesn't. *Newsweek*, May 12, 2003, 45–52.

U.S. Census Bureau. 2002; 2003. http://www.census.gov/population/www/socdemo/fertility.html (accessed October 9, 2005).

Vesely, Rebecca. 2004. New Mothers Test California's Leave Law. *Women's eNews*, August 10, 2004. http://www.womensenews.org/article.cfm/dyn/aid/1944/context/archive (accessed September 3, 2003).

Warner, Judith. 2005a. Mommy Madness. *Newsweek*, February 21, 2005, 42–49.

———. 2005b. *Perfect Madness: Motherhood in the Age of Anxiety.* New York: Riverhead.

Wilson, Marie C., and Ellen Galinsky. 2003. It's About More Than Just Adding Boys to a Girls' Day. *Women's eNews*, April 23, 2003. http://www.womensenews.org/article.cfm/syn/aid/1302 (accessed April 23, 2003).

Index

Left Coast Press Inc. is committed to preserving ancient forests and natural resources. We elected to print *Women In Anthropology* on 30% post consumer recycled paper, processed chlorine free. As a result, for this printing, we have saved:

5 Trees (40' tall and 6-8" diameter)
2,155 Gallons of Wastewater
867 Kilowatt Hours of Electricity
238 Pounds of Solid Waste
467 Pounds of Greenhouse Gases

Left Coast Press Inc. made this paper choice because our printer, Thomson-Shore, Inc., is a member of Green Press Initiative, a nonprofit program dedicated to supporting authors, publishers, and suppliers in their efforts to reduce their use of fiber obtained from endangered forests.

For more information, visit www.greenpressinitiative.org